Using

HTML 3.2, Second Edition

Using
HTML 3.2,
Second
Edition

Todd Stauffer

Using HTML 3.2, Second Edition

Credits

President
Roland Elgey

Publisher
Joseph B. Wikert

Publishing Manager
Jim Minatel

Title Manager
Steven M. Schafer

Editorial Services Director
Elizabeth Keaffaber

Managing Editor
Sandy Doell

Director of Marketing
Lynn E. Zingraf

Acquisitions Manager
Cheryl D. Willoughby

Acquisitions Editor
Philip Wescott

Product Director
Mark Cierzniak

Production Editor
Heather Kaufman Urschel

Product Marketing Manager
Kim Margolius

Assistant Product Marketing Manager
Christy M. Miller

Strategic Marketing Manager
Barry Pruett

Technical Editor
Bill Bruns

Technical Support Specialist
Nadeem Muhammed

Acquisitions Coordinator
Jane K. Brownlow

Editorial Assistant
Andrea Duvall

Book Designer
Ruth Harvey

Cover Designer
Dan Armstrong

Production Team
Troy Barnes, Jerry Cole,
Kathleen Caulfield, Trudy
Coler, Dana Davis,
Toi Davis, Stephanie
Hammett, Natalie Hollifield,
Kevin J. MacDonald,
Angel Perez, Linda Quigley

Indexer
Deb Myers

Composed in *ITC Century*, *ITC Highlander*, and *MCP digital* by Que Corporation.

About the Author

Todd Stauffer is a full-time freelance writer based in Colorado Springs, CO. He's written non stop since graduation from Texas A&M University, where he studied English Literature and Management Information Systems. Since that time, he's been an advertising copywriter, magazine columnist, and magazine editor, all in computing fields.

Todd is currently the Internet columnist for *Peak Computing Magazine*, and host of the Peak Computing Radio Hour on 740AM in Colorado. He's the author of *HTML By Example, Creating Your Own AOL Web Pages, Using the Internet with Your Mac, Using Your Mac, Easy AOL, Using PageMill 2*, and, co-author of a number of other titles, all published by Que. In his spare time, he thinks of new and interesting ways to fund his health insurance and write-off exotic vacations as tax-deductible. He has no cats, although other people's cats are always bothering him.

Todd can be reached via e-mail at **tstauffer@aol.com** or through his personal Web site at **http://members.aol.com/tstauffer/**.

Acknowledgments

This book's first edition was written by Neil Randall, and much of his work remains. He wrote an excellent text that only needed some slight revisions and updates for the latest and greatest on the Web. I owe him a debt for making this project so easy.

Special thanks go to everyone at Que who helped me on a tight schedule. Cheryl Willoughby, acquisitions manager, did her usual calm and collected job of helping me manage to stay sane, eat regularly, and, eventually, get words on a page. Philip Westcott, acquisitions editor, handled the day-to-day flawlessly. Thanks also the Mark Cierzniak for keeping the contents on track.

The rest of the Que staff is invaluable in any project, including production editor Heather Urschel, and technical editor Bill Bruns.

Thanks one more time to the folks at *Peak Computing Magazine* and the *Colorado-Springs Gazette-Telegraph* for giving me the regular checks, encourgement, support, and regular checks.

I'd like to thank my good friends Aaron and Ryan for trying their best to make the baseball playoffs last long enough that I could get a glimpse.

Finally, big thanks to Donna Ladd for support, understanding, and the occassional adult beverage. Like Winston Churchill might have said, this beats having a real job.

We'd Like to Hear from You!

As part of our continuing effort to produce books of the highest possible quality, Que would like to hear your comments. To stay competitive, we *really* want you, as a computer book reader and user, to let us know what you like or dislike most about this book or other Que products.

You can mail comments, ideas, or suggestions for improving future editions to the address below, or send us a fax at (317) 581-4663. For the online inclined, Macmillan Computer Publishing has a forum on CompuServe (type **GO QUEBOOKS** at any prompt) through which our staff and authors are available for questions and comments. The address of our Internet site is **http://www.mcp.com** (World Wide Web).

In addition to exploring our forum, please feel free to contact me personally to discuss your opinions of this book: I'm **mcierzniak@que.mcp.com** on the Internet.

Thanks in advance—your comments will help us to continue publishing the best books available on computer topics in today's market.

Mark Cierzniak
Product Development Specialist
Que Corporation
201 W. 103rd Street
Indianapolis, Indiana 46290
USA

Contents at a Glance

Contents

*The
lowdown
on HTML*

see page 10

*Every Web
page has
the same
basic
structure*

see page 28

*Headings
help the
reader find
what's
there*

see page 39

*Link to
other
Internet
services*

see page 58

Part II: Designing Your Pages for Audience Appeal 81

*In HTML,
you have
five kinds
of lists*

see page 85

*Beyond
the basics:
Animated
GIFs*

see page 114

Part III: Advanced HTML 117

Some great tables served on the Web

see page 150

Part IV: Bells and Whistles 189

CGI in the real Web world

see page 185

The idea behind frames

see page 192

Setting your page up for style sheets

see page 209

Finding (or creating) multimedia stuff

see page 226

Working that thing called Java

see page 233

JavaScript's bold statements

see page 247

What's up in Netscape 3?

see page 265

Part V: My Site's Ready, What Can I Do Now? **275**

And now for Internet Explorer 3.0

see page 270

Announcing your arrival

see page 280

What-You-See-Is-What-You-Get editors (FrontPage, Netscape Gold)

see page 292

Part VI: Appendices 301

Appendix A: A HTML 3.2 Elements Reference 303

Appendix B: World Wide Web Bibliography 345

Index 353

Introduction

Becoming an HTML expert, fast!

Let's say HTML was gardening. If you like to get your hands a little dirty in the computing world—without needing a degree in horticulture—HTML is the place to start. Sure, HTML is a worthwhile job skill, it's the only way to be serious about the Web, and it's a crowning achievement in any college career. But there's one more thing about HTML that you need to know.

It's not programming! It's simple!

Was that two things? HTML is the language of the Web. Its real name is **HyperText Markup Language**, but nobody ever calls it that. It's just "HTML" to folks who know things about how Web pages work. And just a few chapters down the road, you'll be among that select few.

What's so cool about HTML?

HTML is nothing more than a set of codes. Every Web page in the world is done with HTML in one form or another. In fact, the magic of the World Wide Web is that everybody's Web browser—Netscape, Internet Explorer, Mosaic, Lynx, Quarterdeck Mosaic, Emissary, Mariner, MacWeb, you name it—knows what to do with HTML code. That's what browsers do: They display HTML code the way it's meant to be displayed.

Using HTML 3.2, 2nd Edition takes you through the exciting process of HTML authoring. What's so great about it? First, it's not hard to do. You've seen all kinds of pages during your World Wide Web tours, and you probably already have an idea of what you want your pages to look like. To create your own pages, you only need two things: a working knowledge of HTML and access to a computer that's set up as a **Web server**.

Actually, the second of these requirements—access to a Web server—is much more difficult than the first. Part of *Using HTML 3.2*, 2nd Edition shows you how to find such a computer. Basically, you can set one up yourself, or you can rent space on someone else's machine. It's a little bit like owning a home versus renting one, except that you don't pay nearly as much.

You'll need to think about Web servers eventually, because the other truly great thing about HTML authoring is that it lets you make your point to the entire world. Everybody who has access to the World Wide Web has access to your HTML pages, and that's both thrilling and frightening. Thrilling because you can do so much with them, and frightening because you're on stage in front of a potential audience of millions.

It won't cost anything and you don't need software

The way I've approached HTML in this book is the classic way that anyone who's serious should learn it. Without special tools, without WYSIWYG interfaces, and without paying an extra dime on your computer setup. I show you exactly how HTML works, why it makes sense, and why it's so darned easy. And we do it all in a simple text editor like Windows Notepad, Mac's Simpletext, or vi in UNIX.

Later on we take a look at some of the shareware and commercially available tools that are available for making HTML easier. But for anyone who needs to take care of HTML documents on a fairly regular basis, those tools just aren't enough. You need to know *why* things happen the way they do—not just how to push a button.

If you've been looking for an approachable way to really learn HTML like an expert, and you've been turned off by books geared toward a particular program, you've found your book. *Using HTML 3.2*, 2nd Edition is nothing but a friendly look at the world of HTML for all different types of people and computers. Got a Mac? Windows 95 or NT? UNIX? Linux? OS/2? It doesn't matter—HTML works everywhere, the way we'll talk about it.

How this book is structured

I really don't want to beat around the bush too much, so we start with a simple Intro chapter, and then move right on to the basics of a Web page in Part I. In fact, by the end of that part you'll have learned the bulk of HTML, and you'll have a couple of finished pages to your credit.

Part II takes a more detailed look at your Web pages themselves—how to jazz up the text and graphics. Pages have to be more than complete—they need to communicate well, too.

Part III is all about advanced HTML—things like imagemaps, tables, forms, and CGI programming—all the "fun" stuff. The point in Part III is making your Web site more interactive by getting your users involved. That's what keeps them coming back and getting friendly, reading your advertisements, or buying your products.

In the next section, Part IV we explode into the world of bells and whistles for HTML. If you want a *killer* site, you need to wade through these chapters. Just about everything you can imagine is covered in here, including Java, scripting, frames, the new style sheets specification, multimedia, and designing for the latest versions of Netscape Navigator and Internet Explorer.

Then, you're pretty much done. Part V takes a look at what to do when you're ready to publish your page—how to find a Web site and how to attract users. Then we talk about some of those wussy little HTML editors that (honestly) can make things a whole lot easier—once you know what you're doing.

Get through that and you're probably more of an HTML expert than I am. I had to do some research for this book, you know—and I'm sure I'll have forgotten some of it by the time you're done!

Welcome to HTML. The excitement is just beginning.

How to use this book

This book contains a number of special elements and conventions that are designed to help you find important information quickly.

 TIP   **Tips point out extra information.**

 CAUTION   **Cautions serve as warning signs that you might run into trouble.** They might also tell you how to avoid problems.

Q&A ***What are Q&A notes?***

These mainly present answers to trouble-shooting questions.

 Plain English, please!

If a new term or concept is introduced, it will usually be explained in a note like this one. **99**

Another thing to note about this book: A code continuation character (➡) has been used when a code line is too long to fit within the margins of this book. This symbol simply indicates that due to page constraints, a code line has been broken that normally would appear on a single line.

Is a book a product or a service?

I happen to believe that the books I write are more of a service than a product—not because I'm so amazing, but because that's how I feel they should be supported. You bought a book that I wrote, and it says you're going to learn HTML. If you deserve a big ol' "E" for effort, but you can't get past some problem, omission, or a poor explanation, that's my fault.

So here's what I'll do:

tstauffer@aol.com

If you have *any* question, concern, comment, confusion, or cash you'd like to send me, go ahead and do it. I'll answer your question as quickly as possible—I've been up to about 50 e-mails a day recently, but I make a point of answering every question personally (even if I personally answer with a FAQ list, I'll at least try to throw an e-mail smiley in with it).

If you are having trouble, please write me. You paid for it. I'll also be posting frequent questions, errata, and some examples from the book on my Web site at:

http://members.aol.com/tstauffer/

If that changes at some time in the future, I'll make sure you can get to the new site from that URL.

Best of luck, and don't forget we're in this together.

Part I: An HTML Tutorial

1

Introduction to HTML and Web Publishing

● **In this chapter:**

● How Web publishing works

● The lowdown on HTML

● What's up with these different types of HTML?

● All it takes is a text editor

● Saving for posterity and posting

If you've decided you want a Web site, you're in good company. Let's take a quick look at how this whole thing works . . . .

I could go on and on about how the World Wide Web started, what the point was, and why it's become so important to everyday life. But I think you already know that stuff, and I can't see much point in going deep into it one more time. Just to please you history buffs, I've hidden a sidebar in this chapter that hits the high points of the Web's recondite start.

For that matter, I also promise not to use the word "recondite" again, because it really only proves that I, like you, have a thesaurus built into my word processor. Essentially, my purpose here is to show you quickly and painlessly how to use the ever-growing litany of **HTML** commands to create attractive, informative, and useful pages for display on the World Wide Web. And that, I must say, is considerably simpler than it may seem.

 Plain English, Please!

HTML stands for **HyperText Markup Language**, and it's the acronym that suggests the group of little codes you use to create Web pages. Beyond that, you may have noticed that "HTML" is an integral player in the title of this book. So, going deep into an explanation of HTML in this little note would be overkill . . . and cost too much in paper. We discuss HTML from here until Appendix B. **99**

How Web publishing works

First, some ground rules. Rule number one is to completely and utterly abolish the word "programming" from your mind, at least until you get around to JavaScript in Chapter 16. For now, it's very important that you distinguish HTML from programming in your mind, if only because programming is almost always very much harder than is working with HTML. I've taken tons of classes in programming and haven't begun to understand it.

Instead of using the "p" word, I prefer to call people who create Web pages—like you and me—Web authors. I think it has a nice ring to it, as well as—in the computer world—being the terminology that suggests exactly what we're doing. We're authoring pages in a markup language, not programming in a machine language (see Figure 1.1).

A markup language allows you to specify how certain things in a document are going to look. You do that by including little codes in what is essentially a text document, just like any you might create in Windows Notepad or your favorite word processor. In fact, when you create a Web page you do many of the same things you do in a word processor, such as making things bold or turning certain words into headlines.

Fig. 1.1
Notice that the codes for a raw HTML page are readable to humans, if just barely. They result in an attractive Web page.

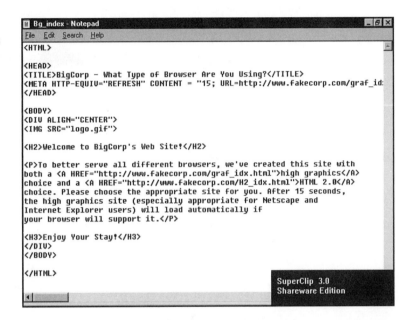

The lowdown on HTML

So what's so special about HTML? It might seem logical for us all to simply send Microsoft Word documents to one another and be done with it. But, there are some things that make HTML a little different from your typical .DOC document:

- *HTML is designed for the Web.* While most word processors are very fussy about little details—such as the particular font you've chosen for text—HTML is designed to work with nearly any sort of computer, anywhere in the world. It's designed to be both easy to transport over the Internet and easy for all different sorts of computers (and people) to read and understand.

- *HTML is an open standard.* We talk more about HTML's standard bearers later in this chapter, but, for now, just realize that HTML is not owned by one particular company. If we used Microsoft's .DOC format, for instance, we might have to pay Microsoft a bunch of cash for the privilege.

- *HTML is readable by humans.* In fact, this is a big part of the design. Have you ever messed something up and accidentally got a glimpse of a Microsoft Word document in a text editor? It ain't pretty. HTML was designed from the ground up so that it makes sense to actual people— not just computer programs.

- *HTML incorporates hypertext.* This one may be the key. If you've spent much time surfing the Web, you know that the little clickable text is the key to moving around on Web pages. HTML is designed so that it's easy for us, as Web authors, to add hypertext to our documents.

- *HTML supports multimedia.* Here's our final good reason for using HTML when we create Web pages…it knows how to work with multimedia. If there's anything that sets the Web apart from other communications mediums—such as newspapers or even electronic mail—it's support for all different forms of media, including sound, images, text, video, and more.

That's HTML in a nutshell. Let's look more closely at those last two, hypertext and the union of hypertext and multimedia on the Web, which are popularly called **hypermedia.**

Hypertext revealed

To me, the word "hypertext" conjures images of librarians going off the deep end. One overcast Wednesday—late in the shift—our intrepid librarian finds that once again the World Book "Ae-Ag" volume has been replaced by a careless patron at the beginning of the Encyclopedia Brittanica section. This time, though, it's too much. It just cannot be tolerated. Our librarian spirals out of control down a miserable little one-lane road to the brink of mental collapse. It's the dreaded…hypertext syndrome.

The hidden sidebar: Web history 101

The Internet began in the late 1960s, but it wasn't until the 1980s that people started to realize how powerful it could be as a communications and information medium. Scientists began to use it extensively as did researchers in other academic disciplines. In the late '80s, those outside of the academic community took notice, but the Net wasn't very attractive: everything was text, and getting information was difficult.

Also in the late 1980s, Tim Berners-Lee and his research team at CERN (European Organization for Nuclear Research in Geneva) began to develop a hypertext system that would work over computer networks. They did it to enable researchers in high-energy physics to share their research with one another. In 1991, they released the idea to the Internet under the name World Wide Web, but even then the idea was restricted. Graphics were foreseen, but everything was still text-only.

1992 brought two important events. First, Marc Andreesen of the National Center for Supercomputer Activity (University of Illinois, Urbana-Champaign) developed a program that could display graphics and make navigating around hyperlinks a simple matter of pointing and clicking with a mouse. That program was Mosaic for the X Windows system, and as soon as it was released, it took the Web by storm. Macintosh and Microsoft Windows versions followed, and Mosaic became the best-known computer program on the planet besides, say, WordPerfect.

The other 1992 event of significance was the U.S. presidential election. During the campaign, then Senator Al Gore spoke of the Information Superhighway, turning the attention of the media to the Internet and the Web.

Businesses began to take note. Suddenly, the race was on to mount bigger and better Web sites, until finally the Web became a business strategy rather than a minor experiment. All kinds of other events from 1992–95 took the Web from a minor convenience to a major communications tool, but it's safe to say that the interest by business has been the driving force.

What's more important is the meaning behind the word. **Hypertext** is special text that you can mark as linked to another Web page. The hypertext is generally underlined and in a different color. Using a mouse pointer, a reader can click on the text. This causes to the reader's Web browser to request the document to which the text is linked, and then load that document in the browser window (see Figure 1.2).

In this way, hypertext makes a Web page more interactive. And, at the same time, it becomes the basis of organization on the Web. This part is interesting because, up until the Web, most things on the Internet were organized hierarchically—generally in menus of some sort. The Web, however, offers a new, more intuitive way to organize information. Actually, it works a little like the way a human mind works.

 Hypertext links are also often called "hot" text or "active" text. Pretend for a moment that this page is a Web page. It's no longer a printed page in a book, even though it kinda looks like a printed page in a book and if you licked your finger and smudged it across the page, you might get ink remnants under your nails. Just go with me, here.

 If you haven't spent much time on the Web, I suggest you put this book down for one solid evening and spend some time surfing. Start at **http://www.yahoo.com/** and click around looking for interesting things. You need to understand the Web before you start creating pages for it.

You're surfing along on this page when you come to a link that says something about `Texas Rangers Baseball`. You click that link, just to see if someone has something good to say about the team. Where do you end up? It could be the sports page over at the `Dallas Morning News`' Web site. Reading along further, you come across a discussion of the Ranger's constant battle with `heat` in the late summer, and you're sent to the Weather Channel's summer forecast.

Over at the Weather Channel, you see a link that talks about trips to different National Forests around the U.S. After reading the travelogue, you click a link to the U.S. Department of the Interior and you finally figure out what the heck that department is.

Fig. 1.2
In most browsers,
hypertext link turn
a new color after
they've been clicked.
Hypertext links are
used to move from
page to page on the
Web.

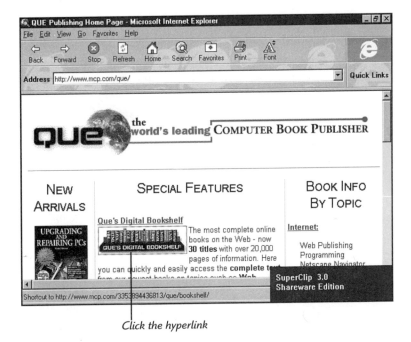

Click the hyperlink

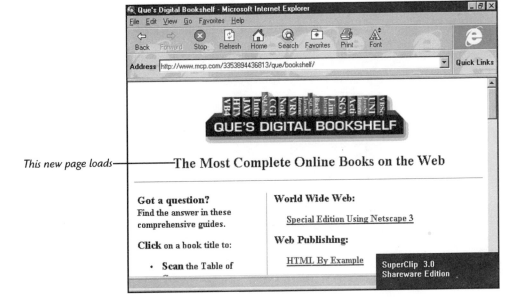

This new page loads

So where did we start and where did we end up? That's hypertext. It's both the charm and the bain of the Web. It's the Choose Your Own Adventure method of document retrieval that's at least partially responsible for the lackluster performance of the international economy over the last few years.

Hypermedia explained

The idea with **hypermedia** is that you can create a link on the page that doesn't load a new Web page—instead, it loads a multimedia document, such as a sound file or a digital movie. When the user clicks one of these links in his Web browser, the multimedia file is downloaded over the Internet, and then the Web browser starts (on the user's computer) a helper application. The helper application then takes over and plays or displays the file for you to enjoy (see Figure 1.3).

This on-demand style of multimedia (where a user has to click a hyperlink before accessing the multimedia file) was, at first, the only way to present video or audio files on the Web. These days, however, some browsers support plug-in technology that allows videos and audio to play as the Web page is displayed in the browser—just as if the multimedia file is part of the document. We talk more about adding plug-in multimedia to your pages in Chapter 14, "Going Nuts with Multimedia and Java."

Fig. 1.3
A helper application displaying a digital video file after a hypermedia link has been clicked.

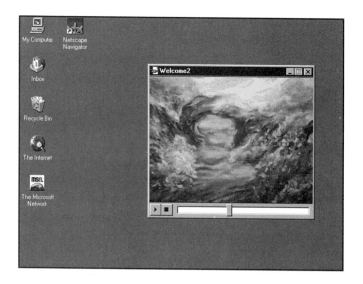

The little numbers after "HTML"

Perhaps you've seen the version numbers folks throw around like so many saucer-shaped trashcan lids just outside of Area 51 in Arizona—things like HTML 2.0, HTML 3.0, HTML 3.2, and so on. Annoying, isn't it? You might have even noticed these annoying, confusing numbers on the outside cover of this very book.

These numbers are versions of the HTML standard as decided by certain uppity people in their little institutions—the kind of folks that occasionally need to get out and see a movie. Actually, I'm only kidding. These days, the people in these standards organizations might be able to afford to produce their own movies, because most of them come from the heavy-hitting Web corporations—like Microsoft, Netscape, Apple, and Sun (see Figure 1.4).

Currently, the standard is pretty much up to an organization called the World Wide Web Consortium (W3C), a group of representatives from the previously mentioned companies (and quite a few others) headed by the creator of the Web, Tim Berners-Lee. One of the ambitions of the group is to create HTML and other standards that everyone on the Web can adhere to, so that anyone with any sort of browser can see most of what's available out there.

Fig. 1.4
The W3C's HTML overview page.

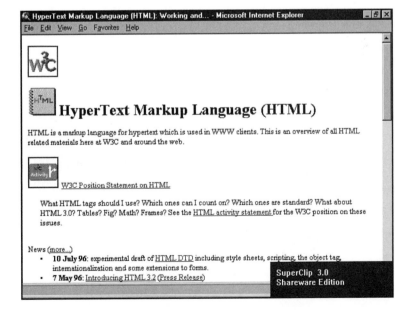

The problem is, not everyone agrees what the standards should be.

TIP **While this book covers just about everything you need to know** about HTML as a whole, you might still be interested in what you can learn about the actual standards from the W3C. That kind of stuff can be found at **http://www.w3.org/pub/WWW/MarkUp/** on the Web. It's a great place to keep yourself up-to-date.

The HTML argument

The battle has been raging ever since Netscape Navigator appeared on the Web scene early in 1995. It's the clash of Madison Avenue and Higher Learning. It's a 20-round, no holds barred, fight to the finish.

Here's a statement to ponder. *HTML is not a page description language.* Whoa?! Isn't that a direct contradiction? After all, the whole point is to describe Web pages for display in Web browsers, right?

The key to the HTML debate is understanding the idea of explicit versus implicit emphasis. The original HTML standard was designed around the notion that all emphasis on a page should be implicit. This means that the Web page author marked text as "a header" or "emphasized," and it was up to the user's Web browser program to decide how that was going to look (see Figure 1.5).

You see, the scientific types have always thought that it was important that HTML commands be implicit—up to the browser—so that everyone had a fair shake at seeing what's on the screen. Their point was that it's more important to communicate things in a less appealing way, as long as all the information gets across.

Fig. 1.5
In this snippet of HTML code, the <EM> marks the text it surrounds as "emphasized," while the <H1> marks text as a "header."

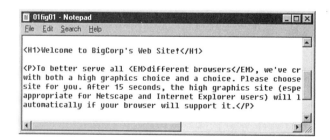

The other school of thought is championed by Netscape, Microsoft, and their ilk. They tend to lean into the explicit camp, where the Web author gets to decide how things are going to look on a Web page—just like you do with a word processor or desktop publishing program. The end result is that everyone can see your pretty designs, text wrapped around graphics, and hear funky sounds—but only if they're all using a compatible browser. Everyone else is out of luck (see Figure 1.6).

Fig. 1.6
Here's the wild and exciting Netscape index page (**http:// www.netscape. com/**) viewed with Lynx, a text-based browser. Pretty, huh?

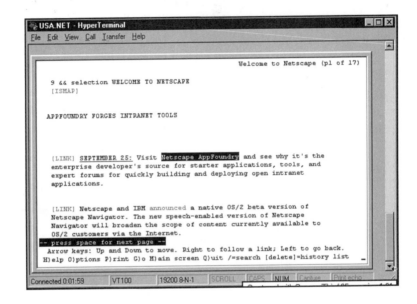

To do this, Netscape and Microsoft did two different things. First, they've become involved in the W3C, just to make sure they have their say in creating the next HTML standard. At the same time, they've continued to create extensions to HTML that only their browsers can recognize—as a way of competing against one another.

So where are the standards right now?

HTML 2.0 yesterday, HTML 3.2 tomorrow

HTML 2.0 is the current standard, and nearly every Web browser out there can read pages that adhere closely to these standard (but limited) commands. Most of these commands are implicit by nature—the standard commands are designed to work with nearly any browser, whether or not it's designed for high-end multimedia computers or text-only terminals in basements on university campuses.

But HTML 2.0 is showing its age. In spite of the fact that it's the current standard, many Web designers choose to add more recent commands to their pages on the assumption that the bulk of Web users have newer browser programs. And some of the new commands are, in a word, cooler.

HTML 3.2 is an emerging standard that requires new browser applications. Although it tries very hard to allow all browsers an equal chance, it includes much more control over the page than does HTML 2.0. For instance, it allows you to center text and images, create tables of data, and add multimedia elements, like video and audio, directly to your Web page. At the time of writing (and for some time to come), HTML 3.2 will be a work-in-progress, although the latest browsers already incorporate nearly the entire standard.

In addition to HTML 2.0 and HTML 3.2, Netscape and Microsoft have both added "extended" commands to HTML that enable you to add certain effects to pages—as long as those pages are viewed in those companies' browsers.

TIP   To learn more about Netscape HTML, head over to **http:// www.netscape.com/assist/index.html** and check out the Help for Authors section. For Microsoft's extensions, try **http://microsoft.com/ workshop/** on the Web.

Q&A   **What ever happened to HTML 3.0?**

HTML 3.0 was never more than a proposed standard, and, at the time, it was proposed by a W3C that didn't have the same level of support for industry corporations that it does now. It never really made it past the drawing board. After the W3C invited participation from the companies that were actually making browsers, the standard changed significantly enough that they decided to scrap HTML 3.0 and give the new standard, HTML 3.2, a higher version number.

Making your design decisions

Robin William's cameo character in the movie *Dead Again* has always stuck in my mind because of one particular line. "There are two types of people in the world: smokers and non-smokers," says the ex-psychologist played by

Williams. "Decide which one you're going to be…and be that." That's kind of what I need you to do with HTML standards.

Are you a traditionalist who believes in getting as close to the standards as possible? Is the most important part of your pages the text, and do you want 99 percent of the World Wide Web to be able to see the full glory of your pages? Then be that…I show you how as we step through the book.

If it's the design of the page—the integrity of the art—that's most important to you, then there's a place for you, too. We look at some of the extensions to the HTML 3.2 standard throughout this book, some of them in special sections marked "Beyond the basics," and others in Chapters 11–15. If you're interested in the tricks to a more advanced (and less accessible) Web page, they're here. Just be aware of the trade-off.

Creating and saving your pages

Believe it or not, creating HTML starts right around this next corner, in Chapter 2. To get ready, let's quickly go through some basics—the tools you need and how you should be saving the pages you create.

Everyone needs a good editor

All you really need to develop Web pages is a text editor. In Windows 95, that's Notepad or WordPad (if you remember to save your files as "Text Only"). Basically, all you need to remember is that HTML pages, while they include the .HTM or .HTML file extensions, are simply regular, boring ASCII text files. Any program that generates ASCII text files will work fine as an HTML editor—even a word processor like WordPerfect or Microsoft Word.

 TIP **If you create an HTML page in a word processor, don't forget to** use the Save As command to save it as an ASCII text file and name the file with a .HTM or .HTML file name extension.

You also need a Web browser to check on the appearance of your Web page as you create it. And to be honest, you're probably best off testing your pages in Netscape, Internet Explorer, or both when possible. Those are the major players—most of your Web visitors will be using one or the other. If you've got another Web browser that you enjoy using, though, go ahead and test in that one as well.

All Web browsers should have the capability to load local pages from your hard drive, just as they can load HTML pages across the Web. Check the menu of your Web browser (if it's a graphical browser) for a command like File, Open (see Figure 1.7).

Fig. 1.7

In Microsoft Internet Explorer for Windows 95, the File, Open command opens the Open dialog box, which contains a Browse command button to open a file from a drive.

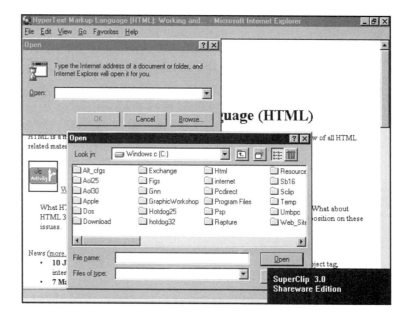

You may have heard of some dedicated HTML editing programs that are designed to make·your work in HTML easier. They do indeed exist, and they can be very useful. Unfortunately, many of them also hide the HTML codes from the designer, so they would be difficult for us to use as we learn how HTML works. After you understand HTML, though, it can be a great benefit to use one of these browsers. Even some other programs, like word processing and desktop publishing applications, have been updated to output HTML codes. I talk about some of them in Chapter 18, "Helpers and Editors for Easier HTML."

Naming your files

After you create your files in a text editor and you're ready to test them in your browser, you first need to save them to your hard drive. The best plan is to create a special directory on your hard drive for your Web site—especially if you're planning on creating more than one page. Then you have a special directory for keeping all your Web files.

All HTML documents should be saved with an extension of .HTM or .HTML, depending on the operating system you use. Only DOS or Windows 3.1 systems should require the three-letter extension. Any other can handle the full .HTML, which is more common on **Web servers** out there.

 Plain English, Please

> A **Web server** is a computer, directly connected to the Internet, that's specially designed to send Web documents to Web browsers that request them. In order to make your documents available to Web users, you need an Internet service provider who's willing to give you storage space on its Web server's hard drive. We talk about finding one in Chapter 17, "My Site Is Ready, What Can I Do Now?"

Structural integrity

The other issue concerns how you're going to save things on your hard drive. For folks creating fairly simple Web sites, it's easy enough to store all your files in one directory. If you've got a whole lot of files to manage, you might want to break things out more, as you can see in Figure 1.8.

Fig. 1.8
Here's a more complicated directory structure in Windows Explorer. It's perfectly okay to break out your Web site by function, as long as you pay careful attention to the file paths you're creating.

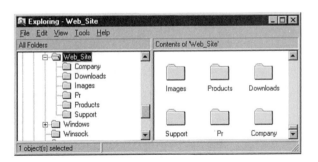

Either way you do it, remember that you need to pay careful attention to the exact names of your directories and sub-directories as we begin to create hyperlinks and add graphic images to our Web pages. You also need to use the exact same directory structure when you send all your files to the actual Web server, so make sure you're not using any long names or weird extensions that your Web server computer won't be able to recognize.

CAUTION **Web browsers are very sensitive to file name extensions, so don't** try to get creative. If you're creating an HTML document, save it with an .HTM or .HTML extension. The same goes for JPEG graphics (.JPG, .JPEG), GIF images (.GIF), and even straight text files (.TXT). I'll be sure to point out the correct extensions throughout the text.

2

In the Beginning: Up Front with Tags, Titles, and Headings

● **In this chapter:**

- ● **A quick game of tag**

- ● **Testing pages in your browser**

- ● **Make a habit of using the *HTML* tag**

- ● **How much can you do with the *HEAD* element anyway?**

- ● **Titles are more than just titles**

Titles and heads might not seem important, but they're actually an integral part of your overall design and organization . . . .

If you read Chapter 1 thoroughly, you're completely versed in the notion of naming and saving your documents. That's pretty thrilling, huh? Now we've got to come up with something that we actually want to save. To do that, we start by taking a look at the HTML commands, or tags, that you use in the pursuit of a Web document.

Once you've gotten the tag thing down, our next step is to look at the most important and basic tags—the tags you include on every Web page you create. Fortunately, at the same time, we create a quick template that will be the basis for all other pages we create in this book. By the time this chapter is over, we'll have created a complete Web page.

Playing tag for fun and profit

You constantly encounter the word "tag" in the HTML world—including in this book. The **tag** is the basic coding unit in the HTML system. Everything in HTML depends on the tags.

 Plain English, Please!

Why call it a **tag**? Remember that HTML is a markup language. That means we're taking a normal text document and marking or tagging certain words or phrases for specific reasons. That's what HTML tags do: They bring attention to certain words in our document so that the user's browser knows to emphasize something, create a hyperlink, or display a graphic. **99**

Tags are enclosed in angle brackets (< and >). For example, the paragraph tag is <P> and the horizontal line tag is <HR>. You can write the tags in either uppercase or lowercase letters (we use uppercase in this book to make it easier to read). Just remember: You need both the opening bracket (<) and the closing bracket (>) to complete the tag. Don't forget to include both. (Normally, Shift+comma gets you the left angle bracket, and Shift+period gets you the right one.)

Your very first HTML code

First, create a folder or directory to store your HTML files, as we discussed in Chapter 1. That'll help you find them as you go along.

Now, in a brand new document in your text editor, type the following:

Hello!<HR>

That's it. Nothing else. Just the word hello, an exclamation point, and HR enclosed in angle brackets (the H and R may be lowercase if you prefer). No carriage return is necessary, but if you want one, go ahead. HTML pays no attention to standard returns.

Next, save the file. Call it FIRST.HTML or FIRST.HTM (DOS and Windows 3.x users must use the three-character .HTM extension). If you're working in a word processor, be sure to select ASCII or text format before saving.

Browsing from home

Now for the fun part. First, load your Web browser. If you have to log on first, do so (some browsers let you work offline). The idea is to load your FIRST.HTML (or FIRST.HTM) file into your browser. This procedure differs from browser to browser, but the point is that we're opening a local file instead of a Web location.

TIP **Memorize, memorize, memorize. This is how you'll preview every** single page your fingers ever tap out in HTML!

In Netscape, for example, choose File, Open File, and then select FIRST.HTML from the directory where you stored it. In Internet Explorer, choose File, Open, and then click the Browse button in the Open dialog box. Other browsers may require different steps.

With FIRST.HTML selected, click OK. If all goes well, you have your first Web page staring at you. All you have is "Hello!" with a long line underneath, but it's a start. Essentially, the rest of this book shows you how to make that first page more attractive. Check out Figure 2.1 for how this looks in my browser.

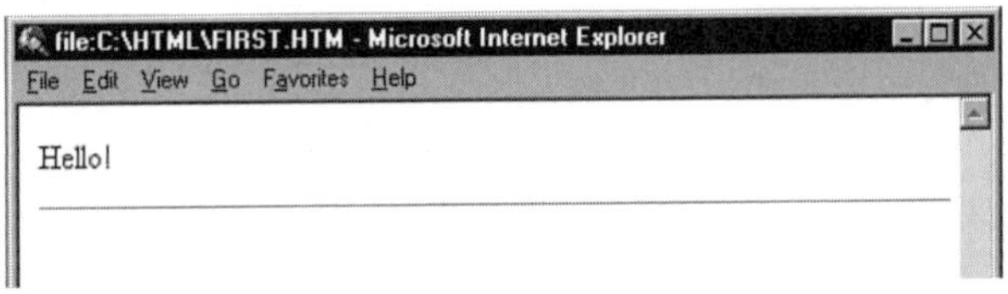

Fig. 2.1
You can use this same process to test every Web page you create.

```
file:C:\HTML\FIRST.HTM - Microsoft Internet Explorer   [_][□][X]
File  Edit  View  Go  Favorites  Help

Hello!
_____
```

Note the following:

- "Hello" needs no coding at all. It's simply a piece of regular text, and browsers display it in whatever font their users have configured for default text. Usually, this is Times New Roman 12 point or something similar, but users can change it.

- The silly looking <HR> tag, which stands for horizontal rule, became a screen-wide line in your browser. The <HR> tag is interpreted by the browser and displayed accordingly. Virtually all browsers know what to do with <HR>.

- You *must* give your HTML document an extension of .HTML or .HTM if you want it displayed properly. If you let your text editor give it an extension of .TXT or .ASC, your browser won't do its job.

Your second HTML code

In Chapter 3, "Entering Text to Your Page," we produce some fairly elaborate HTML code. Right now, just dress up FIRST.HTML a bit to see how things work.

Open FIRST.HTML in your text editor (it's probably already open if you're working straight through this chapter). Now, type <H1> in front of Hello! and type </H1> directly after it (that's the numeral 1 after the H). Leave the <HR> tag as the last element in the line. Your document should look like this:

```
<H1>Hello!</H1><HR>
```

Now save the file again. Make sure it's saved as FIRST.HTML. Reload it into your browser (in many browsers you can just hit the Reload button in the toolbar). You see that "Hello!" is now much bigger and bolder, but apart from that, nothing has changed.

So what happened? With those two small additions, <H1> and </H1>, you transformed "Hello!" from default text to a level-1 heading. Your browser interpreted the <H1></H1> code as a heading and assigned it the font size for level-1 headings. Usually, this is a much larger font than for default text, but again your readers can configure their browsers to display it as they want (see Figure 2.2).

Fig. 2.2
Tags like <H1></H1>
are used throughout
HTML to change the
appearance of text
you type into a Web
document. Now
"Hello!" appears as a
level-1 header in IE.

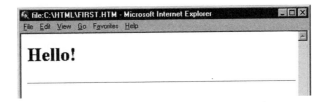

What you just did to this document was easy, but it was one of the most important tasks in HTML coding. You created a container!

Containing your excitement

There are two basic types of tags, which we call **containers** and **empty** tags. As the name implies, containers are designed to hold something—usually text or other HTML commands.

Most of HTML involves placing items inside containers, which have an opening tag and a closing tag. Notice that <HR> has only one tag—it's not a container (it's an empty tag). But the heading tag, in this case <H1>, needs an </H1> on the other side of the item to end the formatting code. The text item "Hello!" is inside this <H1></H1> container, and that tells the browser to make it appear with the level-1 heading font and size.

❝❝ *Plain English, Please*

Why call it an **empty** tag? Because it doesn't act on anything. Empty tags usually perform a very specific task on their own, without focusing on specific text. <HR> creates a horizontal rule, for example, but it doesn't act on any specific text the way that <H1></H1> does. ❞❞

Keep the following points in mind:

- For HTML containers, every opening tag must have a corresponding closing tag. Closing tags are the same as opening tags, except that they have a forward slash (/) in front of them. For example, the opening tag for italics is <I>, and the closing tag is </I>.

- You don't have to put spaces between HTML codes, nor do you have to use carriage returns. Browsers know how to display your text just fine.

They put a carriage return after a heading container (add some text after the heading and before the horizontal rule and see what happens), and another one before the horizontal line. If you want to specify your own spacing, you need to know some further HTML codes. For now, let the browser do its work.

TIP   **In fact, browsers often ignore extra spaces or returns. That can be** a good thing, because it allows you to use returns to make your HTML document easier to read, without affecting how it will look in a browser.

- After you've begun an HTML document, you can keep adding to it and revising it to your heart's content. Just hit the Reload key of your browser and monitor your changes.

With the concept of tags under our belt, lets look specifically at the most common tags in HTML—the document tags. While we're at it, we'll create a template.

Every Web page has the same basic structure

Okay, folks. Here's the first and most basic rule of HTML design. Every page you create must contain the same overall structure, and that structure looks like the following:

```
<HTML>
<HEAD>
<TITLE>The Title of Your Page</TITLE>
</HEAD>
<BODY>The guts of the Web page—text, graphics, links, and so
on.
</BODY>
</HTML>
```

Because this is the structure for any Web page, here's a great little trick. Enter the entire example above, just as shown, in your text editor. When you're finished, save the file as TEMPLATE.HTM or TEMPLATE.HTML. Now, whenever you're ready to create a new page, you can load the template and use your editor's Save As command to create a new page, complete with all the necessary document tags (see Figure 2.3).

Fig. 2.3
Now, whenever I create a new Web page I can start with this simple template.

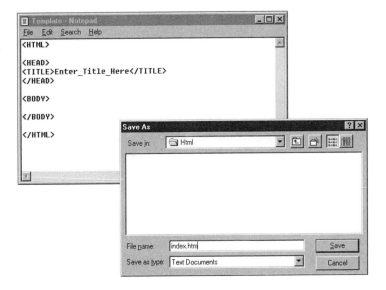

Don't forget the HTML element

The World Wide Web was originally designed as a **platform-independent** technology. Platform independence simply means that Web pages can be read by any browser on any computer system, regardless of what editor was used for their creation.

Q&A How are HTML documents different from other computer documents?

Have you ever changed word processors? Maybe you started out using WordPerfect, but then you bought Word for Windows. The new version of Word could load those WordPerfect documents, but the older WordPerfect couldn't load the new Word documents.

Every document created with a word processor, spreadsheet, and desktop publishing package has a file structure that only the creating program can read. That's why, in the DOS world, they all have different extensions (.DOC, .XLS, and so on). The only way that one program can read a document created with a different program is by using a filter that converts the file.

Web browsers are different. They're all designed for one purpose only: to read documents that contain HTML tags. That's why the Web is so powerful.

The Web browser on your computer can read documents that are stored on any computer. The only requirement is that the documents must be written in HTML and saved as ASCII (sometimes called "universal") text format.

Written properly (that is, using correct HTML tags), Web pages can be moved from server to server or accessed by any regular WWW browser with only slight, often insignificant variations. This saves you innumerable amounts of editing time and increases the availability of your documents. Imagine if we used word processing formats for the Web. You'd have to create and save documents in MS Word, WordPerfect, WordPro, WordPad, and many other formats, and you still wouldn't cover all your users.

The HTML element tags (<HTML></HTML>) contain all other text and tags within the document. The opening tag, <HTML>, is the first thing typed; and the closing tag, </HTML>, is the last, coming at the very end of the document. Most browsers are programmed to ignore any text that appears outside of these two tags.

Getting a *HEAD*

Like people, HTML documents have heads and bodies. Also like people, the body of an HTML document is larger than the head. Of course, the analogy ends right there because the HTML bodies are more significant by a long shot than HTML heads, and that's not supposed to be true with human beings.

As the name implies, the head section of any HTML document precedes the main information (or the body) of the Web page. The tag <HEAD> and closing tag </HEAD> surround the contents of the head section. Text contained between the <HEAD> and </HEAD> tags points to general information about the file and is not displayed as part of the document text itself.

CAUTION   **Although the <HEAD> element and its contents are not displayed as** part of the actual Web page's text, one significant component of the header, the <TITLE>, does appear when the page is accessed.

The <HEAD> element may contain a number of different elements:

- TITLE   Describes the document's name
- ISINDEX   Indicates that the document can be searched

- BASE   Reveals the original URL of the document

- NEXTID   Creates unique document identifiers

- LINK   Displays relationships to other documents

- META   Embeds any additional information

Only the TITLE element is required. The rest are optional and often do not appear in basic HTML constructions. In fact, even complex pages require only the TITLE bar for full World Wide Web functioning. In double fact, all the other ones are really kinda boring.

But it's important to know how all of these function because they can help you produce a richer, more sophisticated Web site. And you want to be prepared if browsers start to demand them.

Your Web page's title

It's as simple as it sounds—the TITLE element names your document, like the title of this book, its chapters, or even the section headers. Every HTML document you create should include a title—and only one title—within the <HEAD> element. Effective use of the <TITLE> and </TITLE> tags results in a descriptive and stimulating sentence that sums up the document content in a concise manner.

 TIP   **The title of any HTML document should label the text screen,** serve as a recording mechanism of documents already viewed, and allow quick document indexing. The title does not, however, assign a file name to a document; this function is performed by the Save As command found in the File menu of your HTML editor.

Figure 2.4 shows the title on the home page for Compaq Computer Corporation (**http://www.compaq.com/**). The <TITLE> of the document is written in HTML as follows:

```
<TITLE>Compaq Online</TITLE>
```

You can see this title in Internet Explorer's title bar (the dark strip at the top of the screen) in Figure 2.4.

Fig. 2.4
Internet HTML codes
(like bold or italics) do
not work because the
<TITLE> is shown in
the browser window's
title bar.

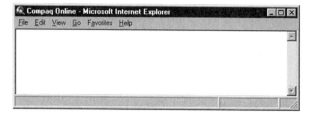

Functional titles

Creating an effective title for your HTML document isn't exactly a technical skill, but it can affect the success of your page on the World Wide Web. You construct an HTML document to send a message to the world, but this solitary message is competing for attention with millions and millions of other pages. The title of your document is one of several elements responsible for attracting an audience and should be given some serious consideration.

On the other hand, the last thing you want to do is take several hours to come up with a good title, especially when the time would be better spent creating effective headers instead. (See Chapter 3 for headers and other useful attractors.)

TIP Your title should be two things: descriptive and functional. It should describe your page's content as closely as possible and should also serve a purpose. If someone decides to add a bookmark or hotlist entry for your page, a properly constructed title will remind him of the exact type of information that your page has to offer—there's nothing more frustrating than a bookmark called "Page 2" or "My Home Page!"

Consider the good and not-so-good titles that you might come across when surfing the Net. Here are some simple suggestions:

- *Avoid generic titles.* If your page is devoted to a study of air and space capabilities for the future, say so. Remember that any page title might be used as a bookmark or entry in a search engine like Infoseek or Lycos.

- *Avoid catchy slogans.* Company names don't always help, either, unless they're very familiar. Remember that your title should indicate the nature of the service or the purpose of the page.

- *No more than 60 characters.* HTML does not limit the length of the TITLE element. However, before you rush off to give your Web pages endlessly descriptive names, keep in mind that the space where the title is displayed (either the viewer's title bar or window label) is limited.

The *<ISINDEX>* tag

If you have a database that you want your readers to be able to search, you need to let them know that searching is possible. This is the function of the <ISINDEX> tag, which prompts your Web browser to display a search box. To make this box work, you have to link it to a searchable item, such as a database, through a **CGI** program.

 Plain English, please!

CGI stands for **Common Gateway Interface**, but nobody calls it that. It's the means by which Web documents collect information from outside the Web. See Chapter 11, "Introduction to CGI," for more on CGIs.

The <ISINDEX> tag begins a chain of communication. When a browser connects to an HTML page containing the <ISINDEX> element in its header, a series of messages are transmitted from page to browser to viewer. First, the <ISINDEX> command informs the browser that the document may be examined using a keyword search. This information prompts the browser to display a search query or string that informs the user that the database can be searched.

 CAUTION <ISINDEX> **does not indicate that you may conduct a search of the** text you are actually reading. Instead, server-side gateway programs designed for full database searches usually send documents containing the <ISINDEX> element to a client. <ISINDEX> automatically inserts a Search box, but it doesn't make the Web site searchable.

The ISINDEX tag is empty (contains no text other than the element name itself), optional, and should be placed in the HEAD portion of any HTML document. An example:

```
<HTML>
<HEAD>
<TITLE>BigCorp's PR Archive</TITLE>
<ISINDEX>
</HEAD>
```

It isn't used as often as it used to be, but you should know about it, just in case you or some sort of a programmer-type working with your site decide it's necessary.

The *<BASE>* tag

Sometimes a document is moved from a location where it has established relationships with surrounding documents and is inserted in a new location. In this new environment, the previously relative addresses are no longer valid. However, if the document is altered to include the <BASE> element and a base address in its <HEAD>, the previously related (linked) documents will once again be found. This element functions to maintain the effectiveness of links and connections throughout the World Wide Web.

 Plain English, please!

> <BASE> tells a Web browser where to find other Web documents in the Web site. It isn't of much use unless you've moved the document to a new directory or machine.

We discuss the <BASE> tag in greater detail after I explain URLs in Chapter 4, "Linking Your Pages." For now, just realize that it goes in the <HEAD> of your document.

What's *NEXTID?*

The <NEXTID> command is not used by humans, WWW browsers, or hypertext servers. Sounds easy so far, right? Instead, <NEXTID> is used by HTML editing programs to label pages with specific identifying numbers. Because we're not using special editing programs, it's not at all interesting to us. But some guy out there in TV Land will call up the Que juggernaut and complain to my boss if I don't at least mention it.

The <NEXTID> command contains a single internal element, N, which gives each page its numeric label. For example, a page with the sequence <NEXTID N=132> is page number 132 to HTML editing programs. The following is an example of what the <HEAD> portion of a document looks like using the <NEXTID> command:

```
<HTML>
<HEAD>
<NEXTID N=132>
<TITLE>title of document</TITLE>
</HEAD>
<BODY>body of document</BODY>
</HTML>
```

TIP In all likelihood, you'll never have to use the <NEXTID> tag. On the other hand, your HTML editor might well add an ID number on its own. Generally speaking, you can safely ignore it.

The *<LINK>* tag

This is probably the easiest of all the optional <HEAD> elements! The <LINK> tag simply displays the relationships your document maintains with other documents on the Net. <LINK> can give directions to related indices and glossaries or to different versions of your current document (graphic and textual drafts). The <LINK> element contains all of the same attributes as the anchor element (discussed in Chapter 4) in HTML construction.

TIP Some Web artists use the <LINK> element to point to preceding or following documents in a series—like a next or previous button. No browsers are yet advanced enough to handle such demands, and <LINK> remains largely unsupported and rarely used throughout HTML invention. Someday, though, browsers might be smart enough to understand this stuff.

Use the following <LINK> format to point to documents related to your page:

```
<HTML>
<HEAD>
<TITLE>title of document</TITLE>
<LINK HREF="file1.htm" TITLE="Title of related document">
</HEAD>
<BODY>body of document</BODY>
</HTML>
```

What's a *META* for?

Put simply, the <META> element takes care of everything else you could ever want to say about your document, including indexing and cataloging information. If present, the <META> option must include the CONTENT attribute as well as either the NAME or HTTP-EQUIV attribute—but never both.

There are a couple of different excuses for using META, each of which is covered in due time throughout the book. Aside from some boring document-related stuff, META can be used to automatically load new Web pages (Chapter 15) or even to help Web search engines like WebCrawler and Yahoo figure out things about your page (Chapter 17).

Next up, the <BODY> of your page. Let's enter some text!

Entering Text and Formatting Your Page

● **In this chapter:**

The main part of a Web page—where you put everything your readers will actually see—is called the body. It can be big or it can be small, but the body had better be right! . . . . ⊳

N o matter what you want to use the World Wide Web for— advertising a business or service, posting weekly results for your softball league games, or publishing the latest family information for relatives in other parts of the world—you'll quickly discover that a Web page is, quite literally, nothing without its body section.

Similar to an artist's canvas, the body of a document displays the results of your creative energies and artistic inspirations. However, keep in mind while painting your "portrait" that HTML is merely a tool for organizing and distributing the information you have already established; what the body contains will always remain a product of your own imagination and labor.

How the body section works

The body section of all WWW documents is defined by the <BODY> element. It has an opening tag, <BODY>, to show where your information starts; and a closing tag, </BODY>, that indicates where the data ends. Inside the body you find text, hyperlinks, headings, graphics, imagemaps, forms, tables, and everything else your users actually see. Figure 3.1 shows how the body tags look in a Web page.

Fig. 3.1
Using the template we created in Chapter 2, you can simply insert your page's text between the body tags.

MONO tags

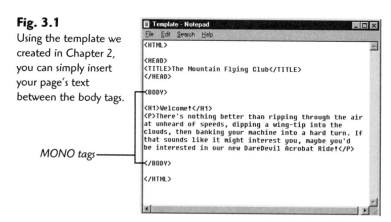

TIP **Although most Web browsers can handle Web pages without the** <BODY> element, you really should use it. As HTML progresses, <BODY> tags will matter a lot more. For instance, you need <BODY> tags to add advanced elements like a background graphic or background sounds to your page. Using the <BODY> tags is a good way to save work later when codes become crucial to your documents.

The HTML code from my personal home page in Listing 3.1 (from **http://members.aol.com/tstauffer/index.html**) shows where the body fits in the overall Web page structure. Notice that it's embedded inside the <HTML> opening and closing tags, which means it's a substructure of <HTML> itself. Almost everything else in your document is contained in the body and thus fits inside the <BODY></BODY> tags.

Listing 3.1

HTML code from my home page

```
<HTML>
<HEAD>
<TITLE>Todd Stauffer on the Web</TITLE>
</HEAD>
<BODY>
<H1>Welcome to my home on the Web!</H1>
…rest of the page
</BODY>
</HTML>
```

Headings help the reader find what's there

Headings are pretty much the first thing HTML authors learn how to write. There are six levels of headings, and browsers generally show a different font size for each level. You can use the varied heading sizes to create a hierarchy of information. The idea is to keep information of equal importance inside headings of equal size, to give larger headings to larger categories, and so on. Figure 3.2 demonstrates this idea.

Fig. 3.2
Headings work like
levels in an outline,
giving you a simple
reference to the
structure of your
information.

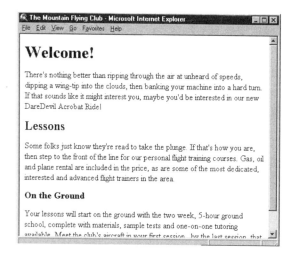

The current HTML standards (2.0 and the ever advancing 3.2) support six
levels of headings: H1, H2, H3, H4, H5, and H6. Each browser has a different definition for each heading level, so that a heading of H1 will look very
different from an H4 heading (see Figure 3.3 to see how the various levels are
displayed). But keep in mind that users of some Web browsers can display
headings in whatever font they want, so it might be wise not to spend an
inordinate amount of time on heading creation.

Fig. 3.3
Here's how Internet
Explorer formats the
various headings;
other browsers vary
in how they display
them.

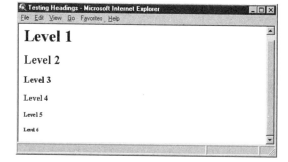

Inserting breaks in your text

Most people don't like reading dense paragraphs on a computer screen.
Instead, they like their on-screen information presented in bite-size chunks
along with headings, graphics, separation lines, and so forth. One method of
separating and chunking information is through paragraph breaks and line

breaks. The <P> and <BR> elements enable you to add white space in your documents to keep information separated.

When you insert a paragraph break <P>, you're telling the browser to end the current paragraph and insert a double space before proceeding with the next cluster of information. Insert a line break <BR>, and you're telling the browser to end the current text here—wherever the line happens to be at the time—and continue the information on the very next line.

 TIP **If you're trying to replicate the function of the Return or Enter** key of your word processor, use <BR> rather than <P>. It gives you more direct control over the spacing on your page.

Using paragraph breaks

The <P> tag separates text into paragraphs for easy reading and visual appeal. While HTML 3.2 defines the paragraph tag as a container—requiring both <P> and </P> tags—browsers still recognize the older HTML standard, which requires only the opening <P> tag. But it's a good idea to use the container format: first because it's becoming essential, and second because it offers some strong formatting benefits. For instance:

```
Thank you for stopping by.<P>
```

is the more common use of <P>, but not the most correct. It's better to use <P></P> as a container, as in:

```
<P>Thank you for stopping by.</P>
```

Figure 3.4 shows how the paragraph tag is used in Web pages.

Fig. 3.4

Enclose text and other elements and objects (such as graphics) between the <P> and </P> tags to group them into a single paragraph.

```
03fig04 - Notepad
File  Edit  Search  Help
<HTML>

<HEAD>
<TITLE>The Mountain Flying Club</TITLE>
</HEAD>

<BODY>

<H1>Welcome!</H1>
<P>There's nothing <B>better</B> than ripping through the air
at unheard of speeds, dipping a wing-tip into the
clouds, then <EM>banking your machine</EM> into a hard turn. If
that sounds like it might interest you, maybe you'd
be interested in our new DareDevil Acrobat Ride!</P>

<P>Some folks just know they're read to take the plunge.
If that's how <EM>you</EM> are, then step to the front of the
line for our personal flight training courses. Gas,
oil and plane rental are included in the price, as are
some of the most dedicated, interested and advanced
```

Quick line breaks

Sometimes you want your text flow to end at a certain point and begin on a new line without separating spaces. The HTML tag that creates these textual breaks is <BR>. This tag is not a container—wherever you put it in a document, it tells the browser to interrupt the content and place the information that follows at the beginning of the next line.

The effect is the same as single spacing (as opposed to paragraph tags, which double space after the container). You can place as many <BR> tags as you want consecutively, and you get as many new lines. This is the surest way of controlling the number of "carriage returns" you put in your document.

The great spacing debate

Different Web authors add space in their document different ways, if only because various browser interpretations have made things a bit confusing. Netscape Navigator, for instance, adds a blank line anytime you enter a <BR> in your document, even if you enter two or more in a row. That's not how it's supposed to work, though. The HTML standard technically only recognizes one <BR> at a time—and many browsers ignore extra <BR> tags.

You might also be tempted to insert consecutive paragraph containers to add space, but that won't work in all browsers.

So what will work in all browsers?

Try using an empty preformatted container with two blank spaces between the <PRE> and </PRE> tags (covered later in this chapter). Most Web browsers read this as acceptable content and generate a blank line. The HTML for creating white space using the preformatted containers is shown below.

```
<BODY>
...insert body of document and end paragraph...
<PRE>

</PRE>
...continue body of document with new paragraph...
</BODY>
```

Figure 3.5 shows how line breaks can be used to create a text listing.

Fig. 3.5
These text effects all use forced line breaks to make the text wrap automatically to the next line for an effect.

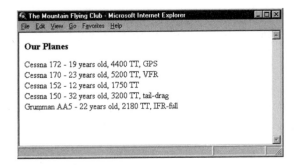

Listing 3.2 shows you how this list was accomplished.

Listing 3.2

Creating lists with the <BR> element

```
<BODY>
<H3>Our Planes</H3>
Cessna 172 - 19 years old, 4400 TT, GPS<BR>
Cessna 170 - 23 years old, 5200 TT, VFR<BR>
Cessna 152 - 12 years old, 1750 TT<BR>
Cessna 150 - 32 years old, 3200 TT, tail-drag<BR>
Grumman AA5 - 22 years old, 2180 TT, IFR-full<BR>
</BODY>
```

Figure 3.6, on the other hand, shows you what happens when the <BR> tag goes slightly wrong. Sometimes, even if you're trying to create an attractive page, you should just let the user's browser do the line breaking. Put <BR> tags on longer sentences and you're bound to hit some snags.

CAUTION **Browsers follow whatever HTML orders you give them—even if the** on-screen output is less than pretty. A line break can look ugly if the text has wrapped because the browser's window is too narrow for your intended line length. The shorter you keep lines of text between <BR> tags (say, 60–80 characters maximum), the better your chances of exact spacing and visual replication in the browser window.

Fig. 3.6
Browsers like Internet
Explorer break the
line at the <BR> tag
regardless of where
the break takes place
on-screen.

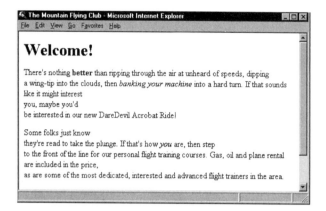

Fig. 3.6
Browsers like Internet
Explorer break the
line at the <BR> tag
regardless of where
the break takes place
on-screen.

More control with preformatted text

If you want to put information on the Web and you already have it in a non-HTML document, you don't have to spend your time retyping. Instead, you can use HTML's preformatted text container tags <PRE></PRE>. This container lets you keep the original formatting of the text, and even regular keyboard-entered returns as line breaks, without the <BR> tag. Other containers, like <BLOCKQUOTE>, give you extra control over the appearance on your text.

The *PRE* element

The preformatted text element, represented by the tags <PRE> and </PRE>, supports blank spaces and lets other tags or links (like the bold and strong text styles and anchors) modify the text. The one catch is that WWW browsers normally render preformatted text in a plain, monospaced font, such as the unattractive Courier (although some browsers let you change this).

Consider the case of poetry. It's not easy to do the following without the <PRE> tags and have it still look like Figure 3.7:

```
<PRE>
Oh Beautiful, for spacious skies,
    For amber waves of grain.
For purple mountains, majesty,
    Above the fruited plains!
</PRE>
```

Fig. 3.7
Using the <PRE>
</PRE> container,
poetry is perfection.

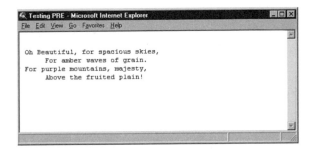

Preformatted text is excellent for items like code examples that you want to indent and format appropriately. <PRE></PRE> tags also enable you to align text by padding it with spaces for table creation. However, because those tables appear in monospaced font, you may prefer to spend the extra time constructing standard HTML table blocks.

The *BLOCKQUOTE* element

Want to indent stuff? The <BLOCKQUOTE> container will handle it. Unlike <PRE>, <BLOCKQUOTE> does not keep any line feeds already present in your text nor does it allow consecutive blank spaces. What it does provide is a uniform indented format.

It's okay to throw other HTML tags in the <BLOCKQUOTE> container, too, such as text styles and line breaks. Figure 3.8 shows how you use <BLOCKQUOTE> in a Web page, and Figure 3.9 shows how Internet Explorer displays this information.

Fig. 3.8
The format your text
already has inside the
<BLOCKQUOTE>
container is ignored
unless you add the
same formatting using
HTML commands.

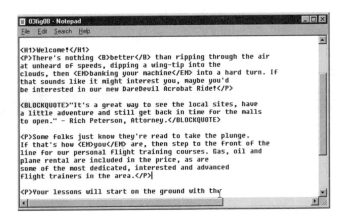

Fig. 3.9
<BLOCKQUOTE> text
uses the regular body
text font (the same
style featured through-
out the rest of your
HTML document) as
well as an even
indentation from the
left-hand margin.

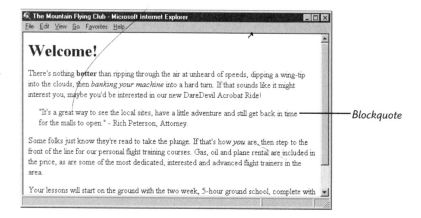

Getting direct control over your text

If you've used any word processor of merit, you'll instantly recognize HTML's physical style elements. Physical styles emphasize your Web page's plain text with boldface, italic, and underlining. These container tags are absolute, which means that every Web browser displays the physical style elements in exactly the same manner.

Although some browsers may have limitations on how they can display logical text styles—such as Lynx, which is a text-only browser—there is no other way for a browser to interpret a physical style. Bold is bold. Italic is italic. Logical styles (covered in the next section) may be flexible, but physical ones are not. Table 3.1 gives you some descriptions of physical styles. Figure 3.10 shows how physical style tags are used, and Figure 3.11 shows how Web browsers display them.

Table 3.1 Physical styles and their meanings

Style	Meaning
<B>	Boldface (where possible)
<I>	Italics
<TT>	Monospaced typewriter font
<U>	Underlined

HTML 3.2 proposed additions

Style	Meaning
<SUB>	Subscript
<SUP>	Superscript

Fig. 3.10
Physical style containers affect all the text between their opening and closing tags.

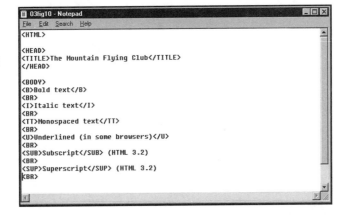

Fig. 3.11
Browsers do not vary in how they display physical styles, and physical styles can be combined for additional effects.

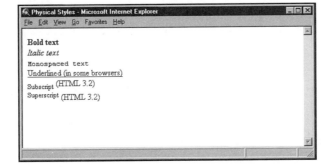

What's so logical about logical styles?

Logical style tags indicate how the Web editor uses the applied text, not how Web browsers should display the document. Just as paragraph and heading tags indicate how a passage is to be used within the document, logical styles allow the browser to decide how to format the text to best fit the rest of your Web page.

Each logical character style has an opening and a closing tag that form a container for the inserted text and restrict the logical application to the contained data. Table 3.2 shows descriptions of logical styles.

Table 3.2 Logical styles and their meanings

Style	Description
<EM>	Emphasized text
<STRONG>	Strongly emphasized text
<CITE>	Text in a citation
<CODE>	Text representing an HTML element sample
<DFN>	Text in a definition
<SAMP>	Text in an output sample, similar to code
<KBD>	Text representing a keyboard key
<VAR>	Text defining a variable or value
<STRIKE>	Struck out text (proposed HTML 2.0)

Q&A *What is the difference between EM and Italics?*

The creation of logical elements such as <EM> and <STRONG> may seem repetitive because the physical styles italic and boldface produce similar effects. The difference between the two lies in their nesting capabilities. Logical highlighting elements may be nested inside of one another, but this is often insensible given the fairly specific meanings assigned to each. Nesting of logical elements is also confused by some browsers that produce inappropriate renditions. Physical styles, on the other hand, can be nested appropriately, and formatting text to appear as underlined, bold, or italic is not an unreasonable request.

One of the interesting points about logical styles is that no matter how you use them, your Web users can view them more or less the way they want. All they have to do is configure their browsers to display each logical style in a particular way.

For instance, if someone likes emphasized text to be in a 24 point Times Roman font, all of the text in <EM> containers will be displayed as 24 point Times Roman regardless of what the rest of the Web page looks like. And the user knows that every Web page that uses logical styles will conform to his own preferences. Figure 3.12 shows how logical styles are written, and Figure 3.13 show Internet Explorer's default interpretation of them.

Fig. 3.12
Unlike physical styles, logical styles can't be used in combinations.

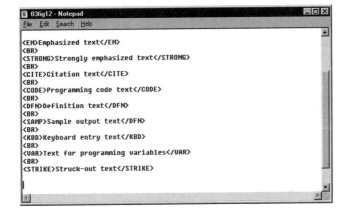

Fig. 3.13
So how do logical styles show up? However the browser wants them to.

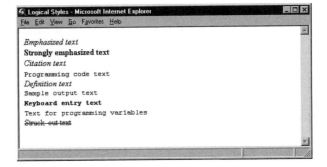

Beyond the basics: Font size

Now part of the HTML 3.2 proposals, the <FONT> container gives you control over how large or small text looks on-screen and what color it will be. For the SIZE attribute, the value is either an actual text size (one through seven) or relative to the normal size of the body text (from +4 down to -4). Here's what it looks like:

```
<FONT SIZE=value>
```

For example, the following creates a "drop-cap" effect:

```
<FONT SIZE=7>W<FONT SIZE=3>elcome!<BR>
```

To change the entire document's basic font size, use the HTML 3.2 empty tag `<BASEFONT SIZE=value>`. Again, the value can range from one through seven (the standard browser text size is three).

Figure 3.14 shows a document using different text effects. Remember, these are only visible for readers using HTML 3.2 and Netscape-compatible browsers like Internet Explorer.

Fig. 3.14
Don't get too elaborate with your text. A single effect at the appropriate time will have much more impact than a Web page loaded with all sorts of text effects (which only shows that you lack a critical eye).

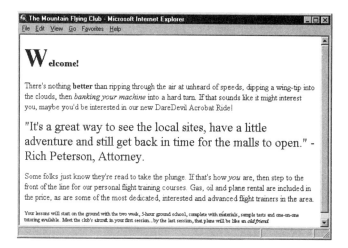

Horizontal lines break up the page

There really isn't much to say about horizontal lines except that they're popular. The `<HR>` tag places a shadowed line across the width of the Web browser's window. If the reader changes the size of the window, the line resizes to match. The `<HR>` tag is an empty tag and does not require a closing element for functioning. Horizontal rules insert a paragraph break before and after the line (see Figure 3.15).

Fig. 3.15
Use horizontal rules to break up text and keep from overwhelming your readers with endless paragraphs of info.

Beyond the basics: HTML 3.2 line attributes

The HTML 3.2 specification provides additional functions for horizontal rules. These give you control over the weight of the line, its length, and the location of the hard rule within the browser's window. You can also drop the "etched" look of the line in favor of a solid black rule. Table 3.3 lists the Netscape parameters and what they do.

Table 3.3   HTML 3.2 extensions to *<HR>*

Extension	Description
SIZE	Sets thickness of horizontal line
WIDTH	Sets width as a measure of pixels or percentage of viewer window's width
ALIGN	Allows line to be justified left, center, or right within the viewer window
NOSHADE	Changes appearance of horizontal line to be solid black with no "etched" effect

Figure 3.16 shows how you can use these extensions to the <HR> element in your Web pages.

Fig. 3.16

If a browser does not recognize the HTML 3.2 extensions, it ignores them

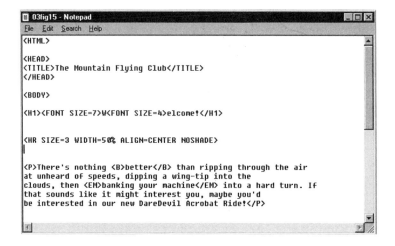

Figure 3.17 shows how Internet Explorer displays the extensions.

Fig. 3.17

Controlling the appearance of your lines adds a creative touch to Web pages.

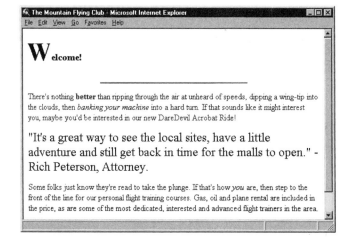

Linking Your Pages to Other Internet Services

● **In this chapter:**

- Dissect the URL— the Internet's ZIP code system

- Create hypertext links and anchors

- Create links within Web pages

- How do I use menus in Windows?

- Link other Internet services into a page

The Web is based on the concept of hypertext, and virtually all Web documents contain hyperlinks to other Web documents. It's the hyperlinks that make the Web so easy to use · · · · ·

Hyperlinks are the basis of the World Wide Web. They should also be the core of your Web pages. By clicking these links, your readers can move within your own web or transport instantly to any other part of the Web. In fact, they can go to just about any part of the Internet itself, even to those resources that aren't part of the Web. Hyperlinks make the "world wide" part of the Web possible, and they're what most Web users are seeking from your pages.

Before you learn about hyperlinks, though, you need to learn about URLs.

Local links versus distant links

Confused over this whole local and distance thing? Let's look into this a bit.

When I say a resource is "local," I'm trying to suggest that it's in the same place as the current Web document. On my home page, for instance, I've created some local links to graphics that are part of my Web site. In this case, local means those resources are on the same server computer as my home page.

A distant link, then, would be a link to a page, graphic, or multimedia file that is somewhere else on the Internet. On my page, again, I have links to Que's site, which is presumably located somewhere in Indiana, near or at headquarters. All I need is an URL, and I can create a link that sends my users off to Que's Web presence.

Now here's where the confusion comes in. A file on your hard drive—whether a Web page or a graphic—is only local if your hard drive happens to be part of a Web server.

For most of us who dial up Internet providers, our hard drives aren't part of a Web server. (In fact, that'd be a security risk, especially if you don't want people reading your Quicken files.)

Instead, we have to upload all the files we want as a part of our Web sites to our Web server. That includes graphics, Web documents, and multimedia files. When they're on the Web server's hard drive, they're ready to be referenced as local files.

Of course, you can have a test site on your hard drive—in which case, all related files should be on your PC's hard drive, too. But when you're ready to publishing on the Internet, you'll have to send everything up to your Web server.

Bottom line: Your Web pages, once on the Internet, can't access your hard drive at home or work, unless your system administrator tells you otherwise.

The Uniform Resource Locator (and what that means)

Every hyperlink contains a **Uniform Resource Locator**, or **URL**. The URL is the address of the Web page. It's the thing that appears in the Location or URL box near the top of your browser. It's also the thing that shows up (with most browsers) at the bottom of the screen when you move the cursor over a hyperlink.

The URL consists of two major items: the protocol and the destination (although they have all kinds of other names).

The protocol tells you what kind of Internet resource you're dealing with. The most common protocol on the Web is http://, which retrieves HTML documents from the Web. Others include gopher://, ftp://, and telnet://.

The destination can be a file name, a directory name, or a computer name. An URL such as **http://members.aol.com/tstauffer/index.html** tells you exactly where the HTML document is located and what its file name is. If the URL is **ftp://ftp.netscape.com/**, the URL is telling the browser to log in to the FTP site on the machine named netscape.com.

 TIP **Fortunately, you don't have to type many URLs. But sometimes,** when you can't figure out how to click your way to a site, you'll want to anyway. And typing them is a great way of experimenting. If you want to see if your favorite company has a Web site, for instance, try typing http:// www.*companyname*.com/ in the Location box (but substitute the company's name for *companyname*).

Now that you know how URLs are formed, it's time to learn how they're used.

Putting hyperlinks to use

On the Web, you see some text that's highlighted, underlined, or in a different color—that text is probably a hyperlink. You'll know it is for sure if your cursor changes shape when you move it over the text. This means that the text is clickable, and if you click it you'll probably be rewarded with a new page.

How does the computer know what to send next? The answer is in the URL. You may have a link on a page that says, "Click me to get the winning lottery numbers," and as long as the URL associated with the hyperlink is correct, your browser will retrieve the document with those winning numbers. The URL tells the browser what protocol to use and where on the Net to find the file to retrieve.

Web page links

Most hypertext links by themselves are part of what's known as an **anchor element**. This anchor, `<A HREF></A>`, surrounds the text that describes what the link points to. The URL itself must be in quotes, and it must immediately follow the definition of the anchor.

A link in HTML takes the following format:

```
<A HREF="URL">put your link text here</A>
```

So, if you want to link the text "Prices for aircraft rental" with the HTML document called RENTAL.HTML that resides in the hanger on the www.myserver.com machine, the HTML code would look like this:

```
<A HREF="http://www.myserver.com/hanger/rental.html">Prices
for aircraft rental</A>
```

 CAUTION **It's a good idea to make sure that your link or anchor includes a** text string explaining where the link takes the reader. Otherwise, you'll have what is known as a hidden link. These can be fun, but they are not generally what you want.

You may be wondering about linking to Web pages that are on the same machine or about linking to other parts of the present page. These are both common occurrences. In most cases, you'll be building a series of pages that make up a "site" and you'll want to store them all on the same server. But most important, you want to link the pages to one another. If you are doing this, you don't have to include the machine name in the URL. For instance, if the file MOREINFO.HTML is in the same directory and on the same machine as the page containing the following HTML code, the URL shown will work fine:

```
<A HREF="moreinfo.html">Get More Information</A>
```

TIP Try to make your link descriptive, too. Links that say things such as "Click here" or "Follow this link" don't give the user enough information about what he is getting into.

Linking within documents

If you want to include a link that takes the user to a different part of the page that he is already on, use a # and an anchor name. Your HTML will look something like this:

```
<A HREF="#phone">Phone Number Listing</A>
```

Clicking this HTML would cause the page to scroll in the browser until the part of the page that has the target name "phone" is showing on the screen. This means that something has to be targeted; the following HTML shows how this is done:

```
<A NAME="phone">You can contact any of our staff at the
following numbers:</A>
```

This target anchoring or URL fragment identification can be used for linking to specific places on other pages as well. If you have a link to a page that is very extensive, but your users will only be interested in a specific part of that page, you can use a target anchor so they will automatically go to that part of the page (see Figure 4.1).

Fig. 4.1
Anchor names and target links are a common way to move around on a large page of definitions or similar items.

Target links

Targeted section

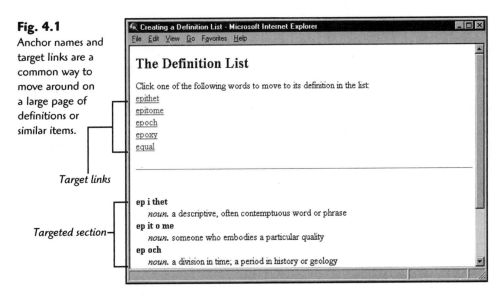

However, if the page is someone else's, you'll have to hope that that someone will be willing to embed the target name where you need it.

Now that you've read about how URLs and hyperlinks are formed, you should try building a few yourself. When you've mastered it, keep reading, and you'll learn how to link other Internet resources into your Web page.

Link to other Internet services

URLs are so flexible that you can use them to create links to practically anything on the Net. You can create links to e-mail, FTP, Gopher, Usenet news, Telnet, and the search engine WAIS. This makes it possible for Web pages to put related information together. In other words, your readers no longer have to fire up individual Internet programs to get to the information you want them to see.

Partially for this reason, in fact, the Web browser has become the single most important Internet tool. From your browser, you can do just about everything else you can do on the Net. This allows Internet users the simplicity of accessing information using just one piece of software. Figure 4.2, taken from **http://www.yahoo.com/Business_and_Economy/Companies/Computers/ Software/Databases/WAIS__Inc_/**, demonstrates how browsers display URLs of several different types.

Fig. 4.2
The arrow is pointing to a link that, at the bottom of the screen, reads wais://wais@wais.com, a wide area information server (WAIS).

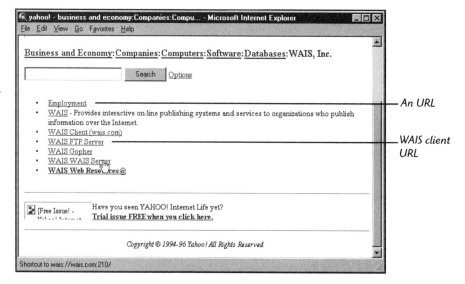

As an example of how this works with other Internet services, here's the HTML code for the list shown in Figure 4.2.

```
<HR>
<A HREF="http://www.wais.com/newhomepages/
jobs.html">Employment</A><BR>
<A HREF="http://www.wais.com/">WAIS</A> - WAIS, Inc. provides
interactive on-line publishing systems and services to orga-
nizations who publish information over the Internet. Our
three main goals are: to develop the Internet as a viable
means for distributing information electronically, improve
the nature and quality of information available over net-
works, and offer better methods to access that
information.<BR>
<A HREF="telnet://wais@wais.com/">WAIS Client (wais.com)
</A><BR>
<A HREF="ftp://ftp.wais.com/pub">WAIS FTP Server</A><BR>
<A HREF="gopher://gopher.wais.com/">WAIS Gopher</A><BR>
<A HREF="wais://wais.com:210/">WAIS WAIS Server</A><BR>
<A HREF="/Computers_and_Internet/Internet/World_Wide_Web/
Databases_and_Searching/WAIS/"><B>WAIS Web Resources@</B></A>
<I>(25)</I><BR>
<HR>
```

Each of the items begins with an anchor <A HREF>. The first item is a standard link to a Web document, as signified by the http:// protocol designation. Below that, in order, are links to Telnet, FTP, Gopher, and WAIS resources. In each case, http:// is replaced by the protocol and address for that resource.

CAUTION **Links to other Internet tools are great things, but be careful when** using them. Your readers must have their Web browsers configured properly to make use of some of them. Many browsers need a separate Telnet program, for example. Most browsers do FTP and Gopher on their own, but only a few handle Usenet newsgroups. Browsers can be configured to launch external programs, but don't assume your readers have done this. Make it very clear in pages that link to non-Web tools that they're doing so.

One click e-mail

E-mail is, without a doubt, the most widely used tool on the Net. E-mail lets two or more people send electronic letters to each other and talk about anything they want. When designing a Web page, many authors like to include a link to their e-mail address. This lets people who are reading your page send comments to you about it. If you have a lot of information on your page that comes from different sources, put links to them, too.

Putting an e-mail link in an HTML document is pretty easy. All you need is a valid e-mail address, which is made up of four parts: the username, the @ symbol, the machine name, and the domain name. The username is the name you typed when you first logged on to the computer. The machine name is the name of the computer on which your account resides. The domain name indicates the company, school, or organization that gives you access to the Net. (Table 4.1 gives a short list of the most common domains available.)

Table 4.1   Some common domains

Domain	When Is It Used?	An Example
com	Companies that are trying to make money	General Motors (gm.com)
edu	High schools, colleges, and universities	University of Southern California (usc.edu)
gov	Government or government–related entities	The White House (whitehouse.gov)
org	Special (usually nonprofit) organizations	X Consortium (x.org)
net	Internet service provider	Inforamp (inforamp.net)
xx	Countries (xx can be any 2 letters)	ca (Canada)au (Australia)fr (France etc.)

Here's an example of a valid e-mail address. It happens to be mine:

tstauffer@aol.com

My username is tstauffer and the domain name is aol.com.

After you have a valid e-mail address, you just put mailto: in front of it. An example of an e-mail link is as follows:

```
<A HREF="mailto:tstauffer@aol.com">Send me mail!</A>.
```

Figure 4.3 shows an example of a mailto: link. Many authors like to "sign" their home page by putting an e-mail link at the bottom.

Fig. 4.3
When a user clicks an
e-mail link on your
home page, he'll be
able to write messages
with his browser.

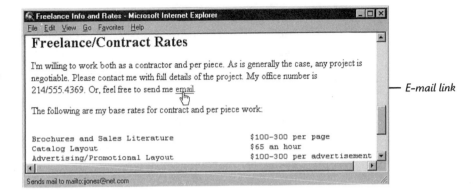

— E-mail link

Creating a link to an FTP site

FTP (File Transfer Protocol) is mostly used to copy files between computers. Users of FTP have to log on to remote computers, often as guests, and
get whatever files they want. Most guest accounts use the userid of "anonymous," and the password is often the guest's e-mail address.

The only thing you need to put in a link to an FTP site is the name of the site:
type ftp://site/ between the quotes for an anchor (see Figure 4.4). So if a valid
FTP site is **ftp.microsoft.com**, the link would look like the following:

```
<A HREF="ftp://ftp.microsoft.com/">MIcrosoft's FTP Site</A>
```

Fig. 4.4
In most browsers, a list
of hyperlinks to files
results from an FTP
URL. Just click to
download the file.

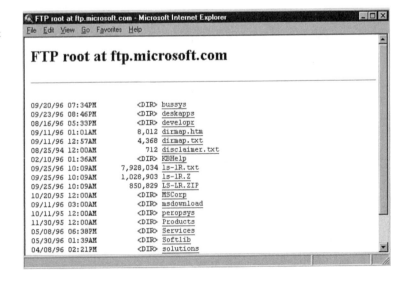

TIP   **If you're building a Web site for a company that has a lot of files** to make available, it's a good idea to put the files on an FTP server, and then just include a link to that server on your Web page. This prevents your Web page from becoming cluttered with download links.

 Plain English, please!

Internet users throw around the word **anonymous**, and it's hard to spend more than an hour surfing the Net without coming across it. When you log on to an anonymous FTP site, type anonymous as the userid (logon name) and your e-mail address as the password.

Users can type in any e-mail address, but many servers only accept the valid address from which the FTP request is coming. The reason for creating anonymous logon capabilities is so people who want to download public files don't have to wait to be assigned a userid and password. It's basically the same thing as having a guest logon.

If you're inviting your readers to download a particular file from your site, you should specify the path for them. That is, put in the exact combination of directories to get to the file directly. This keeps users from trying to go through weird (and sometimes unknown) directories.

For example, let's say you have a program (PROGRAM.EXE) in your home directory (/users/myself/) that you want people to access. A link to it might look something like the following:

```
<A HREF="ftp://ftp.mycom.com/users/myself/program.exe">My
program</A>.
```

This tells the Web browser to connect with FTP, go directly to the correct directory, and immediately begin downloading the file.

Gopher servers

Before the Web came into existence, one of the most popular ways of storing and accessing information was through Gopher sites. **Gopher** is basically a collection of text-based menus that store information in a hierarchical format (see Figure 4.5). These same menus can also refer to other Gopher "holes" on other computers throughout the Net.

Gopher is very similar to the Web except that it doesn't have any built-in multimedia capabilities, such as graphics or sound. You can incorporate a link to a Gopher site on your Web page by simply adding an anchor around the computer's address, and putting gopher:// in front of it. So a Gopher link would look like the following:

```
<A HREF="gopher://marvel.loc.gov">The Library of Congress</
A>.
```

Fig. 4.5
Browsers jazz up an otherwise plain-text Gopher interface and clearly distinguish menus from files for Internet users.

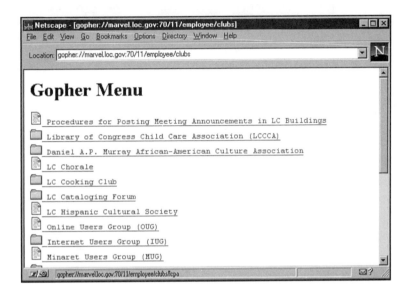

Link to newsgroups

A very popular activity for people who access the Net is reading and contributing to Usenet news. **Usenet** news is just a large collection of groups in which people talk about certain topics. You can think of Usenet as a high school or university and the newsgroups themselves as clubs that you can join.

The topics that are discussed usually relate to the name of the newsgroup, although unrelated flame wars are not uncommon. You may want to point people to a newsgroup because your home page relates specifically to what goes on in that group. Or, if you think that the users might have more questions than you can answer, you can include a link to a related newsgroup in the hope of decreasing the amount of e-mail you receive.

Whatever the case, putting in a link to a Usenet newsgroup is different from most other hypertext tags (see Figure 4.6). To put in a link to a newsgroup, simply enter news: followed by the newsgroup name in the anchor. A typical newsgroup link would look like the following:

```
<A HREF="news:alt.tv.mad-about-you">Check out the Mad About
You newsgroup!</A>.
```

Fig. 4.6
The Mad About You newsgroup pops up in Netscape when you click the example Usenet link.

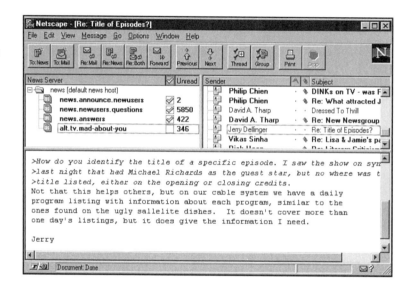

Log on to remote computers with Telnet

Sometimes you'll want the user to be able to directly access other computers, which is what the **Telnet** link is for. The Telnet link actually establishes a connection with another computer and asks the user for a logon name and password.

The syntax for a Telnet link is pretty straightforward: you just type telnet:// followed by the remote computer's address. A typical Telnet link would look something like the following:

```
<A HREF="telnet://mycomputer.com/">Log on to my computer!
</A>.
```

Q&A **What's the difference between Telnet and Web links? Why don't I just use a regular http link to get the user to the other computer?**

Telnet is quite different from Web links in that it actually turns the user's computer into a simple terminal and allows the user to log on and run software on the remote machine. The user is no longer really using his own system when he participates in a Telnet session. Telnet sessions are great for connecting your users to remote libraries and allowing them to browse through the libraries' online catalogs, for instance.

TIP **You can tell users what logon name to use for guest accounts. All** you have to do is specify the logon name they should use followed by the @ sign before the machine name. So, if you want a person to access your computer with the logon name of "guest," the HTML code would be:

```
<A HREF="telnet://guest@mycomputer.com/">Log on to my sys-
tem</A>
```

When the browser sees this, it notifies the user of the correct logon name.

Beyond the basics: the <BASE> tag

Now that you've seen how to create hyperlinks, we're about to make things a whole lot easier . . . at least, in some cases. How? By showing you how to use the <BASE> tag for **relative URLs**.

 Plain English, Please!

We've actually already dealt with **relative URLs**—they're the URLs that don't include an Internet address, like HREF="index.html". Early in this chapter, I mentioned that you can use a relative URL if the file you're linking to is in the same directory as the document that will include the link. <BASE> enables us to take that one step further. **99**

Base is added to the <HEAD> of your document, like this:

```
<HEAD>
<BASE HREF="http://www.mycom.com/mydir/">
</HEAD>
```

If included in the <HEAD>, the <BASE> element contains only the HREF attribute that holds the base URL of the document. The base URL provides the browser with a slightly different reference for relative URLs. It also allows you to avoid using complete URLs, so that the Web site can easily be moved if necessary.

Now, if the above <BASE> example were part of our Web document, a relative URL in that document:

```
<A HREF="products.html">Our Product Catalog</a>
```

would actually reference the URL http://www.mycom.com/mydir/ products.html in order to find the new document. Add the base URL and the relative URL together and you have the complete link.

 Q&A   ***What happens if my page doesn't have a <BASE> URL statement?***

If you decide not to include the <BASE> element in your HTML documents, browsers assume that the base URL is the same as the URL that was used to access the page.

 CAUTION   **Although the BASE command is effective for moving pages, be** aware that many browsers, such as MacWeb and Lynx, do not recognize the command and use the default exclusively.

5

Adding Graphics to Your Page

● In this chapter:

A picture's worth a thousand words? Then stop all that typing! . . . .

Back in the old days (like two years ago), graphics and the Internet just didn't get along. The Net was text, text, and more text. To see a graphic you had to know all about file transfers, download protocols, and image viewing software. The Net was as graphically rich as your phone book's white pages.

Now the Web is **graphics**. More and more Web pages rely primarily, or even exclusively, on attractive, colorful graphics to the extent that many pages have nothing at all to offer users with non-graphics browsers. Turning off your browser's graphics option these days is a little like watching TV with only the sound on: you might get by, but you'll hardly be impressed.

 Plain English, please!

> **Graphics** are pictures. They can be drawings, photographs, or computer paintings. They can even be pictures of text. In computer talk, graphics are files of a specific kind. They're binary files (made up of ones and zeros) as opposed to text or ASCII files. This means that your favorite text editor won't be able to read them properly, and you'll need a graphics viewing program instead. The best-known graphics types are GIF, JPEG, TIFF, PCX, and BMP. There are several others as well. **"**

You can create Web pages without graphics. They'll work, and some people will thank you. Then again, when was the last time you saw a Calvin Klein ad without graphics? Or a billboard? Or a top-flight magazine? Or a tapestry? Even the staid old New York Times has beefed up its graphics—perhaps the publisher realizes that even the steadiest reputation in the world won't keep readers for long. For better or for worse, we live in an age of images, and if you hope to attract Internauts to your Web site, you'd better add graphics to your arsenal of Web skills.

Adding graphics

You don't see many professional documents without graphics. There's a reason for this: Designed properly, a picture really can be worth a thousand words. Through television and magazines, we've come to expect graphical presentation of information. Heck, you might have noticed that even this book has a graphic image every once in a while. Your Web readers will expect this as well.

TIP **Nearly all graphics on the Web are either in GIF or JPEG format. If** you need help understanding these formats, check out Chapter 7, "Making Graphics, Text, and Color Work Together."

Graphics help your Web pages

Here are a few of the enhancements your graphics will provide:

- They break text into digestible "chunks," making the page easier to read.

- They separate content so that the reader knows when a new subject has been started (or when a transition has been made).

- They provide content that is not available via text, such as a picture of your pet or your latest watercolor masterpiece.

- They add color, humor, and excitement to the medium.

- They demonstrate the author's creativity.

CAUTION **Keep in mind, at all times, that these are enhancements for your** reader, not for you as designer (even the last point). As with everything else, only the customer matters. Poorly designed graphical Web pages are almost always the result of the author not considering the reader's point of view—and wasting their time.

Now it's time to move on to the production of graphics in HTML. By the end of this chapter, you'll be well on your way to producing your own images—and very effectively, as well.

The *IMG* element lets you insert graphics files

Let's start with a picture. Figure 5.1 shows a graphic added with the IMG (image) element of HTML. In this case, it's an **inline** image.

Fig. 5.1
A simple HTML
command allows you
to include images on
your pages.

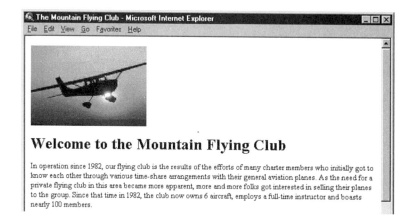

When you want to insert a graphic file on a Web page, you actually do so with an URL, just as you might create a hypertext link. The URL is the specific location on the Internet where the graphic file is located. It can be on the same Web host computer that your Web page is on, or it can be on a host somewhere else on the Internet.

❝❝ *Plain English, please!*

Inline images are graphics files that appear exactly where you place them, along with text, on a Web document. (In a moment we discuss the other kind, floating images.) The basic difference is that inline images aren't aligned against a margin—they are anchored in the text of the page. Floating images can be made to stick to the left or right margin. ❞❞

To create the URL pointer for your image, use the IMG element. This element acts as a placeholder in your text where the browser will put the graphic. IMG is an empty container with the following syntax:

```
<IMG SRC=image_URL>
```

IMG is the HTML image tag; it appears with all inline images. SRC means source and refers to the location of the image (it's on some hard drive somewhere in the world). The actual URL for the image file replaces the words image_URL.

The image_URL can be a full URL with full machine name (e.g., **http://members.aol.com/tstauffer/me.gif**). Alternatively, it can refer to the graphics file's relative URL; in this case, you refer to the file's location relative to the directory where the Web page is.

The following is sample HTML code for adding an inline graphic to the page:

```
<P>I just thought you might be interested in seeing this
graphic I've created
for myself in PhotoShop. <IMG SRC="image1.gif"> I was actu-
ally a bit surprised
at how easy it was to create. I'm not artist, but there are
enough filters and
special effects in PhotoShop that it makes it possible for me
to create something
this professional looking without being absolutely sure of
what I'm doing!
</P>
```

Notice the `<IMG SRC>` command is using a relative URL—actually, it could have just as easily been a complete URL like:

```
<IMG SRC="http://www.mycom.com/todd/image1.gif">
```

Both are similarly useful, but you only need to use a complete URL if the image you're loading resides elsewhere on the Internet. If it was in a subdirectory, then something like:

```
<IMG SRC="/graphics/image1.gif">
```

will work just fine. See Figure 5.2 for an example of how this looks.

Fig. 5.2
The <IMG> tag in action. Notice that the graphic appears within the text—that's inline.

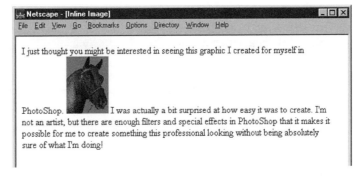

Q&A *My inline graphic is too big. Do browsers automatically resize graphics files according to the width of the window the way they wrap text?*

No. In fact, be careful when you create wide graphics; many people do not run their browsers full-screen (or can't set their screen size larger than VGA or 640 x 480), and graphics wider than five or six inches may get cut off by the side of the browser window. Most image manipulation programs (like Paint Shop Pro or PhotoShop) allow you to resize your graphic images.

Aligning text next to images

On their own, Web browsers don't do much to help text and graphics share space on a Web page. The text in Figure 5.3, for example, looks tiny when lined up along the bottom of the image. It's not very attractive, partly because

Fig. 5.3
Web browsers treat images like a character in the line of text and don't wrap text along side the graphic.

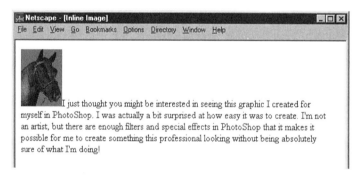

the white space beside the graphic is fairly useless.

Fortunately, you can do something about this. IMG comes with an attribute called ALIGN. ALIGN determines how text and images interact with one another on a Web page. Specifically, ALIGN controls how text that's placed in your HTML code on the same line as an image will line itself up along the vertical sides of the image.

The ALIGN attribute is written as:

```
<IMG ALIGN=value SRC=image_URL>
```

The possible values for ALIGN are shown in Table 5.1.

Table 5.1   Standard *ALIGN* values

Value	Effect on Text
TOP	Aligns the bottom of the text to the top of the image
MIDDLE	Aligns the bottom of the text to the middle of the image
BOTTOM	Aligns the bottom of the text to the bottom of the image

The BOTTOM value is the default for IMG and does not need to be specified if it's what you want to use. When using any of the standard values, Web browsers leave white space around the text on the line, and the text wraps down to the next line beneath the bottom of the image. Figure 5.4 shows how each standard alignment includes a variety of image alignments used in HTML code.

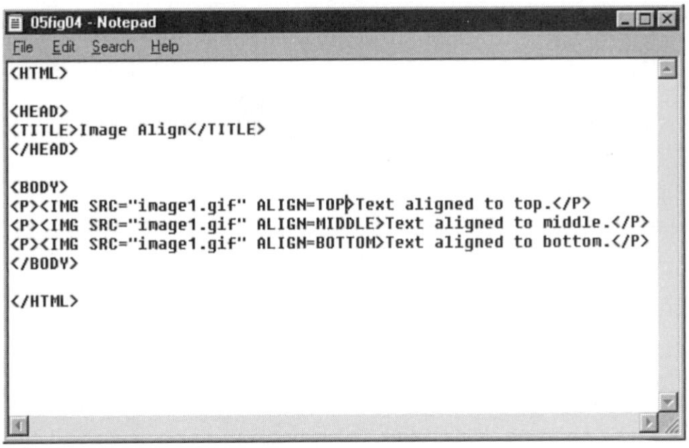

Fig. 5.4
Only one ALIGN command *is* allowed per line of text, or you'll confuse the browser.

```
05fig04 - Notepad
File  Edit  Search  Help
<HTML>

<HEAD>
<TITLE>Image Align</TITLE>
</HEAD>

<BODY>
<P><IMG SRC="image1.gif" ALIGN=TOP>Text aligned to top.</P>
<P><IMG SRC="image1.gif" ALIGN=MIDDLE>Text aligned to middle.</P>
<P><IMG SRC="image1.gif" ALIGN=BOTTOM>Text aligned to bottom.</P>
</BODY>

</HTML>
```

Figure 5.5 shows how Netscape handles each of these attribute values.

Fig. 5.5
Only the text on the current line follows the selected ALIGN option. Text on the next line in the browser drops underneath the inline image.

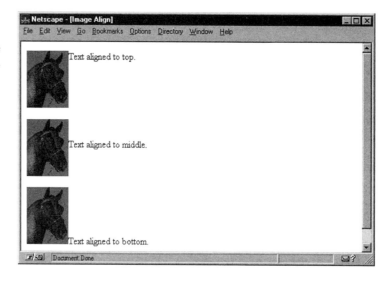

HTML 3.2's floating images

The HTML 3.2 proposal provides more ALIGN values for a new type of image called a floating graphic. No longer tied to one line of text (with all of that awkward white space), these graphics float against one of the margins, and text wraps along the entire height of the image.

The two ALIGN values are LEFT and RIGHT, and they specify which margin the image will float against. Figure 5.6 shows how easy it is to use these extensions in your Web page IMG links.

The LEFT and RIGHT values determine to which margin the graphic aligns.

In Figure 5.7, you see how Netscape displays floating images.

Two other design attributes are available for HTML 3.2 and Netscape-compatible pages. To control the amount of spacing between text and floating images and between the edge of the window and the images, use the attributes VSPACE and HSPACE. VSPACE defines the space (or gutter size, for those of you familiar with page layout) above and below a floating image, and HSPACE controls the space to the right and left of a floating image. Figure 5.8 shows the VSPACE and HSPACE attributes at work in an HTML document.

Fig. 5.6

The LEFT and RIGHT values determine to which margin the graphic aligns.

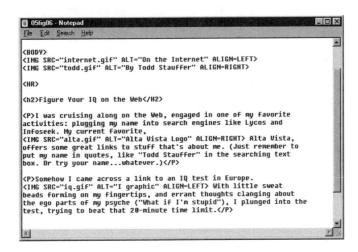

```
05fig06 - Notepad
File  Edit  Search  Help

<BODY>
<IMG SRC="internet.gif" ALT="On the Internet" ALIGN=LEFT>
<IMG SRC="todd.gif" ALT="By Todd Stauffer" ALIGN=RIGHT>

<HR>

<h2>Figure Your IQ on the Web</H2>

<P>I was cruising along on the Web, engaged in one of my favorite
activities: plugging my name into search engines like Lycos and
Infoseek. My current favorite,
<IMG SRC="alta.gif" ALT="Alta Vista Logo" ALIGN=RIGHT> Alta Vista,
offers some great links to stuff that's about me. (Just remember to
put my name in quotes, like "Todd Stauffer" in the searching text
box. Or try your name...whatever.)</P>

<P>Somehow I came across a link to an IQ test in Europe.
<IMG SRC="iq.gif" ALT="I graphic" ALIGN=LEFT> With little sweat
beads forming on my fingertips, and errant thoughts clanging about
the ego parts of my psyche ("What if I'm stupid"), I plunged into the
test, trying to beat that 20-minute time limit.</P>
```

❝❝ *Plain English, please!*

Sometimes the blizzard of cryptic abbreviations in a coding language makes you forget that they actually make some sense (well, now and then). ***VSPACE*** means vertical space, ***HSPACE*** means horizontal space. So <IMG ALIGN=LEFT HSPACE=10> simply means, "Align this image and put 10 pixels of space to the left of it.' ❞❞

Fig. 5.7

Floating images are detached from the surrounding text so that the text can flow around the image.

Netscape - [Aligning Images]
File Edit View Go Bookmarks Options Directory Window Help

On the Internet ————————————————— by Todd Stauffer

Figure Your IQ on the Web

I was cruising along on the Web, engaged in one of my favorite activities: plugging my name into search engines like Lycos and Infoseek. My current favorite, Alta Vista, offers some great links to stuff that's about me. (Just remember to put my name in quotes, like "Todd Stauffer" in the searching text box. Or try your name...whatever.)

Somehow I came across a link to an IQ test in Europe. With little sweat beads forming on my fingertips, and errant thoughts clanging about the ego parts of my psyche ("What if I'm stupid"), I plunged into the test, trying to beat that 20-minute time limit.

I emerged from the test, clicked for my score and was pleasantly shocked. "Wow," I thought. "That's high." But was it right?

Document: Done

Fig. 5.8

The values of VSPACE and HSPACE are in pixels; a good gutter value is somewhere around five.

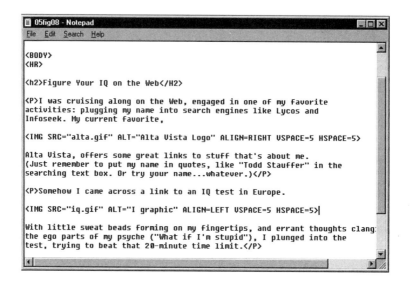

If you compare Figure 5.7 to Figure 5.9, you'll see the difference that VSPACE and HSPACE can make. Figure 5.9 shows how Netscape puts the gutter space around a floating image.

Fig. 5.9

VSPACE and HSPACE always control both sides of an image—you can't give a side more or less space than its opposite.

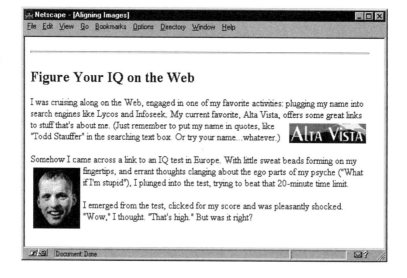

Remembering our text-based friends

Odd though it may seem, not everyone on the Internet has access to Netscape, Mosaic, Internet Explorer, or any other graphical browser. Of the 20 million plus audience available to you on the Net, a sizable percentage still use browsers like UNIX's Lynx, which is extremely capable but doesn't display graphics. Other users keep the graphics feature of their browser turned off. But these people want access to your Web pages as much as anyone else. And if your Web site is about information, you don't want to disappoint them.

So how can you accommodate these users, even when you use graphics in your Web pages? HTML provides a simple solution: IMG's ALT attribute (ALT means alternative). ALT defines a text string that replaces the image in browsers without graphics support. This text is often displayed in a box (to separate it from the surrounding body text). Here's an example:

```
<IMG SRC="plane.gif" ALT="Our Cessna 172">
```

Figure 5.10 shows the ALT text as displayed in Internet Explorer when the Download Images option is turned off.

Fig. 5.10
Your ALT text should be fairly short, and should describe the picture to someone who can't see it.

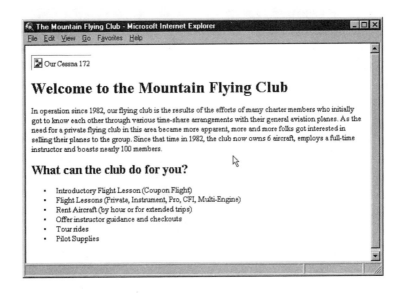

Other fun with *<IMG>*

HTML 3.2 provides two more extensions for the IMG element. The pair, WIDTH and HEIGHT, are designed to make your Web site faster reading.

WIDTH and HEIGHT help solve one of the Web's continually nagging problems. When people click a link to your Web pages, their browsers generally wait until all the inline images are loaded before going back and filling in the text around them. The WIDTH and HEIGHT attributes alleviate this wait.

By telling the browser the pixel dimensions of the images in your Web page, it can mock up the layout and lay in the text before starting to retrieve the images. If you are the reader and want to click a text link before the image finishes loading, you're free to do it. Figure 5.11 shows a Web page with the dimension attributes.

CAUTION Although WIDTH and HEIGHT **can be used to resize the appearance** of an image, they do nothing to the actual file size of the graphic, which means the user has to wait the same amount of time for the image to download. See Chapter 7, "Making Graphics, Text, and Color Work Together," for hints on making your images download more quickly.

Fig. 5.11
WIDTH and HEIGHT values are arbitrary, but they should match your image's actual measurements so it looks right on-screen.

```
05fig11 - Notepad
File  Edit  Search  Help
<HTML>
<HEAD>
<TITLE>The Mountain Flying Club</TITLE>
</HEAD>

<IMG SRC="C152.GIF" ALT="Our Cessna 172" HEIGHT=150 WIDTH=200>

<H1>Welcome to the Mountain Flying Club</H1>
In operation since 1982, our flying club is the results of the efforts of m
members who initially got to know each other through various time-share arr
with their general aviation planes. As the need for a private flying club i
more apparent, more and more folks got interested in selling their planes t
that time in 1982, the club now owns 6 aircraft, employs a full-time instru
100 members.<P>

<H2>What can the club do for you?</H2>

<UL>
<LI>Introductory Flight Lesson (Coupon Flight)
<LI>Flight Lessons (Private, Instrument, Pro, CFI, Multi-Engine)
<LI>Rent Aircraft (by hour or for extended trips)
<LI>Offer instructor guidance and checkouts
<LI>Tour rides
```

Figure 5.12 shows Netscape's interpretation with a graphic partially displayed.

Fig. 5.12
Netscape sets aside white space for the graphic, then loads it a bit more quickly with WIDTH and HEIGHT set.

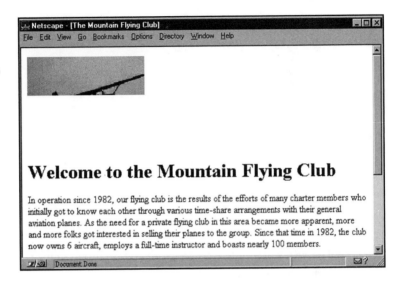

Beyond the basics: Clickable images

Now that we've seen how to create hyperlinks, and we've seen how to add images to our pages—why not combine the two? I guess we can call them "hyperimages," uh, if we have to.

The HTML code for that would be:

```
<A HREF="URL"><IMG SRC="picturename.gif"></A>
```

As you can see, this simply replaces the "Click here . . . " text with the file name of a graphic. The image appears on the screen, and the reader clicks the image rather than a line of text (see Figure 5.13).

One more HTML 3.2 addition: *BORDER*

HTML 3.2 adds one more attribute for <IMG>, which is generally only useful when you've made the image a clickable graphic: BORDER. Increasing the border makes it more obvious that the image is a link, and decreasing it makes it less obvious. BORDER is set, by default to a value of 1, which looks like a normal border. Setting it higher simply makes the border look kinda

Fig. 5.13
Here's a clickable graphic image. Click it to load the next Web page.

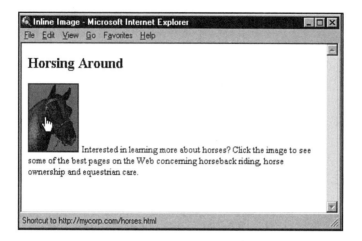

pudgy. Not many Web authors use it because, to be quite frank, it doesn't do much.

To use BORDER, add it to your IMG statement and give it a numerical value. Here's an example:

```
<IMG SRC="plane.gif" ALT="Our Cessna 172" BORDER=4>
```

Q&A

If I remove the border, won't that make it look just like an ordinary inline image?

Yes, exactly. The value BORDER=0 removes the telltale border around the image and, as a result, potentially confuses your readers. If you want to remove the border for aesthetic reasons, be sure to include text inside the <A HREF> anchor so people will know they can click it.

A potential design reason for removing the border would be to offer a bonus for any reader who takes the time to move the mouse around and figure out that the graphic is actually a link. But are you sure you want them to work that hard?

Part II: Designing Your Pages for Audience Appeal

I Have This List, See...

● **In this chapter:**

- ● **Hit the mark with bulleted lists**

- ● **You can count on your numbered lists**

- ● **The versatility of definition lists**

- ● **Can lists be combined?**

I do lists. You do lists. Letterman does lists.
So does Guinness. The Web does lists, too,
and it's your job to put them there . . . .

W ant a challenge? Try to get through two hours of your waking life without encountering a list. Any kind of list. Sure you could avoid watching Letterman. Or at least avoid the Top Ten segment. But that's late at night, and by that time you'll have run into all sorts of lists. Pick up the newspaper, and you see lists of stories and editorials. Read the ads, and you see lists of components, prices, and store locations. Grab a can of spaghetti sauce, and you find a list of ingredients. And then there's your own lists: groceries, phone numbers, things to do, and—something we should all have—things *not* to do.

Lists are popular because they work. Bulleted lists add pizzazz to a presentation and prove to the audience that you actually have several points to make. Numbered lists set things in order and are superb for offering a process of instructions. Lists cut to the chase, eliminating unnecessary verbiage while organizing things into categories and hierarchies. It's hard to imagine getting through life—or even a single day—without them.

Blessed is the list maker?

Lists aren't the be-all and end-all of civilization. Yes, they're everywhere, but they're often misused. The purpose of lists is to present specific points of information quickly and clearly. Bulleted lists of five items work well; bulleted lists of 15 items don't. And a numbered list of 35 instructions has little value.

Keep these things in mind when you're thinking about creating your Web lists. The Web is filled with useless lists designed by HTML authors who just didn't think and certainly didn't test. Make sure your readers know that you understand the important functions of lists of all kinds.

One other point: A page with nothing but lists is a page with no intelligence. For a list to be effective, it must be short, to the point, and chunked. What does **chunked** mean? Your readers can only take in so much information at a time (and on the Web, it's even more important because users whip through these pages, reading them off a computer screen); it's your responsibility to offer it to them in digestible chunks. Small lists, logical categories, and headings all make a very real difference.

In HTML, you have five kinds of lists

Think about the lists you see every day. Dos and Don'ts, instructions and warnings, to-do and to-buy, topics and arguments. Lots of lists look the same, but the range of formats is extensive. On any given day, you see lists with items separated by bullets, numbers, or just plain spaces. You see annotated lists (in which each item contains a paragraph or so of explanation), indexes, tables of contents, menus, and so on.

The Web lets you create five different kinds of lists, and although you can't use them to re-create all the lists you find in the world, you'll find them immensely useful nevertheless. The list types are:

- **ordered lists** <OL>, a.k.a. numbered lists
- **unordered lists** <UL>, a.k.a. bulleted lists
- **definition lists** <DL>, a.k.a. glossary lists
- **menu lists** <MENU>, a.k.a. rarely-used bullet lists
- **directory lists** <DIR>, a.k.a. file name lists

In fact, you don't need to learn all five types. Only three list types are regularly found on the Web: ordered, unordered, and definition. Menu and directory lists are specialized types of unordered lists, and whether they display differently from normal unordered lists depends on your Web browser. As it turns out, most browsers ignore these last two—at least, they fail to render them differently from regular <UL> bullet lists.

As a result, I cover only the three main types in this book—ordered lists, unordered lists, and definition lists.

Lists by the number: Ordered lists

TIP **Use numbered/ordered lists when you want to emphasize the** order of something. In a set of instructions, for instance, step 1 must be done before step 2, and the numbers help your reader follow along. The same holds true for rankings: You want to show them in order beginning with the best.

The HTML element for ordered lists (or more easily remembered as **numbered lists**) follows the basic rules for all HTML lists: It is a container element using the beginning and closing tags <OL> and </OL>. Each item within the list is identified by the item tag <LI> (which stands for **list item**).

The syntax for numbered lists is:

```
<OL>
<LI>List item one
<LI>List item two
</OL>
```

Each <LI> represents a single item within the list.

Figure 6.1 shows a numbered list displayed in Internet Explorer.

Fig. 6.1
Numbered lists are useful for numbering of items ("top ten") or instructions.

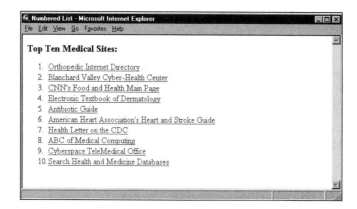

The HTML code for the numbered list in Figure 6.1 is as follows (from **http://www.i-med.com/wm/topten/**):

```
<H3> Top Ten Medical Sites:</H3>
<OL>
<LI><A HREF="http://www.slackinc.com/bone/
➥orthonet.htm">Orthopedic Internet Directory</A>
<LI><A HREF="http://www.bvrhc.org/">Blanchard Valley Cyber-
➥Health Center</A>
<LI><A HREF="http://www.cnn.com/HEALTH/index.html">CNN's Food
➥and Health Main Page</A>
<LI><A HREF="http://telemedicine.org/stamfor1.htm">Electronic
➥Textbook of Dermatology</A>
<LI><A HREF="http://www.intmed.mcw.edu/
➥AntibioticGuide.html">Antibiotic Guide</A>
<LI><A HREF="http://www.amhrt.org/heartg/ac7.htm">American
➥Heart Association's Heart and Stroke Guide</A>
```

```
<LI><A HREF="http://www.holonet.net/homepage/1d.htm">Health
➥Letter on the CDC</A>
<LI><A HREF="http://www.bmj.com/bmj/abcmc/abcmc.htm">ABC of
➥Medical Computing</A>
<LI><A HREF="http://www.telemedical.com/">Cyberspace
➥TeleMedical Office</A>
<LI><A HREF="http://www.charm.net/~ibc/sleuth/
➥medi.html">Search Health and Medicine Databases</A>
</OL>
```

Notice that each element within the list starts with the `<LI>` empty tag (there's no corresponding `</LI>` tag). The entire list is surrounded by the `<OL>` and `</OL>` container tags. This list looks complex because each element is a hyperlink (and lets face it, hyperlinks look pretty ugly in ASCII code), but it could just as easily be a simple list of colors or funny sayings. What's important here is that the list items themselves can contain just about whatever HTML code you can dream up.

These lists work much the same as the numbered lists in your word processor. You don't number each item manually; you just put in the information and your browser adds the numbers for you. If you add a list item, the browser renumbers the entire list.

Each `<LI>` tag signals the browser software to start a new line for the item, so no other line-ending tags (like `<BR>`) are necessary.

TIP **You can use almost all of the formatting HTML tags inside lists.** One of the most useful is the paragraph tag `<P>`, which enables you to separate text within a list item. You can only start a new list item with `<LI>`, however.

CAUTION **Avoid using headings in your list items; they don't look very good,** and it's (technically) the wrong way to use heading tags. Also, pay attention to your closing tags in lists, especially when you use nested lists (lists inside of lists). Forgetting a tag can do amazingly horrible things to the appearance of your page.

Bullets over bandwidth: Unordered lists

By far the most common type of list on the Web is the unordered list. But almost nobody actually calls these things **unordered** lists; instead, they call them **bulleted** lists. Why? Because the items in an unordered list are preceded by **bullets**—big black circles that have become a staple of overhead transparencies, PowerPoint presentations, and books like this one.

Unlike numbered lists, bulleted lists don't have an obvious order to them. That is, the second bulleted item isn't necessarily more significant than the fifth—unlike numbered lists, in which item two is almost always more important (or earlier in a process) than item five. In fact, this lack of order tells you why they're called **unordered.** It's not because the items aren't put in some kind of order, it's just that the order doesn't matter.

 TIP **Most Web page designers use bulleted lists rather than numbered** lists because they look better. In fact, there are so few numbered lists on the Web that you might never actually put one in place. Nonetheless, they're good to know about because a well-designed numbered list can help present information to your reader more usefully. In reality, though, bulleted lists are often chosen over numbered lists for nothing more than aesthetic reasons.

The tags for bulleted lists are <UL> and </UL>. As with numbered lists, each list item begins with the <LI> tag. Also like numbered lists, each item can include other HTML elements, including additional sublists (nested lists). And don't worry about line breaks—your browser inserts a line break whenever it finds a new <LI> item tag.

Each browser uses its own internal bullet icons for these list items. You can't control these. As an example, Figure 6.2 shows Internet Explorer and Netscape Navigator displaying the same list. Despite the difference in bullet styles, the HTML code is exactly the same.

Fig. 6.2
Bullets display differently in different browsers, depending on the browser's built-in bullet styles.

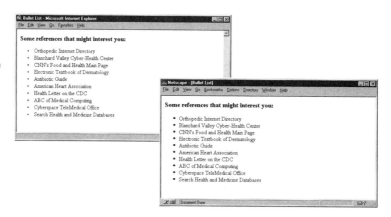

Except for the change in container tags from <OL></OL> to <UL></UL>, the HTML code for bulleted lists is exactly the same as the code for numbered lists. You can even put bulleted lists within bulleted lists, as seen in the following code:

```
<UL>
<LI>Introduction
<LI>Chapter One
      <UL>
      <LI> Section 1.1
      <LI> Section 1.2
      <LI> Section 1.3
      </UL>
<LI>Chapter Two
</UL>
```

Figure 6.3 shows what this code looks like in Netscape. The second item includes a sublist, which has been "nested" in the second <LI>. Notice that the entire sublist is actually part of the second <LI> of the original list. The different bullets are actually a default behavior in Netscape.

Fig. 6.3
This HTML page contains two bulleted lists: the main list (solid circles) and the sublist (squares).

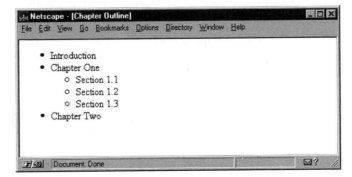

Double duty: Definition lists

Now that you know how to construct numbered lists and bulleted lists, it's time to break the news that neither is as useful or as powerful as **definition** lists (<DL>). Sometimes called **glossary** lists, definition lists are used to create lists that look like glossary entries in which a term or phrase is accompanied by an indented definition paragraph. This is a great tool to use when you need to list items with extensive descriptions (such as real estate listings or items in a retail catalog).

Figure 6.4 shows a short definition list introducing the members of a fictional corporate Board of Directors.

Fig. 6.4
Definition lists are good for any list that needs two different elements, like names and descriptions.

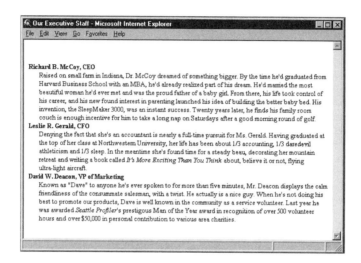

The HTML code for the definition list shown in Figure 6.4 is as follows:

```
<DL>
    <DT><STRONG>Richard B. McCoy, CEO</STRONG>
    <DD> Raised on small farm in Indiana, Dr. McCoy dreamed
of something bigger. By the time he'd graduated from Harvard
Business School with an MBA, he'd already realized part of
his dream. He'd married the most beautiful woman he'd ever
met and was the proud father of a baby girl. From there, his
life took control of his career, and his new found interest
in parenting launched his idea of building the better baby
bed. His invention, the SleepMaker 3000, was an instant
success. Twenty years later, he finds his family room couch
is enough incentive for him to take a long nap on Saturdays
after a good morning round of golf.
    <DT><STRONG>Leslie R. Gerald, CFO</STRONG>
    <DD> Denying the fact that she's an accountant is nearly
a full-time pursuit for Ms. Gerald. Having graduated at the
top of her class at Northwestern University, her life has
been about 1/3 accounting, 1/3 daredevil athleticism and
1/3 sleep. In the meantime she's found time for a steady
beau, decorating her mountain retreat and writing a book
called <I>It's More Exciting Than You Think</I> about, be-
lieve it or not, flying ultra-light aircraft.
```

```
<DT><STRONG>David W. Deacon, VP of Marketing</STRONG>
<DD> Known as "Dave" to anyone he's ever spoken to for
more than five minutes, Mr. Deacon displays the calm friend-
liness of the consummate salesman, with a twist. He actually
is a nice guy. When he's not doing his best to promote our
products, Dave is well known in the community as a service
volunteer. Last year he was awarded <I>Seattle Profiler</I>'s
prestigious Man of the Year award in recognition of over 500
volunteer hours and over $50,000 in personal contribution to
various area charities.
</DL>
```

As you can see from this code, definition lists do not follow the same format as numbered and bulleted lists (or any other HTML elements, for that matter). The definition list is enclosed inside a container labeled <DL></DL>. Inside the definition list, a <DT> tag is used to indicate the header for the item or items (the <DT> can include a URL reference), and the <DD> tags indicate each separate list item. Both <DT> and <DD> are empty tags—they don't need closing tags to contain their information.

The important point about definition lists is that they make your information appear very attractive and very well organized. You can have one <DD> item for each <DT> heading, or you can have several. This heading-item feature gives definition lists a professional appearance.

In other words, definition lists have three elements—<DL>, <DT>, and <DD>—rather than two like unordered and ordered lists. <DT> presents the headline, while <DD>s make up the actual items.

In the previous HTML code, there are three headings, each with one item. To be more technical, each <DT> has one corresponding <DD>. It's entirely possible to include several <DD>s with each <DT>, and you can have numbered or bulleted lists inside the <DT> listing. You have a great deal of design flexibility with definition lists, which is why they're so great.

 **CAUTION** **Make sure your heading is short enough to fit on a single line; if it's too long, it will wrap down onto the next line without indenting, and it will look pretty ghastly.**

Figure 6.5 shows how a definition list can be used to create an online catalog with HTML. Figure 6.6 shows how Internet Explorer displays these text lists on-screen.

Fig. 6.5

Notice that it's perfectly acceptable to have an image as your <DT> item, followed by <DD> and descriptive text.

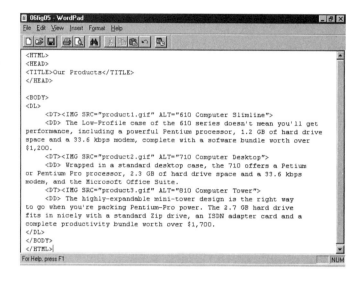

Fig. 6.6

Here's our catalog listing, with images as the "term."

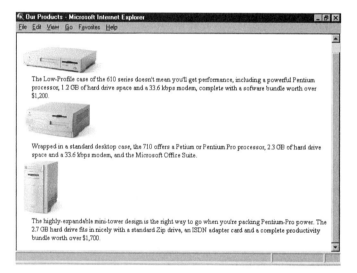

Browsers vary in how definition lists look in the Web pages they display. For instance, Mosaic has a tendency to use a double-space between terms, but Netscape does not. All this means is that readers may be able to read Mosaic definition lists easier, but Netscape users will be able to see more of the definition list information on-screen at any given time.

Q&A

I've got a very long list. Is there anything I can do to make it take up less space?

Yes there is. All the lists we've discussed allow you to add the attribute COMPACT, as in <OL COMPACT>. Of course, all browsers render things differently, but any browser that recognizes the COMPACT attribute will force the list to take up less space by placing the line items closer together.

Combining similar and different lists

If you think of HTML elements as the rules of Web authoring, then it stands to reason that sometimes you've just got to break the rules. Not all of your information is going to fall into neat categories and packages. Unless you're a writer for David Letterman's "Top Ten List," your world is not so tidy.

Combining types of containers and elements goes a long way to making your Web pages dynamic and interesting. Instead of forcing your content into a narrow form (like a bulleted list), experiment with combinations of lists that work together to deliver your message.

If you have a numbered list, and one of the list items is a list itself with no specific order to it, insert a bulleted list. Browsers are smart enough to indent the bulleted list within the numbered list, which gives your Web page a smart look and better communication capability. Figure 6.7 shows you how easy it is to put containers into containers, letting different lists work for you.

Fig. 6.7
When you create your page, you can indent your code to make it easier to read, but browsers don't take their on-screen formatting cues from these indentations— they rely on interpreting your codes.

```
06fig07 - WordPad                                          _ 6 X
File  Edit  View  Insert  Format  Help
<BODY>
<DL>
        <DT><IMG SRC="6001.gif" ALT="6001 Computer Slimline">
        <DD> The Low-Profile case of the 610 series doesn't mean you'll get
performance, including a powerful Pentium processor, 1.2 GB of hard drive
space and a 33.6 kbps modem, complete with a sofware bundle worth over
$1,200.
                <UL>
                <LI> 180 MHz Pentium Processor
                <LI> 16 MB RAM
                <LI> 1.2 GB Hard Drive|
                <LI> 33.6 kbps Modem
                <LI> Software bundle
                        <UL>
                        <LI> MS Works
                        <LI> Windows Plus Pak
                        <LI> Card Creator
                        <LI> 20 more titles
                        </UL>
                </UL>
        <DT><IMG SRC="7001.gif" ALT="7001 Computer Desktop">
        <DD> Wrapped in a standard desktop case, the 710 offers a Petium
or Pentium Pro processor, 2.3 GB of hard drive space and a 33.6 kbps
modem, and the Microsoft Office Suite.
For Help, press F1                                         NUM
```

Figure 6.8 shows how Internet Explorer displays this mix of containers.

Fig. 6.8
Lists embedded in
other containers may
"inherit" certain style
and formatting charac-
teristics. Again, it's up
to the browser to
determine what the list
looks like on-screen.

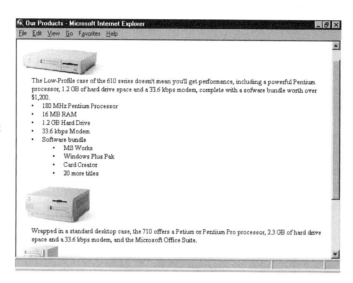

In the original HTML specifications, lists were the most important organiza-
tional tool available. To a large degree, they still are. While you certainly
don't want to overuse them, lists offer you the possibility of categorizing
your material and setting it down on the page so that anyone can find what
he wants.

Experiment with lists. Find out what kind of information needs a numbered
list, and what kind works best with a bulleted list. If you want sophisticated
list designs, learn definition lists well. Not only will your readers expect lists
on your page, but they're also the most effective way to organize a great deal
of information in a small amount of space.

Beyond the basics: List extensions

As you might expect, it was Netscape that pioneered most of the attributes to
alter the appearance of list tags. Now, these extensions have been included in
the HTML 3.2 specification and should be supported by more and more new
browsers. This help is in the form of <OL> and <UL> **attributes** that allow you
to create lists as complete and complex as multi-level outlines.

Plain English, Please!

Many HTML tags have **attributes** or extra commands that can be added to those tags that affect the appearance or behavior of the tag. In all cases, the attributes for a tag appear inside the tag itself, like the attributes SRC and ALIGN that we used in Chapter 5 with the <IMG> image tag.

Numbered list add-ons

In order to create more effective numbered lists, you have the option of changing the numbering system and the start number for a given sequence:

- You can set the numbering style, ranging from Arabic numbers (1, 2, 3, 4) to letters (a, b, c, d; or A, B, C, D) or even Roman numerals (i, ii, iii, iv; or I, II, III, IV).

- You can set the first number in the sequence so that it's not necessary to start with 1.

Table 6.1 shows the enhancements to ordered lists that are possible when designing for HTML 3.2-compatible browsers.

Table 6.1   HTML 3.2 extensions to ordered (numbered) lists

Attribute	Description
TYPE=A	Sets markers to uppercase letters
TYPE=a	Sets markers to lowercase letters
TYPE=I	Sets markers to uppercase Roman numerals
TYPE=i	Sets markers to lowercase Roman numerals
TYPE=1	Sets markers to numbers
START	Sets beginning value of item markers in the current list

These attributes are written just like ordinary tag attributes, placed directly after the main tag itself. For example:

- `<OL TYPE=A>` produces a lettered list with items "numbered" A, B, C, D, and so on.

- `<OL TYPE=I>` yields a list that uses Roman numerals; items will be numbered I, II, III, IV, and so on.

- `<OL TYPE=a START=4>` displays a list with a lowercase Roman numeral in front of each list item starting with iv (the Roman numeral for 4).

Obviously, these extensions give you more options for displaying items in lists. It's a good thing, too; numbered lists are unexciting by their very nature, and they need this help to make them work like traditional outlines—the most obvious use for `<OL>`.

 TIP **If you want to change the value of a particular list item, use the** `VALUE=#` attribute to the `<LI>` tag, where # is an actual integer. The rest of the list will renumber itself from that point on.

When you create multiple lists, consider using a mix of `<OL>` list styles. By doing so, you can help users easily distinguish between different types of information. Figure 6.9 shows a source page that includes a list using mixed markers, and Figure 6.10 shows the final product as it appears in Netscape.

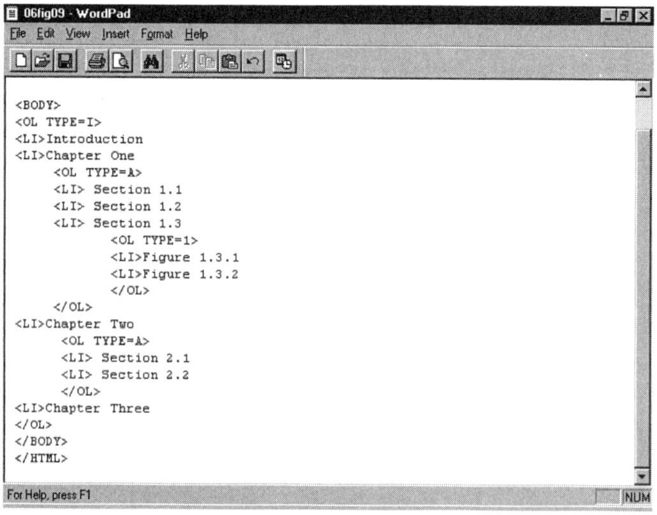

Fig. 6.9

You can put lists with different types of markers inside other lists (even if the list is not the same type, such as an ordered list inside a bulleted list).

```
06fig09 - WordPad                                    _|6|X|
File  Edit  View  Insert  Format  Help

<BODY>
<OL TYPE=I>
<LI>Introduction
<LI>Chapter One
      <OL TYPE=A>
      <LI> Section 1.1
      <LI> Section 1.2
      <LI> Section 1.3
            <OL TYPE=1>
            <LI>Figure 1.3.1
            <LI>Figure 1.3.2
            </OL>
      </OL>
<LI>Chapter Two
      <OL TYPE=A>
      <LI> Section 2.1
      <LI> Section 2.2
      </OL>
<LI>Chapter Three
</OL>
</BODY>
</HTML>

For Help, press F1                                   NUM
```

Fig. 6.10
Mixing list types can provide a nice looking list, as well as keep different lists separate from each other.

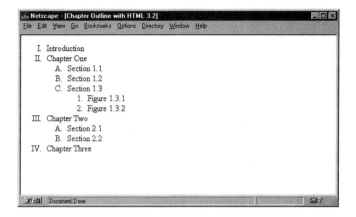

Bulleted list add-ons

Netscape refused to take those default bullets lying down and its support in the industry influenced the W3C to add these attributes to HTML 3.2. From the folks that brought you Roman numerals, then, come enhancements for bulleted lists.

Remember all that stuff about the browser (not the Web author) controlling what the bullets in a bulleted list actually look like? Well, if you write for an HTML 3.2-compatible browser, you can choose the bullet styles yourself— as if you hadn't guessed.

The new bullet styles are as follows:

- **filled circles** <UL TYPE=disc>

- **filled squares** <UL TYPE=square>

- **open squares** <UL TYPE=circle>

Hardly a cornucopia of bullet varieties, but a little better than a measly little black dot. How do they look? Pretty much as you'd expect. Figure 6.11 demonstrates how to use these bullet types in your lists, and Figure 6.12 shows you what a Netscape user sees when she views Web pages with these special markers.

Notice from the above list that the TYPE designation for open squares is "circle." Looks like the Webster people will have to add another definition entry to their next revision, eh?

Fig. 6.11

Mixing bullet types helps readers distinguish different types of information.

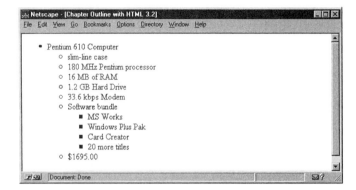

Fig. 6.12

Three bullet types are displayed here: open squares, filled squares, and filled circles (bullets).

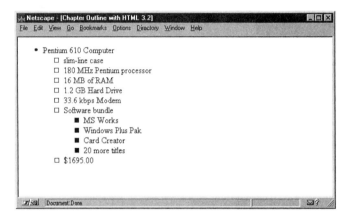

Making Graphics, Text, and Color Work Together

● **In this chapter:**

- ● **Keep your pictures clear**

- ● **The size of the graphics matters**

- ● **Making interlaced and transparent GIFs**

- ● **You can even use pictures of text**

- ● **Create graphics that help with navigation**

- ● **How can I add color to my pages?**

Communicating graphically is both fun and challenging. Graphics can help eliminate the problems of global communication, but that doesn't take text completely out of the equation. . . . . ▶

W hen the World Wide Web appeared on the Internet a few years ago, users applauded the medium's potential for worldwide communication. Soon thereafter, users began to realize that miscommunication could result as well. Part of the problem was that Web pages had text, and because they logged in from all over the world, not all Web users knew the same language. Then, as graphics became more commonplace, users started to see the value of visual representation as accurate and persuasive communicative devices.

But graphics are definitely a two-edged sword. Too much emphasis on graphics, and you can obscure the meaning of your page. By the same token, too many graphics can also make a page travel slowly over the Web, forcing your reader to sit and ponder a blank screen. It's a balancing act—you want to include images, but only when they have a clear purpose.

Figure 7.1 displays some of the hazards that surface with the use of graphical communication: Users can become lost and bored, and may eventually tune out a confusing Web site entirely.

Fig. 7.1
Absolut Vodka's home page is aesthetically pleasing and professional, but could be confusing for the first-time reader. Where do you click?

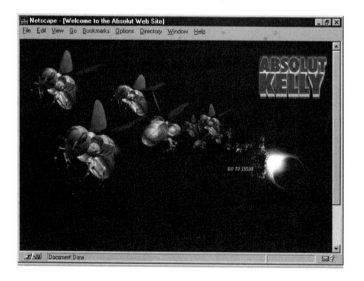

Choose your images for clarity

Clear images communicate their function almost instantly. But that's not to say that creating clear images is necessarily easy to do (witness the confusing "button bars" on many popular computer applications). Some commonly designed symbols, such as the question mark, can make it easier for you as a Web author. In fact, icons in general are often a clever way to get a point across graphically, without hitting the user over the head (see Figure 7.2).

Toolbar

Fig. 7.2
Microsoft's Web site relies on a toolbar of clear graphics at the top of the page. It's attractive, but not overwhelming.

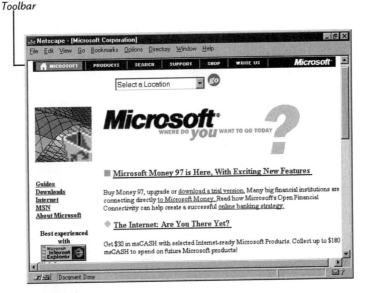

TIP **Most users understand that clicking a graphical button containing** a question mark transports them to a Help page.

If your graphics are attractive, but don't quite stand on their own, adding a little text isn't cheating. Text can be added two ways: graphically, within your image manipulation software, or via HTML. Figure 7.3 displays a World Wide Web page that combines images with graphical text to ensure clarity.

Fig. 7.3
C-Net Online uses text and related graphics to ensure the clarity of their functions.

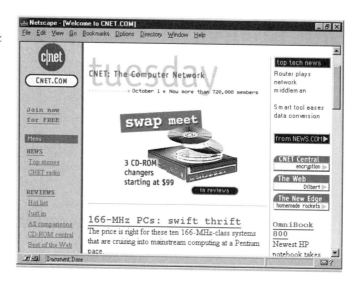

Clarity is the key to the success of your design—confusing pages are tossed aside as quickly as they appear in favor of other, more effective sites. As you create Web pages and the images that will be used on-screen, focus on whether your ideas and intentions are clear. If you have any doubts about your icons, add descriptive text to the image for clarity.

Icons: Fooling the eye with graphics

Perhaps overlooked too often by Web authors, icons are a great way to give your page a graphical "feel" without weighing the page down with large images that force your user to wait endlessly.

Icons are not, however, easily created. Unless you're a strong commercial artist, you may find that creating your own icons is an exercise in futility. It's not much fun to try and boil an idea down to about one square inch of space.

But, icons are also the norm in today's graphical computing world, and they make a lot of sense to

users who might be new (and lost) on your site. So what's the answer? Some kindly souls have made collections of icons available for download on the Web. Check out this listing at Yahoo for links to tons of graphic icons you can right-click and download in Netscape or IE:

http://www.yahoo.com/
Computers_and_Internet/Internet/
World_Wide_Web/
Page_Design_and_Layout/Icons/

What about the size of the graphics of my pages?

Among other things, the World Wide Web is a mass distributor of images. Art portfolios, photo journals, and concert shots clog the Web and often trap users anxiously downloading half a megabyte of graphics. Graphics archives do serve a functional purpose on the Web, but the organization and distribution of these typically large sites often leave something to be desired.

How, then, can you distribute large graphics files without losing your somewhat impatient audience? How can an online art gallery post its latest show on the Web? How can a real estate broker give you a proof sheet for each home listing? The answer is simple: Use smaller images. There are two measurements of size on the WWW: the amount of the screen that an image requires, and the storage space the image's file fills.

 TIP If you're scanning images into your computer for use on the Web, they generally only need to be at a resolution of about 72–75 dots per inch (dpi). That's the dpi on typical computer monitors, so graphics look good at that resolution. More dots (like the 360 dpi of inkjet printers) is overkill for a computer monitor, and it makes the image file larger.

Make the picture smaller

All that any WWW user can hope for is speed and results, and if possible, speedy results. To facilitate this need for efficiency, consider using on your page small **thumbnail** images that link to other Web documents, which in turn contain the full-sized graphics.

❝ *Plain English, please!*

Thumbnails are tiny graphical representations that link to a full screen reproduction of the initial image. Thumbnails are usually .5–1 inch square and run about 5–10 kilobytes each in storage size. Even the slowest Web user can tolerate 10–12 thumbnails on a single Web page, but if you have many more than 12, consider breaking them up into categories with a separate Web page devoted to each. Figure 7.4 shows how the "Travels with Samantha" Web site uses thumbnails as links to the corresponding full-sized images. **❞**

Fig. 7.4
This site presents over 220 full-sized JPEG images as inline thumbnails, allowing readers to retrieve only the full-sized images they want to see. Often, thumbnails are even smaller than this.

Remember, though, that you need to have two copies of the image, and the smaller copy needs to have been made smaller in an actual image manipulation program, not just with the <IMG WIDTH= HEIGHT=> attributes. That's the only way you'll create a smaller image *file* that will transmit more quickly over the Internet.

Put 'em in smaller files

As you must realize by now, smaller images mean faster retrieval. Even a novice Internet surfer quickly comes to appreciate how fast compact graphics load in his browser. To minimize the size of your graphics, consider using **JPEG** formatting. JPEG coding compresses images to one-third or one-fifth of the total size of GIF styles.

CAUTION   **Before converting all of your larger GIF files to JPEG format,** remember that during compression, JPEG removes the information it perceives as the least important to the image's final quality. The higher the compression, the greater the loss, which creates the potential for patterns to appear in solid or gradient colors.

To further reduce the size of your images, highlight your graphics with only a limited number of colors. Every image you create has a palette of colors that may be added for animation and aesthetic appeal. GIF files support palettes of up to 256 colors, while JPEG files have access to over 16 million different shades.

TIP **Graphics manipulation programs often have commands that allow** you to choose 16, 64, 256, or other color palettes. Some even allow you to choose a palette that only includes the colors you've actually used. Look for choices like these to make your image files smaller.

By removing the palette entries for colors that do not appear in your image, you can reduce the amount of file space reserved for the palette information. Limiting your images to fewer colors (64 or 100 for GIFs and 1–2,000 for JPEGs) dramatically reduces the size of your files. Programs like Photoshop, Paint Shop Pro (**http://www.tucows.com/**), and xv give you control over the palette information of your graphics files.

Q&A *Bottom line...Do I use GIF or JPEG for Web page graphics?*

Both. GIF is good for images that require few colors, less detail, or lower-end computer generated images—like icons, images that are basically graphical text, or computer drawings. JPEG is better for images with more color levels and detail—like scanned photos.

Creating interlaced and transparent GIF graphics

Because HTML offers only limited manipulation and handling of graphics, you need to run a more advanced image manipulation program to get the most out of your graphics. The creation of both interlaced GIFs and transparent GIFs requires such special handling from external sources.

With **interlacing**, a browser displays the graphical image in stages, presenting the file information to the reader as soon as it is read. The image revealed to the user displays a "horizontal blinds" effect, with pieces of the picture folding over one another as if slatted blinds were being closed.

TIP **In many image manipulation programs, interlacing both GIFs and** JPEGs takes no more effort than selecting an "interlacing" option when you save the image using the File, Save command.

Users might also see interlaced images as low-resolution, chunky graphics that refine themselves with each successive pass. This is somewhat like watching a blurry slide come into focus with an automatic slide projector. Figure 7.5 shows the horizontal blind effect.

Fig. 7.5
The larger the file size, the longer the browser takes to retrieve the file and show it "in focus."

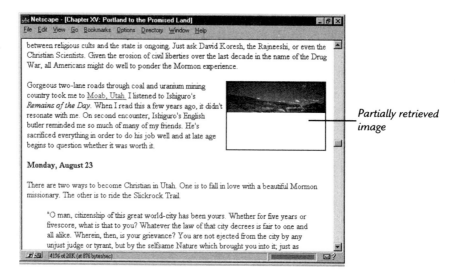

Partially retrieved image

To construct **transparent** images, assign one of the palette colors to the background of your **GIF89a** file as a transparent channel (many image manipulation programs have this capability). When a GIF89a-compatible browser loads the file, the transparent portions of the image are replaced by the information behind them (often the color of the background or the background bitmap). Transparency constructs graphics that float on top of the background and are not defined by a standard square picture frame (see Figure 7.6).

 Plain English, Please

GIF89a is one of many graphics formats—it's the most recent of CompuServe's GIFs formats, sporting advanced capabilities such as transparency, interlacing, and animation. Most graphics programs let you create graphics in GIF89a format or convert other types to GIF89a. **"**

Graphics can be saved as GIF89a files using a graphics tool, such as LView Pro (**http://www.lview.com/**) or xv. Separate utilities, like the Mac's Transparency and GIF converter programs, are designed solely to create transparent images.

Fig. 7.6
Every instance of the transparent palette entry shows through to the background, so don't choose a color that is found in the graphic itself.

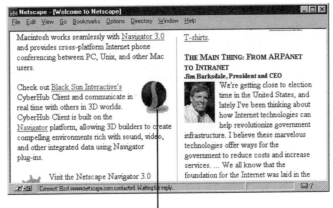

A transparent image

Consider transforming your text into graphics

Although you, as a Web author, have little control over how browsers display your font applications, pictures of text add a stimulating effect to the visual display of information. "Pictures of text" are really just graphics files—you create fancy text in a graphics program and save it as a graphics file. Figure 7.7 displays text that has been inserted in the Web document as a graphical image.

CAUTION **Inserting pictures of text raises some vital considerations** concerning display capacity and image size.

First, text-only browsers display only the ALT text string—and that's only if it is supplied by the author. Remember that using pictures of text may diminish a large portion of your potential audience.

Second, the extra time required for downloading the pictures of text can be unappealing to users (to say the least). To solve this problem, keep the number of colors in your text and enhancements to five or so, and use transparency to let the background shine through around your text graphic. Keep it simple.

Fig. 7.7
The Slate (**http://
www.slate.com/**) site
uses subtle graphical
text along with browser
text to give a more
magazine-like
appearance.

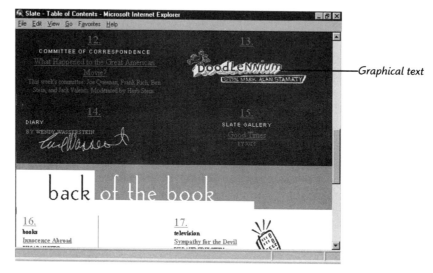

—*Graphical text*

Give your readers some buttons to navigate by

Given two topics we've already covered—clickable graphics (in Chapter 5) and the libraries of icons available through Yahoo—you have very little excuse to avoid adding navigational buttons to your pages. These little clickable icons are an exceptional way to help users move around on your site. But don't just give them buttons for "next" and "previous." It's important to let them jump straight to your home page and any other important pages.

TIP **Navigation graphics provide authors with the freedom to pick and** choose which controls appear on which pages while ordering and aligning them in any number of ways. Figure 7.8 displays a WWW page with separate navigation graphics.

Aligning graphics with <BR> is as simple as:

```
<IMG SRC="news.gif"><BR>
<IMG SRC="thrills.gif"><BR>
<IMG SRC="arts.gif"><BR>
<IMG SRC="cafe.gif"><BR>
<IMG SRC="movies.gif"><BR>
```

Fig. 7.8

These navigational graphics may be aligned horizontally or vertically (using <BR>, for instance).

 Q&A *I've got my images aligned nicely on the left side of the page, but my text keeps appearing below the images. How do I get text to appear next to my icon controls?*

There are a couple of different ways. If you use a single graphic image for your control icons, you can use the ALIGN=LEFT attribute for the <IMG> tag, and your text will flow around the graphic. If you're using a <BR> list of a series of <IMG> tags, you want to lay out your page using HTML tables, as discussed in Chapter 9, "Tabling Your Data."

There are an abundance of navigation-style icons and buttons available for public use on the World Wide Web. Refer to Appendix B, "World Wide Web Bibliography," for a list of graphic resources on the Web. Figure 7.9 shows a Web page that provides a navigation imagemap. (Imagemaps are coming up next in Chapter 8, "Imagemaps for Eye-Catching Hyperlinks.")

It's really the intelligent use of graphics that will set your pages apart from the droves of others that aren't quite good enough. If your users notice that your pages are visual, useful, and a bit snappy when they load, they'll reward you by visiting often and reading a bit more of what you have to say. You've already mastered the basics of HTML, and you can slap together a page. Don't forget to take the time with your image manipulation program to create the best, smallest, and smartest graphics you can.

Fig. 7.9
Using imagemaps as navigational tools enables users to stray from the typical "square button syndrome" to a more whimsical style that incorporates text and composite graphics within the Web page.

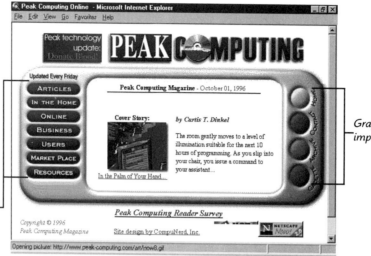

Graphical buttons for important links

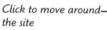
Click to move around the site

Putting graphics in the background

You've probably been waiting for me to bring this one up. It seems like folks have a lot of fun putting an image of some sort in the background of their page. It definitely adds personality, if that's what you're striving for.

The HTML 3.2 way to change the background into a graphic is to use the BACKGROUND attribute for the body tag, as in the following example (see Figure 7.10):

```
<BODY BACKGROUND="paper.gif">
```

Fig. 7.10
A background graphic will tile itself to fill the page. Remember to keep it light enough to show black text well, unless you also plan to change the color of the text.

The Mountain Flying Club - Microsoft Internet Explorer
File   Edit   View   Go   Favorites   Help

Welcome!

There's nothing **better** than ripping through the air at unheard of speeds, dipping a wing-tip into the clouds, then *banking your machine* into a hard turn. If that sounds like it might interest you, maybe you'd be interested in our new DareDevil Acrobat Ride!

Some folks just know they're read to take the plunge. If that's how *you* are, then step to the front of the line for our personal flight training courses. Gas, oil and plane rental are included in the price, as are some of the most dedicated, interested and advanced flight trainers in the area.

Your lessons will start on the ground with the two week, 5-hour ground school, complete with materials, sample tests and one-on-one tutoring available. Meet the club's aircraft in your first session...by the last session, that plane will be like an *old friend*.

Done

Adding a little color

If you'd like to go crazy and take complete control of the look of your Web page, it's time to break out some of the color commands. As always, realize that only HTML 3.2-compliant browsers will notice all this colorful fun—but more and more of the latest browsers do.

Coloring your canvas

Let's start by coloring the background. Using the BGCOLOR attribute for the <BODY> tag, you create a background color by specifying a 6-digit hexadecimal number. This attribute takes the following format:

```
<BODY BGCOLOR=#rrggbb>
...HTML Document...
</BODY>
```

The #rrggbb number represents the two-digit hexadecimal number for red, green, and blue values of the color you want added to the background of your document. An example of this is the following, which would turn the background of your page black:

```
<BODY BGCOLOR="#000000"
```

Background graphics: Size matters

There's an interesting little paradox with background graphics. I've constantly told you that graphics files should be as small as possible to speed their downloading over the Internet. And, the same is true for background graphics, most of the time.

The exception is the fact that once a background graphic is downloaded to the Web browser, it's actually displayed a little quicker if it's *physically* bigger (e.g., 3 inches × 4 inches, instead of 2 inches × 3 inches). That's because the Web browser has to "tile" the image behind the Web page. The bigger the graphic, the fewer the tiles.

If you're using the same background graphic for *all* of your pages, then it's okay to send a file that's a little on the large size—both physically and in terms of kilobytes. After the background is in the browser's cache, it will load rather quickly.

If you use a different background on every page, though, the cache effect won't help as much. In that case, you'll still want to keep your graphics fairly small.

Similarly, `#ffffff` would be a white background, `#ff0000` would be red, `#00ff00` would be green, and so on.

TIP **Here's a quick refresher in hex numbers. Hexadecimal means** base-16, as opposed to base-10 (normal counting numbers), so each column in a hex number represents a multiple of 16, not 10. The right-most column (we called it the "one's place" in grade school) needs single-digit numbers past nine in order to allow us to represent hex numbers.

Unfortunately, our numbering system doesn't have single digits past nine. (10, which is past nine, is a two-digit number in base-10. See?) So, we use letters—the first six of the alphabet. An *F* in the right-most column represents the value 15, and an *F* in the 16's place represents 240 (15×16). So, the hex number FF is equal to 255 (240+15).

By the way, because all this is remarkably confusing, nearly all these attributes will also accept a lot of typical color names (such as "yellow" or "light blue"). You might try them first.

Making text readable in a color world

After you've changed the background colors in your document, you may need to change the foreground (text) colors to make them readable. The default for most graphical browsers is black text, aside from hypertext links. If you change your background color so that it's also black, you'll have a communication problem.

TIP **There are a number of pages on the Web to help you pick colors** for backgrounds and links. Try **http://www.bga.com/~rlp/dwp/palette/ palette.html** and **http://www.phoenix.net/~jacobson/rgb.html** to start.

To change the main text color, you use the TEXT attribute to the <BODY> tag, which takes the following format:

```
<BODY TEXT="#rrggbb">
...HTML document...
</BODY>
```

In this code, `#rrggbb` represents another series of three two-digit hex numbers. An example appropriate for the black background would be the following, which turns the text white:

```
<BODY TEXT="#FFFFFF">
```

It's also possible the change the colors used to represent hypertext links in HTML, using three different attributes: `LINK`, `VLINK`, and `ALINK`. These represent an unvisited link, a visited link, and an active link, respectively.

To change these, you'd use the following format:

```
<BODY LINK="#rrggbb" VLINK="#rrggbb" ALINK="#rrggbb">
...HTML document...
</BODY>
```

Once again, the numbers are three two-digit hex numbers that represent the red, green, and blue values of the desired color. The default values are blue for `LINK`, purple for `VLINK`, and red for `ALINK`. These values may also be overriden by the user if they've set different colors in their browser's preferences settings.

 TIP **How can you see an "active" link? If you notice, a link turns a** different color right after you click it—basically, just so you know you've been successful in selecting it. The `ALINK` value is also the color of a hypermedia link while the file is downloaded to the user's computer.

Creating colorful words

So far all the color commands we've seen for text have been rather global in scope—but it's actually possible to change the color of individual words (or sentences, paragraphs, etc.) with a quick swipe of the `<FONT>` container tag. Here's how it works:

```
<FONT COLOR=RED>This text is red.</FONT>
```

The value for the `COLOR` attribute can be one of those confusing and boring `#rrggbb` hex numbers, or it can be a simple, delightful, intuitive color name. Take your pick.

Beyond the basics: Animated GIFs

The GIF89a specification—which as I mentioned earlier has the capability to display gradually (interlacing) and offers transparent backgrounds—has another special capability that has recently taken the Web by storm. With GIF89a it's possible to store a number of images in a single GIF file, and then scroll through those images automatically. That capability, with the right graphics program, enables you to create animated and slide-show GIFs.

Animated GIFs are currently only fully displayed in Netscape 2.0 (or above) and IE 3.0 or above. Other browsers may begin to support them, but, for now, browsers that don't support animated GIFs either show the animation once, or just show the first or last image in the animation.

To create an animated GIF, you need a program designed to handle the multiple-graphic feature of GIF89a. The shareware GIF Construction Set for Windows (Alchemy Software, **http://www.mindworkshop.com/alchemy/gifcon.html**) is a great example of a program that walks you through the creation of animated GIFs.

 TIP Mac users should check out the shareware GifBuilder (Yves Piquet, available Mac archives, like MacWorld Software **http://www.macworld.com/software/**), which offers straightforward animated GIF functionality.

Creating an animated GIF with the GIF Construction Set is simple—the hard part is creating the frames or "cells" for the animation in another program. If you're working in Paint Shop Pro, for instance, you create a number of different images to represent the movement for your animation, as shown in Figure 7.11.

 CAUTION Unless you want a "strobing" effect on your animation, you should keep every frame you create the same size, with a solid-colored background.

With the frames of your animation created, the GIF Construction Set (GCS) makes things simple with the Animation Wizard. Fire up GCS and choose <u>F</u>ile, <u>A</u>nimation Wizard. Follow the on-screen instructions to create your animation.

The GIF89a format stores information like how many times to loop the animation, how long to wait between frames, and what frames occur in what order. All it takes, then, is a program capable of getting that information from you, and saving it in the correct format.

Fig. 7.11
Each cell of the animation needs to be created individually to create the illusion of movement.

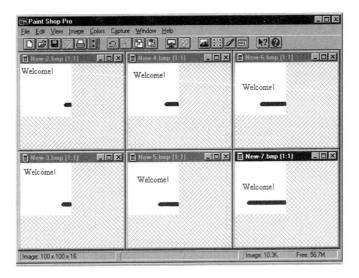

The GCS window shows you the order in which images appear in the animation, and it allows you to change certain variables (such as LOOP and CONTROL) by double-clicking their name in the listing. When you're ready to see the masterpiece you've created, click the View button. If things are moving like you think they should, you're done. Choose File, Save to save your new animated GIF.

 Plain English, Please!

In GCS, **LOOP** enables you to determine how many times the GIF animation will repeat itself before stopping. **CONTROL** enables you to set the amount of time that the image will display a particular frame before moving on in the animation.

 Animated GIFs don't always have to be animations. A flashing "billboard" or slide-show effect is possible if a number of different images (generally the exact same size) are added—with a CONTROL delay between each—to the animated GIF file.

Part III: Advanced HTML

8

Imagemaps for Eye-Catching Hyperlinks

● **In this chapter:**

- ● **What's an imagemap?**

- ● **Client-side versus server-side**

- ● **Good imagemap design**

- ● **Boring but necessary imagemap syntax**

- ● **How to write the imagemap's map files**

- ● **Specify clickable regions on your imagemap**

- ● **Available tools for creating map files**

Imagemaps are just graphics with more than one link inside, but they've become one of the most popular HTML features of all. . . . . ⊙

Hyperlinks reflect the way we think and act—they're nonlinear, spontaneous, and intuitive, working more like a human brain and less like a computer. With hyperlinks, it's possible to spend hours following a diverging path of interests and whims, exploring whatever information you happen to come across. Pictures make great hyperlinks, especially when you can assign separate hyperlinks to different parts of the picture. That's precisely what imagemaps let you do.

Just what is an imagemap?

An **imagemap** is a Web picture that contains clickable regions, or **hot zones**. When you click one region, you access one Web page. When you click another part of the image, you get an entirely different Web page. This is what differentiates imagemaps from simple hyperlinked "clickable" graphics (see Chapter 5). A clickable graphic is a picture that has only one associated hyperlink. An imagemap is a picture with two or more associated links. Where you click determines where the hyperlink will take you.

 Plain English, Please!

> Hypertext is often called hot text, so the regions on an imagemap can rightly be called **hot zones**. When you create an imagemap, you define different parts of the graphic to be hyperlinks. Each region is assigned its own URL. Click in that particular zone and the relevant URL is loaded. **99**

Imagemaps work as a team effort between the user's browser and a program on the page's Web server that processes where the mouse click occurs in the image (its pixel coordinates for you techie-types—discussed later in the chapter). Figure 8.1 shows an example of a simple imagemap used as a control center for Apple Computer's Web site.

Fig. 8.1
Apple's imagemap
interface isn't terribly
fancy, but it's
consistent and it loads
quickly in a browser.

Imagemap for controls

Fire up your browser and head for **http://www.compaq.com**, **http://www.whitehouse.gov**, or **http://www.apple.com**. When the imagemap
graphic (the interface control) has loaded, watch the status line at the bottom
of your browser as you move your mouse cursor across the graphic. What
you see is a display of coordinates rather than a destination URL. That's how
you can tell that the image is an imagemap (see Figure 8.2). The coordinates
have been defined by the Web author to link to specific URLs. You learn how
to define these coordinates in this chapter.

Many Web sites have navigational toolbars—clickable text and function
buttons—as integral parts of all the site's Web pages, so that when a user
wants to go to the home page, he clicks the part of the picture that has a
house on it. This is great because the imagemap is used over and over again,

Fig. 8.2
The browser can tell
where—exactly—the
user is pointing the
mouse on a page.

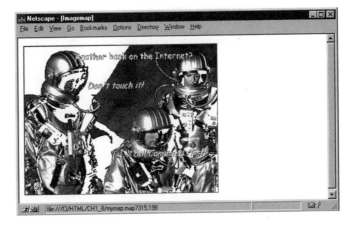

and the user becomes familiar with the navigational imagemap very quickly. Figure 8.3 shows a great example of an imagemap that is unambiguous and easy to use.

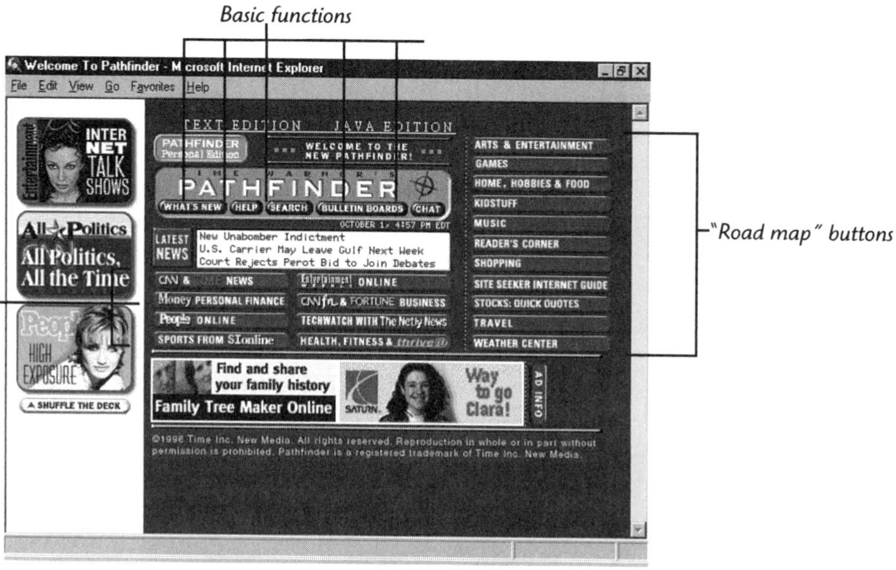

Fig. 8.3
Time Warner's Pathfinder home page includes a "road map," clickable text, and function buttons—all in one inline image.

Imagemaps are similar to other visual, graphics-based interfaces, such as Microsoft Windows or the Mac OS. Computer games often have complex graphical interfaces that encourage you to click objects or screen areas to accomplish tasks or receive information.

Client-side versus server-side

Let's stop here for a second and address something else you may have seen around the Web. Sometimes you'll be waving the mouse over a graphic that you know is an imagemap—but instead of coordinates, you see URLs. What's up with that?

When you see URLs in the status bar you're dealing with a **client-side** imagemap. With the latest HTML 3.2-compatible browsers, it's possible for you to actually create a map that isn't

designed to use the Web server at all—instead, it figures out the coordinates *and* the URL, and then loads the page when the user clicks.

Currently, it's Netscape, Internet Explorer, and Spyglass Mosaic that support client-side imagemaps—in my opinion, they'll be the first way to create maps in the near future. For now, I show you how to cover all the bases with both types of maps in the last section of this chapter, "Beyond the basics: Client-side imagemaps."

In each instance, the program that processes the mouse click varies depending on the software running on the Web server. The most popular imagemap is from NCSA, which is used with the NCSA Web server software. Another is MapServe, a package available for the Macintosh. Most newer Web server packages have imagemap support built in.

Q&A *Is it necessary to have a graphical Web browser to use imagemaps?*

Sure is—at least with server-side imagemaps. Without a browser with graphic support capabilities, someone who visits your Web page has no way to access or read your imagemaps. Even using ALT text links is tricky and clunky. If you want to cater to these users, you want to at least offer a "text-only" menu that duplicates the links of the imagemap. It could be just below the imagemap graphic, or perhaps at the bottom of the page. Your text menu could look something like this:

```
<A HREF="index.htm">Index</A> ¦ <A
HREF="products.htm">Products</A> ¦ <A
HREF="service.htm">Service</A> ¦ <A HREF="help.html">Help</A>
```

This is a very typical way to support both graphical and text-only browsers on the same page. Of course, this is entirely up to you. You don't have to cater to nongraphical browsers, but you'll alienate this particular group of users if you don't.

How do I create an imagemap?

The rest of this chapter outlines in detail how to create imagemaps. To put the process in perspective before we get into the specifics, here are the basic steps:

1 Select the graphics file you want to use as the basis for your imagemap.

2 Decide how you want to divide the image into regions, and decide which regions will lead to which Web pages.

3 Using a special program, map out the regions or hot zones for the image (in effect, you're overlaying shapes on the image). The program then creates a **map definition file** for use on the Web server.

Plain English, Please!

A **map definition file** is a regular ASCII text file that includes information about the coordinates of each hot zone that you create, and its associated hot zone. Only rarely would you hand-code a map definition file—you'll almost always rely on a special program that lets you draw the hot zones graphically. It then creates the definition file.

4 Assign URLs to each region.

5 Store the map file and the image file on a computer that functions as a Web server.

6 Write the HTML code for your Web page that will display the imagemap.

As you can see, imagemapping isn't an easy procedure. But practice, as they say, makes perfect, and nowhere is this more apparent in HTML design than in the creation and storage of imagemaps.

 Q&A *Do I really have to put my imagemap on a Web server?*

Unfortunately, yes, at least for server-side imagemaps. You can't create an imagemap on a stand-alone computer (PC, Mac, or UNIX), not even if that computer is connected to the Internet. The machine must be set up as a Web server because imagemaps are *served*, not just viewed (as graphics files are). The graphics file will be stored in your regular space on the Web server—the map information file (more in a moment) may need to be stored in the CGI-BIN directory or elsewhere on the "back end" of the server.

For client-side, you don't have to have the imagemap on a Web server, because all the processing is handled by the Web browser. (See "Beyond the basics: Client-side maps" at the end of this chapter.)

Start with an appropriate image

The image you use depends on what you need it to do. If you want to create a navigational toolbar that has links for a home page, e-mail, and an FTP resource, you might want to create a long rectangular graphic and include icons of a house, a mailbox, and a file folder.

If you want to use your company's logo, you can do that, too (as long as it can reasonably be divided into different sections), and graphically edit it to contain words that can then be linked to different pages. If your site is divided up by information pertaining to different geographical regions, you may want to use a geographical map, so that people can click the region they are interested in.

In fact, it's with imagemaps that artists really start to shine through on the Web. If you're a graphic artist, create a graphic that's appealing, corporate, or just plain cool (if you have the freedom) that can be used to navigate the site. The graphic still needs to be reasonably small (file-size wise) but this is your chance to really be creative.

Supported graphic file formats

Imagemaps generally use a file format you've already been introduced to—the GIF format. JPEG files may also become commonplace for imagemaps, but for now you should convert your digital pictures to GIFs to be certain they're fully supported.

TIP **There are many commercial, shareware, and freeware graphics** programs available today. Almost all of them have the capability to convert digital pictures from one file format to another. If, for example, you have a BMP file, you can usually convert it to a GIF file by opening it in a graphics program such as Paint Shop Pro, choosing the Save As option, and then changing the file format to GIF (or GIF89a) before you save it.

Imagemap GIFs can be in either GIF87a or GIF89a formats, and they can also be interlaced. (Chapter 7 explains what these formats are and how to use them.) Images can also be transparent or regular. A transparent image has no visible background, and looks as though it is floating on the page.

Take care that you don't create imagemaps that are too wide for the typical browser window, or you may find that your readers can't see or use some of the options on your imagemap. They may even have to horizontally scroll in order to use the entire graphic, and that can be extremely annoying.

Q&A *How do I know whether my image is too wide?*
There isn't really any way to tell if it might be too wide on different browsers other than by trying all of them out. However, the one thing that

makes a big difference for how large an image appears is the video resolution of the machine on which the browser is running. Older machines with slower video cards often run at a lower resolution such as 800–600 or 640–480. These resolutions cause everything on the screen to be larger. If your picture works fine at 1024–768, but is too large when you switch your resolution down to 800–600, you may want to rethink your sizing. Also, you're better off having a picture that is too long vertically than too wide horizontally, because people are used to vertical scrolling on the Web.

The *ISMAP* attribute starts the imagemap process

ISMAP is an attribute to the <IMG> tag. Essentially, it tells the Web browser that this is an imagemap, so it needs to make note of the coordinates of the user's click. The browser doesn't have to know if the user has clicked a clickable region or not—that's a job for the Web server's imagemap program. The syntax for using an ISMAP is:

```
<A HREF="MAP_file_URL"><IMG SRC=image_URL ISMAP></A>
```

The MAP_file_URL is the location of the related database of clickable regions and their actions, and image_URL is the inline image being used in the Web page.

For example, if your image is called *picture.gif* and is located in the /web/ pictures/ directory on your server, and the map definition file is called *picturemap* and is located in /cgi-bin/mapfiles/, your HTML tags would look like this:

```
<A HREF="http://www.server.com/cgi-bin/mapfiles/
picturemap"><IMG SRC=http://www.server.com/web/pictures/
mymap.gif ISMAP></A>
```

Figure 8.4 shows how the imagemap is added to a Web page's code, and Figure 8.5 shows how Internet Explorer displays the new imagemap.

If your imagemap does nothing at all, it may be because it's not
actually on a Web. Server-side imagemaps must be downloaded from a Web
server into your browser in order to work. Check with your Internet provider
to see how you might develop a Web site on their server, and then add the
imagemap to that site. (You'll probably at least need permission to put the
map definition file on the server.)

Fig. 8.4
Sometimes your map
definition file needs to
be on the "back side"
of the server (perhaps
in the cgi-bin
directory). Check with
your ISP or Web server
administrator.

Fig. 8.5
Some browsers don't
display imagemaps with
colored borders like
other images inside
anchor links, which
have borders to show
they are "clickable."

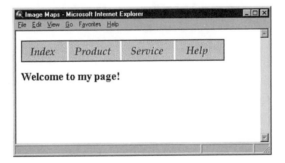

Every server-side imagemap actually requires two files—the map definition
file and the graphic file. In many cases, you can simply store both files in
your Web directory—but not always.

Some Web servers are picky about where you store the map
definition file—and some aren't. Your best bet is to ask your Web server
administrator where you should store the definition file.

TIP **A clickable region in an imagemap is a kind of hyperlink, but it** may not be encased in a definite visible border the way inline image hyperlinks are. Unless the imagemap makes it clear without explanation, it's always a good idea to tell users they should click the imagemap.

How to create the imagemap file

It's possible to create a map definition file in any word processor or text editor, as long as you remember to save it as a text file. Comments may be incorporated into map files using leading # characters to make it obvious what it is you are trying to do. This is a good idea, because somebody else may come along and modify the map file you've created.

The problem is, it's really more trouble than it's worth. Unless you're completely intent on the self-satisfaction that a proud accomplishment— like creating ASCII text files that map servers can understand—will bring, I'd suggest using a Windows, Mac, or UNIX program to solve this problem for you.

Using special programs to define the map

Each platform has its own tools that do the job. If you are a professional graphics user and have PhotoShop on your computer, it will do the trick. Most people aren't that serious about creating images, and they should rely on one of the available shareware tools.

Microsoft Windows users have two good options: Mapedit (**http://www.boutell.com/mapedit/**), a 16-bit Windows 3.1 utility, and MapThis! (**ftp://ftp.winsite.com/pub/pc/win95/netutil/** then look for mpths120.zip or a newer file), a 32-bit tool for Windows 95 users. Mapedit and MapThis! let you mark out your clickable regions by drawing directly on your inline image. You can then create your map files—complete with URLs. Mapedit even lets you change and move the clickable regions you create.

TIP **On the Web, imagemaps must be created with a lot of care so** readers don't get lost or overlook available hyperlinks because they didn't recognize something as being "clickable." Ask a friend to point out all the different clickable regions on your imagemap to ensure that it's clear.

UNIX users are crazy not to use xv (**http://csep2.phy.ornl.gov/csep/XV/ XV1.html**), an X Windows viewer and editor that does everything you might want with your graphics—format conversions, interlacing, and transparency—as well as finding your pixel coordinates. You have to track your coordinates by hand (xv doesn't make a list for you) but as an all-purpose tool, it's one of the best.

Mac users should look for a tool called WebMap. This program lets you draw the clickable regions right on top of your image and then define the "action" (the URL for the hyperlink) for each region. The program then saves all the information into your map file for you. Figure 8.6 shows a typical WebMap session.

Fig. 8.6
WebMap is a recommended graphical environment for creating a map definition file on a Macintosh.

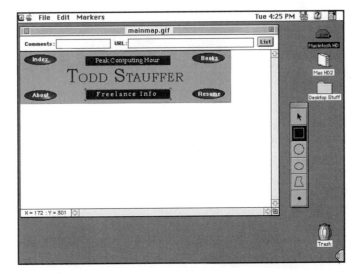

More information about WebMap is available online at the URL **http:// www.city.net/cnx/software/webmap.html**.

Other programs for coordinates

What if you don't have one of these tools, or what if the package doesn't automatically create the map file for you? In this case, you have to record the pixel coordinates by hand, and then type up your map file and insert it into your map file directory. But how do you determine the coordinates? Most graphics packages have a coordinate listing.

For example, in Paint Shop Pro, you simply open up the image and point your cursor at the pixel you want as one of your coordinates; the coordinates can be read off the bottom of the screen. (This is shown in Figure 8.7.) It's kind of a pain compared to the packages that do it for you and write the map file automatically, but at least it works.

Fig. 8.7
To determine the coordinates of the smaller rectangle in this large image, you simply put the cursor over the corner of the rectangle and take note of the coordinates (87,36) shown at the bottom.

The completed map definition file

Whether you're using a graphical program or creating your map definition file by hand, there are a few things you should know. After it's completed, you can look at it in a text editor, if desired, to make sure everything seems correctly lined up and ready for the Web server. Every map definition file will have a listing of shapes and coordinates along with comments about the file (see Figure 8.8).

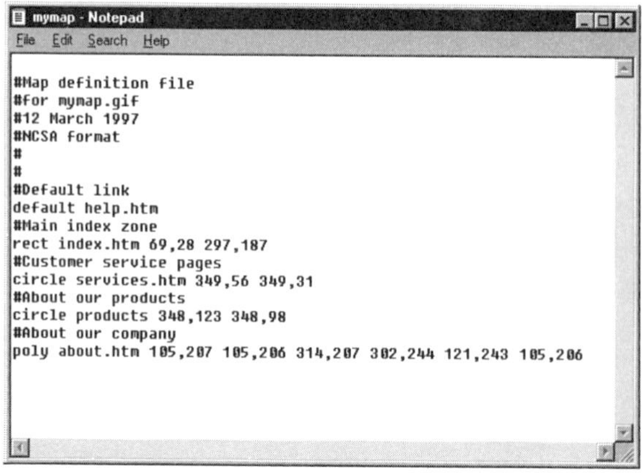

Fig. 8.8
A typical map definition file. Each entry line (starting with a shape) is a separate hot zone.

The components of a standard map file entry are:

```
shape URL x1,y1 x2,y2 . . . xn,yn . . .
```

Here, *shape* is the type of clickable region (circle, rectangle, polygon, or oval); *URL* is the URL to send back to the browser (either another Web page, an FTP connection, Gopher connection, and so on); and *x1,y1* is the list of coordinates that describe the exact location of the hot spot in your inline image.

Each clickable region type uses a different number of pixel coordinates to define their shapes (see Table 8.1).

Table 8.1 Defining clickable region methods

Method	Type	Required coordinates
circle	circle	2 pairs: center edgepoint
oval	oval	2 pairs: upper_left, lower_right
rect	rectangle	2 pairs: upper_left, lower_right
poly	polygon	"polygon" means "many-sided"; up to 100 pairs can define the vertices ("points") of the shape
point	a point	1 pair: the_point

The point method is useful as a "closest to" input (it's pretty hard to click a specific pixel in an image). If two points are defined in your map file, the one that is selected is the one that the mouse click is "closest to" (as measured by a straight line).

The map files also include a line that states the default URL for mouse clicks that are outside any of the listed clickable regions. Be careful, though, not to include a default URL in the map file for an imagemap that has a point hot spot—any clicks that are not in other clickable regions (like circles or rectangles) will be "closest to" the point, and the default URL will never be used.

If you decide to code this file by hand, put one clickable region definition on each line in your map file to make it easier to read and troubleshoot in case of problems.

Here's what happens with the actual map files

Browsers are programmed to wait for mouse clicks. When you click, your browser sends information to the Web server where the HTML page actually resides. In the case of an imagemap, the browser sends the coordinates of the map segment that was clicked on. The imagemap program or server software responds in accordance with the map file that is included in the Anchor tag. The file is primarily a list of links that correspond to each of the clickable regions in the imagemap. If the coordinates sent do not match any in the list, the software returns the default URL value, which is usually a page saying something like, "You haven't clicked anything. Please try again."

TIP Avoid pages that tell people they've either made a mistake or have not accomplished anything. You're just wasting their time making their browser download another page that is irrelevant to what they want to do. One good idea is to have the default area point to the current page, so that a mistake gives them another try at the imagemap.

WWW tools: MapMaker

Available at URL **http://www.tns.lcs.mit.edu/cgi-bin/mapmaker**, this Web service helps you create an imagemap for any existing inline image on a Web page already up on the WWW. It asks for the URL of your page and then maps the clickable regions you fill in (see Figure 8.9).

Fig. 8.9
After you enter your clickable regions and action URLs, click the complete imagemap button to compile the new map file and save it to your hard drive.

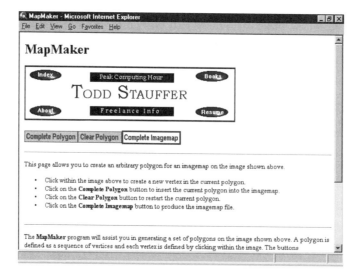

This Web service is provided by Professor David Tennehouse and the Telemedia, Networks and Systems Group at the MIT Laboratory for Computer Science.

Beyond the basics: Client-side maps

It's my opinion that we'll be moving quickly to a point where only client-side imagemaps are necessary. It just makes more sense to have the browser do the work, instead of bothering with a special map server program on the Web server computer. Client-side imagemaps require a bit more code, but, fortunately, we already have all the tools we need at our disposal.

The HTML for a client-side map is a little different than server-side, adding a new attribute for <IMG>: USEMAP. The USEMAP attribute excepts an internal-document URL, as in:

```
<IMG SRC="picture.gif" USEMAP="#mapdata">
```

The name of the USEMAP link doesn't have to be mapdata, it can be anything you want it to be so long as it matches up with the name assigned to our new HTML tag: <MAP></MAP>. <MAP> is where you store the coordinates for the imagemap, as in:

```
<MAP NAME="mapdata">
<AREA SHAPE="RECT" COORDS="x,y,x1,y1" HREF="index.html">
<AREA SHAPE="CIRCLE" COORDS="x,y,r" HREF="service.html">
<AREA SHAPE="POLY" COORDS="x,y,a,b,c" HREF="products.html">
</MAP>
```

The <MAP> tag and its contents serve the same purpose as the map definition file for a server-side imagemap, except that the <MAP> tag is actually in the same HTML document as the <IMG> for the imagemap. It doesn't really matter where—you can put the <MAP> tag and info anywhere you want in the same document as the USEMAP attribute.

 TIP **Actually, you can put the <MAP> tags in another document, but you** need to change the USEMAP attribute to reflect it. Something like USEMAP="http://www.fake.com/maps.html#mapdata" would work fine.

Here's an important difference between server-side and client-side: there are only three shapes for client-side maps. You've got rectangles (`RECT`), circles (`CIRCLE`), and polygons (`POLY`) to play with. So how do you get the coordinates for these shapes? Use one of the map definition programs we talked about earlier in this chapter. You won't need the text file—just the numbers generated for the file. Plug them directly into your `<MAP>` data and you've got a working client-side imagemap (see Figure 8.10). Just remember to use only those three shapes. No `POINT` or `OVAL` allowed.

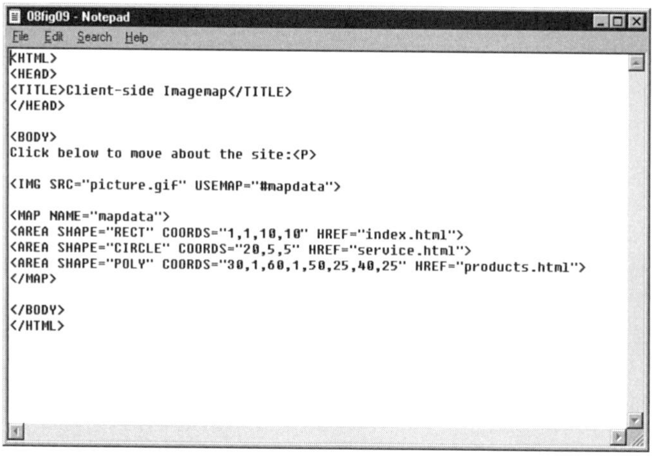

Fig. 8.10
Here's all the code I need for a client-side imagemap.

```
08fig09 - Notepad
File  Edit  Search  Help
<HTML>
<HEAD>
<TITLE>Client-side Imagemap</TITLE>
</HEAD>

<BODY>
Click below to move about the site:<P>

<IMG SRC="picture.gif" USEMAP="#mapdata">

<MAP NAME="mapdata">
<AREA SHAPE="RECT" COORDS="1,1,10,10" HREF="index.html">
<AREA SHAPE="CIRCLE" COORDS="20,5,5" HREF="service.html">
<AREA SHAPE="POLY" COORDS="30,1,60,1,50,25,40,25" HREF="products.html">
</MAP>

</BODY>
</HTML>
```

TIP **You can even create a "default" hot zone that catches any clicks** outside of the hot zones you define. Using `RECT` (if your entire image is rectangular) just enter the coordinates for the entire graphic ("0,0,100,100" for instance) and make this the *last* entry in the `<MAP>` data. Give it an URL to whatever you want to be the default—usually your index page.

Want the best of both worlds? It's even possible (and encouraged, when you have access to your Web server and administrator permission) to use both client- and server-side imagemap technology at the same time. All it takes is some ingenious HTML:

```
<A HREF="http://www.company.com/cgi-bin/mapfiles/
picturemap"><IMG SRC=http://www.company.com/web/pictures/
picture.gif ISMAP USEMAP="#mapdata"></A>
```

Do you see it all in there? There is an `<IMG>` set up for both client- and server-side processing. Any browser that recognizes client-side technology goes with that first; others won't understand the `USEMAP` attribute, so they'll stay away from it and opt for the `ISMAP`—server-side process—instead.

9

Tabling Your Data

● In this chapter:

- What are tables good for?

- Using tables well

- How to build a table in HTML

- Examples straight from the web

- Using tables for page layout

HTML tables can display all sorts of information, making a lot of information easier for the user to read. Tables are so flexible, in fact, that they can be used to format your pages to look as if they've been prepared with a desktop publishing program . . . . ▶

I f the word table conjures up an image of a boring form of data full of statistical information found in the appendices of long documents, do I have a surprise for you! Tables are at the root of some of the most attractive and flexible Web pages. That's because HTML allows tables to contain everything from pictures and links to even video and sound files.

Putting a table of information on the Web offers a number of interesting possibilities, but also a number of constraints. The overall effect can be quite impressive and very useful.

So, what are tables good for?

HTML tables are good for nearly anything that tables on paper are good for—sales figures, tables of contents, you name it. Because of the Web's limitations, it's true that some standard table ideas simply don't translate well. But, on the other hand, with the multimedia capabilities of the Web, information you wouldn't normally associate with a table or spreadsheet works very well in tables.

Tables that do not work well on the Web are those that are extremely large or those that contain paragraph after paragraph of text. This is because Internet users are confined to the viewing size of their monitors. Of course, browsers do allow users to scroll both horizontally and vertically.

 CAUTION **A table that extends beyond the physical limit of the screen can** be difficult to actually use because the headings will easily fall out of view. Tables also limit the ability of the browser to reformat text to fit the window, so, if your table's too big, all your users will be forced to scroll.

Think of a table that contains product and price information. It sounds pretty standard. But when you add to that information a picture that is hyperlinked to an even larger picture and perhaps a full description of the product, the possibilities begin to become clear. A video of a product demonstration or a sound clip of music can easily become very valuable elements of a table. Figure 9.1 shows an obvious candidate for hyperlinked table elements.

Fig. 9.1
Some tables translate really well into HTML and onto the Web. The Periodic Table of Elements is a natural candidate, allowing users to link to information about the different elements.

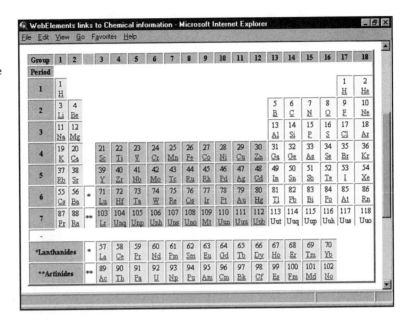

 TIP The HTML code that is used to construct tables is not overly complicated, but it can get a little unwieldy. Luckily, many HTML editors available on the Internet come with built-in tables features, and they're getting increasingly powerful.

Start small and work your way up

A table in HTML is wrapped up by the <TABLE> and </TABLE> container tags. From there, it is easiest to think of a table as defined by its individual cells. You determine the maximum number of rows and columns your table will have. Then you define your cells one by one. Cells are defined from left to right in rows and then from top to bottom.

66 *Plain English, please!*

Rows, columns, and **cells** are the standard terms for talking about tables. If you've worked with spreadsheets, you already know about them. Rows go across the screen while columns go up and down. Every place where a row and column intersect is a cell. A table that has 10 rows and three columns has 30 cells. 99

Deciding what your table will look like

Before you begin designing your cells, you may want to specify some characteristics for the whole table. For instance, you can specify whether or not it will have a border and how wide that border will be. This is done by including the BORDER=# attribute within the opening <TABLE> tag. If you add the BORDER attribute without a number (e.g. <TABLE BORDER>), most browsers will default to a value of one. A value of zero (e.g. <TABLE BORDER=0>) or leaving out the BORDER attribute will create a table with no border at all. Larger numbers mean thicker borders.

You can determine, in the <TABLE> tag, how wide your table will be with the WIDTH attribute. By default, the width of a table is based on the width of each of the columns in that table. The width of each column (unless otherwise specified) defaults to be just wide enough for your widest data element or picture.

This can result in a table that looks cramped. By specifying that your table is to take up 90 percent of the space between your margins, for instance, you can include a lot of nice white space. This is done by adding the width attribute to the opening <TABLE> tag, as follows:

```
<TABLE BORDER=2 WIDTH=90%>
```

You might also set a table's WIDTH to a fixed number, like 600, which keeps it a uniform size, but ensures that it will fit on a 640x480 (standard VGA) monitor.

```
<TABLE BORDER=0 WIDTH=600>
```

Finally, for even more control over how your table looks, you can set the CELLSPACING and CELLPADDING attributes within the table tag. CELLSPACING specifies how much space is between cells; the default is two. CELLPADDING specifies how much space is between a cell wall and the contents of the cell. The default is one— you probably won't want to set it to zero or your text will run into the cell and table borders. The following is an example of a complete <TABLE> tag:

```
<TABLE BORDER WIDTH=90% CELLSPACING=4 CELLPADDING=5>
```

Okay, now you're ready to move on and define some cells!

TIP Remember, everything except <TABLE **is optional. It's perfectly** reasonable to have nothing but <TABLE in the first line of your table definition, if you so desire. (Or if all those attributes seem a bit too trivial for you to bother with.)

The data cell and the heading cell

There are two main table elements: the data cell and the heading cell. The tag that defines a data cell is <TD>, and it can be matched up with a complementary <TABLE, but it doesn't have to be. Both the heading cell tag and the TD tag have a number of attributes: ALIGN, VALIGN, COLSPAN, and ROWSPAN.

TIP The only major difference between data cells and header cells is the fact that text in header cells is boldface. That and the fact that you need to use <TH></TH> to create a header cell.

Alignment of cells

ALIGN specifies the alignment of the cell's contents, and it can take the value of CENTER, JUSTIFY, DECIMAL, RIGHT, or LEFT.

- If the ALIGN attribute is not defined, your contents default to LEFT alignment in most browsers.

- The JUSTIFY value of the ALIGN attribute justifies the textual contents of your cell (forces the contents to align to both left and right margins, like a newspaper column), but only if it is practical. For instance, it won't justify a single word by spacing between characters to fit the cell.

- The DECIMAL value aligns everything with whatever character you specify as a decimal point.

You specify a decimal point in your <TD> or <TH> tag by writing dp="(whatever symbol you want to use to align)". For example, if you want everything within a particular cell to align to a slash, use the following:

```
<TD ALIGN=DECIMAL DP="/">Cowboys/Falcons</TD>
```

This can be really useful for displaying nearly anything that you want aligned to a particular character, including, of course, money.

Spanning cells

The COLSPAN attribute determines how many columns wide that cell will be—the **default value** is one. The ROWSPAN attribute specifies how many rows deep your cell will be. The default for ROWSPAN is also one.

 Plain Enlish, Please

Default value is the value that comes into play if you don't specify a different value. In this case, you get one column width unless you specifically tell HTML to give you more.

Vertical alignment

The VALIGN attribute can appear inside a TR, TH, or TD cell, and it controls whether text inside the cell is aligned to the top of the cell, the bottom of the cell, or vertically centered within the cell. If used in the TR tag, it specifies that all the cells in the row should be vertically aligned to the same baseline.

This all may seem a bit confusing at first, but a quick example should clear things up (see Figure 9.2).

Fig. 9.2
Some cells span more than one column or row, and data within the cells can be aligned in different ways.

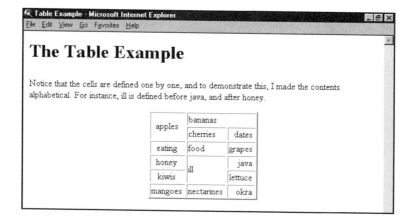

The data in Figure 9.2 doesn't really mean much, but it's a simple example that makes the HTML easy to understand. The code is in Listing 9.1.

Listing 9.1

A sample HTML table

```
<H1>The Table Example</H1> <BR>
<P>Notice that the cells are defined one by one, and to
demonstrate this,
       ➥I made the contents alphabetical.  For instance, ill is
defined
 before java, and after honey.
<BR><BR>
<DIV ALIGN=CENTER>
<TABLE BORDER=2>
<TR><TD ALIGN=CENTER ROWSPAN=2>apples
<TD COLSPAN=2>bananas  </TR>

<TR><TD ALIGN=LEFT> cherries
<TD ALIGN=RIGHT>dates  </TR>

<TR><TD ALIGN=CENTER>eating
<TD>food
<TD ALIGN=RIGHT>grapes  </TR>

<TR><TD ALIGN=CENTER>honey
<TD ROWSPAN=2>ill
<TD ALIGN=RIGHT>java   </TR>

<TR><TD ALIGN=CENTER>kiwis
<TD ALIGN=RIGHT> lettuce  </TR>

<TR><TD ALIGN=CENTER> mangoes
<TD>nectarines
<TD ALIGN=RIGHT>okra </TR>
</TABLE>
</DIV>
```

TIP   **It's a good idea to sketch your table out on paper ahead of time**
to make sure that ROWSPAN and COLSPAN specifications make sense.
Otherwise, you could end up with something like that shown in Figure 9.3.

Listing 9.2 shows the first few lines of the HTML for the table in Figure 9.3.
You can see where the column addition went wrong.

Fig. 9.3
The HTML for this table specified one too many columns in the COLSPAN attribute of the first cell of the second row.

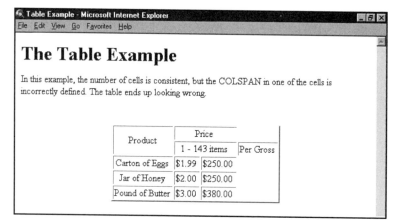

Listing 9.2

First lines for Figure 9.3

```
<TR><TD ALIGN=CENTER ROWSPAN=2>Product
<TD ALIGN=CENTER COLSPAN=2>Price </TR>

<TR><TD ALIGN=CENTER COLSPAN=2> 1 - 143 items
<TD ALIGN=RIGHT>Per Gross  </TR>

<TR><TD ALIGN=CENTER>Carton of Eggs
<TD ALIGN=RIGHT>$1.99
<TD ALIGN=RIGHT>$250.00  </TR>
```

Q&A

Why isn't my table appearing properly in my browser? Part of one of my cells isn't showing up.

You probably have defined your table in a way that causes two cells to overlap. You may have a cell that is three rows deep, and in that third row, you've got a cell that is two rows wide and overlapping your deep cell. The only way to avoid errors like this is by planning ahead and double-checking. Overlapping errors are rendered differently by different browsers, so it isn't always obvious that this is a problem.

Remember to use the WIDTH attribute in your table tag to give your table lots of white space and to make it easy to read. Figure 9.4 shows the same table you have been working with, but made a little bit more appealing with the addition of the WIDTH attribute.

Fig. 9.4
The WIDTH attribute of the table tag allows you to make a table wider than its default. The default, otherwise, makes each column only as wide as its widest cell.

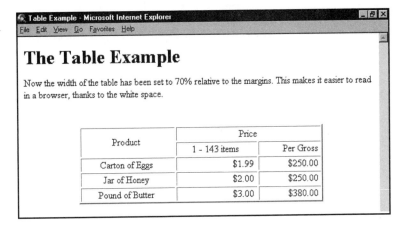

Table rows

The <TR> and </TR> tags are the table row tags, and they tell the browser that the cells defined after the <TR> and up to the next </TR> tag are all the cells in a single row. It is the existence of this tag that makes the </TD> and </TH> tags rather useless. Table data and table heading cells are considered closed when the browser reaches the next <TD>, <TH>, or </TR> tag. Therefore, the contents of every cell will be followed by the introduction of the next data or heading cell or by the end of row tag. So you really never need to include the complementary tags <TD> and <TH>. Here are two sample rows from earlier:

```
<TR><TD>apples <TD>bananas </TR>
<TR><TD> cherries <TD>dates </TR>
```

Each row needs to be explicitly defined, and you want the same number of columns in each row (using COLSPAN can cut down on the number of column entries, but things still need to add up). Make sure every row has a </TR> tag to keep things nice and tidy in your table.

 This is just like the HTML list tags we discussed in Chapter 6.
Recall that there was no </LI> tag for the <LI> list items, because each new <LI> tells the browser to add a new item. A </OL> or </UL> tag, just like and "end-of-the-row" tag </TR>, is necessary.

Captions

A table can also have a caption, using the <CAPTION> container tag. This is always a good idea and can be especially useful if put at the bottom of a table. You'll often introduce a table with some text preceding it, so a user scrolling down will catch a glimpse of the introductory text and then see the table.

The caption, then, can be used to be more specific about the table—perhaps attributing the information to its source or discussing the measurements you're using in the table.

By default, the caption actually appears above the table, so you'll need to specify otherwise in the caption tag as follows:

```
<CAPTION ALIGN=BOTTOM>This is the caption</CAPTION>
```

Okay, so let's have a look at a table that has a good number of rows, columns, headings, and a caption. Figure 9.5 is a good example of how to use headings and captions.

Fig. 9.5
The <TH> tag tells a browser that the specified cell is a heading cell and should therefore have special formatting.

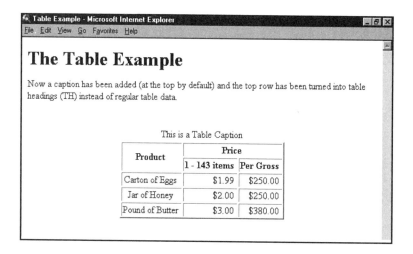

Listing 9.3 shows the HTML for the table in Figure 9.5.

Listing 9.3

Code for Figure 9.5

```
<CENTER><TABLE BORDER=2>
<CAPTION>This is a Table Caption</CAPTION>
<TR><TH ALIGN=CENTER ROWSPAN=2>Product
```

Listing 9.3 Continued

```
<TH COLSPAN=2>Price </TR>

<TR><TH ALIGN=LEFT> 1 - 143 items
<TH ALIGN=RIGHT>Per Gross  </TR>

<TR><TD ALIGN=CENTER>Carton of Eggs
<TD ALIGN=RIGHT>$1.99
<TD ALIGN=RIGHT>$250.00  </TR>
```

What else can I do with tables?

Want to put graphics in a table cell? Cool. Multimedia elements can easily be contained within a table. A cell can contain a picture, a link for a movie clip, or a link for a sound clip. Of course, if a cell can contain multimedia links, it can also contain hypertext links, which are very useful.

For tables that contain a number of brief elements and then a row or column filled with paragraphs of text, it's often a better idea to include a link to that text instead of the text itself. This not only saves space, but it keeps the table from looking really weird.

What about other HTML elements? Any HTML that can appear between <BODY> tags can also be put into a table cell. That includes lists, forms, imagemaps, and even another table.

Page layout with tables

In fact, embedding a table within a table is a good example of creative page layout. This works when you have a number of different pictures, text, lists, and tables that you want to show on different areas of the screen. In this case, you define a table with all of your contents, but without a border. Make your WIDTH=100%. Then when you embed a table, define the nested table with borders. You'll have a great screen layout. Imagemaps are also really good elements for a page that has a table layout. ESPN's SportsZone (**http://espnet.sportszone.com/**) is a great example of this, as you can see in Figure 9.6.

Fig. 9.6
Using an `imagemap` within a table can make your home page resemble the layout of a newsletter or magazine.

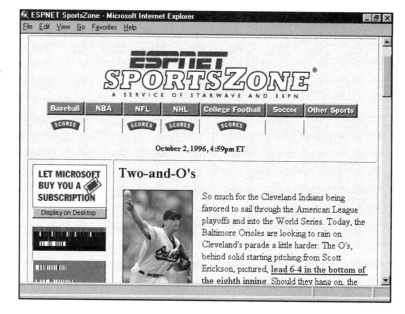

The HTML from Figure 9.6 is quite extensive. Consider a more simple example that should give you something to go on:

```
<TABLE BORDER=1 CELLPADDING=5>
<TR ALIGN=JUSTIFY>
<TD> A bunch of text <P> <TD> <IMG SRC="animage.gif"> <TD>
More text
</TR>
<TR>
<TD COLSPAN=2> <H3>Headline</H3> Paragraph of text <P> <TD>
Image or icon
</TR>
</TABLE>
```

Perhaps you can see where I'm going here. Even without nesting tables, you can create a page that allows you to compartmentalize your page into different sections. You'll need to play with it, but it's not a bad way to spend a few minutes—especially if Web design's limitations find you a bit frustrated.

Just for fun and ideas, Listing 9.4 shows the first bit of Figure 9.6 to give you an idea of what's involved. Notice the client-side imagemap being used in the top of the table. (*Note:* a lot of Java and Javascript has been eliminated from the listing for the sake of clarity. For a more complete view, use the View Source command in your browser while you're viewing the SportsZone home page.)

Listing 9.4

HTML code for Figure 9.6

```
<TABLE BORDER="1" VALIGN="top" CELLPADDING="8">

<TR>
<TD COLSPAN="3" ALIGN="CENTER">
<BR>
<A HREF="/img/logos/front.map">
<IMG SRC="/img/logos/h0913.gif" border=0 alt="ESPNET
SportsZone"
WIDTH=533 HEIGHT=138 USEMAP="#frontmap" ISMAP></A><P>
<B><FONT SIZE="-1">October 2, 1996, 4:59pm ET</FONT></B>
</TD>
</TR>

<TR>
<TD VALIGN="top" ALIGN="center" WIDTH="128" ROWSPAN="2">

<A HREF="/img/login/day1.map"><IMG SRC="/img/login/v1001.gif"
WIDTH="127" HEIGHT="823" BORDER="0" ALT="Log-in"
USEMAP="#day1map"
ISMAP></a>

</TD>

<TD COLSPAN="2" VALIGN="top">

<H1>Two-and-O's</H1>

<IMG SRC="/editors/media/photo/mlb/1002cle.jpg" HEIGHT=160
WIDTH=120 HSPACE=8 ALIGN=left ALT="Photo of  Erickson">

So much for the Cleveland Indians being favored to sail
through the American League playoffs and into the World
Series.  Today, the Baltimore Orioles are looking to rain on
Cleveland's parade a little harder.  The O's, behind solid
starting pitching from Scott Erickson, pictured, <a href="/
mlb/961002/scoring/clebal.html"><b>lead 6-4 in the bottom of
the eighth inning</b></a>.  Should they hang on, the host
Orioles will take a commanding 2-0 lead in the best-of-five-
games series. Stay tuned.

</TD>
</TR>
```

It is important to remember that not only can a table contain many different HTML elements, it can also be part of many HTML elements. For example, a table can be part of a list, a form, or even part of a blockquote.

TIP **Don't forget that you can look at any page on the Web to see how** it works with the Edit, View Source (or similar) command in your Web browser application.

Q&A *I have a table that has a paragraph in one of the cells, but it's not wrapping the way I want it to. Can I do anything about this?*

Yes. You can set your table data tag to contain the NOWRAP attribute. This means that you have to manually insert line break tags (<BR>) at the points where you want the text to wrap. This isn't usually recommended, but if you need to use it you can. The tag looks like the following:

```
<TD NOWRAP>(paragraph with line breaks here)</TD>
```

Some great tables served on the Web

Web authors and designers have gotten very serious about tables in the last year, taking them from a Netscape-only technology to a standard method for presenting data and laying out entire Web pages.

One of the most well-known pages that has a table as its whole home page and table of contents is the Zippo News Service page (**http://www.zippo.com/**). In this case, the home page is a table made to look like the front page of a newspaper with part of each column containing a story headline and maybe a few brief sentences. But of course, instead of turning to the page that contains the full article, you simply click the link. The nice part about the Zippo table is the incorporation of pictures and inline hyperlinked images. Figure 9.7 shows the Zippo page.

The HTML source for this page is pretty intense. The listing below isn't everything it takes to put out the Zippo front page, but it should give you an idea of how the rows and cells were created to give things a newspaper feel (see Listing 9.5).

Fig. 9.7
The Zippo News Service page uses a table as its home page and incorporates hyperlinks and pictures into the scheme. This works great for advertising.

Listing 9.5

HTML code for Figure 9.7

```
<CENTER><TABLE BORDER=4 CELLPADDING=5 WIDTH=640>

<TH COLSPAN=3>
<CENTER><A HREF="zcopy.htm">
<IMG SRC="name.gif" border=0></A></CENTER>
<CENTER><STRONG>Extra - Zippo Introduces <A
HREF="direct.htm">Direct Read News</a> - A Daily News Exclu-
sive ! <BR><A HREF="isp.htm">ISPs</a> that provide Super
Zippo to their membership<BR>
</STRONG>
</CENTER>

</TH>
<TR>

<TD VALIGN=top WIDTH=200>
<CENTER><A HREF="http://www.pointcom.com"><IMG
SRC="5perct.gif" border=0></A>
```

continues

Listing 9.5 Continued

```
<A HREF="http://www.mckinley.com/"><IMG SRC="vert4sta.gif"
border=0></A></CENTER>
<HR>
<A HREF="http://drn.zippo.com/news-bin/wwwnews?*"><IMG
SRC="withev.gif" ALIGN=RIGHT BORDER=0></a>
News With<A HREF="http://drn.zippo.com/news-bin/
wwwnews?*"><STRONG> Everything</STRONG></a> On It. All news
Direct Read News groups carried on Zippo.
</TD>

<TD VALIGN=top>
<A HREF="http://www.cmp.com/NetGuide/home.html"><IMG
SRC="nguide.gif" border=0></A>
<HR>
<CENTER><A HREF="rules.htm"><IMG SRC="nrz.gif" border=0></
A></CENTER><P>
<A HREF="rules.htm">No Waiting</A> -You can enjoy Original
Zippo right now with -<P><CENTER><A HREF="rules.htm"><IMG
SRC="nim.gif" BORDER=0></CENTER>
<HR>
<CENTER><A HREF="gallery/zgallery.htm"><IMG SRC="gallery.gif"
BORDER=0></A></CENTER><P>
<STRONG>October Issue - The Daily News </STRONG>This October
showcase features a whole new group of <A HREF="gallery/
zgallery.htm"> Poetry and Prose</A> from a variety of differ-
ent Usenet and Internet based poets.<BR>
<HR>
</TD>

<TD  VALIGN=top WIDTH=200>
<A HREF="http://drn.zippo.com/news-bin/
wwwnews?alt.politics.*"><IMG SRC="patrihat.gif" ALIGN=left
border=0></a>
<A HREF="http://drn.zippo.com/news-bin/
wwwnews?alt.politics.*"><STRONG>Politics</STRONG></
a><BR>Elections '96. Tired of the brain drain from nightly
news ? Can't get enough of C-SPAN ? Right, Left, Center and
International coverage.
<HR>
</TD>

</TR>
</TABLE></CENTER>
```

Another well-known example of table usage on the Web is found on the TV1 listing in The Gist site (**http://www.thegist.com/**). TV1 is a service dedicated to providing television information over the Internet. One of the most often accessed pages on the site is "What's On Tonite!" From here, you can get a listing of what all of the major broadcast and cable stations are showing for any day. TV1 shows this information in your choice of formats, and one of the best ways to examine the information is by reading the time-station grid shown in Figure 9.8.

Fig. 9.8
TV1 on The Gist uses a table to let users find out what's playing on all the major television channels at any time. Notice the hyperlinks that take a user to episode descriptions or movie details.

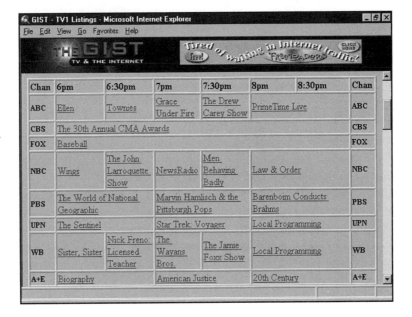

Beyond the basics: Coloring your table

Originally created by Microsoft for Internet Explorer, the BGCOLOR attribute for table tags has since been adopted by others, like Netscape, and rolled into the HTML 3.2 standard proposal. It's a pretty good idea, allowing you to color code rows or individual cells to make things stand out, just like the ledger paper and financial printouts of old (and not quite so old).

The BGCOLOR attribute accepts three two-digit hex numbers (representing red, green, and blue levels) or a color name and works with the <TABLE>, <TR>, and <TD> tags (see Listing 9.6).

Fig. 9.9

Using color in IE tables.

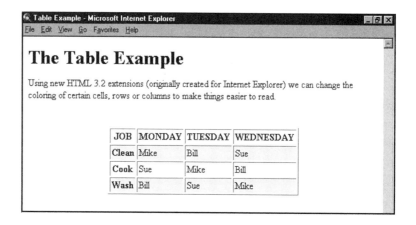

Listing 9.6

IE table extensions

```
<TABLE BORDER=1 CELLSPACING=2 CELLPADDING=2>
<TR><TH>JOB</TH><TH>MONDAY<TH>TUESDAY<TH>WEDNESDAY
<TR BGCOLOR=yellow><TH>Clean<TD>Mike<TD>Bill<TD>Sue<
<TR><TH>Cook<TD>Sue<TD>Mike<TD>Bill
<TR BGCOLOR=yellow><TH>Wash<TD>Bill<TD>Sue<TD>Mike
</TABLE>
```

As you can see in Figure 9.9, you can do more than just change the background color of tables for aesthetic reasons. As accountants and engineers have known for years, it's easier to communicate information in tables when you're able to shade different rows to make it clear what data is related to what other data and headers.

The other attributes, BORDERCOLOR and BORDERLIGHT, are used to change the color of the border in IE tables. In order for them to be effective, you need to use the BORDER attribute to the <TABLE> tag. (The BORDERCOLOR and BORDERLIGHT attributes may be used with the <TR> or <TD> tag if you want to change border colors in mid-table). Both accept either three two-digit hex numbers or a color name. The following is an example:

```
<TABLE BORDER=3 BORDERCOLOR=blue BORDERLIGHT=lightblue>
```

The BORDERCOLOR value affects the top portion of IE's 3D style table border. The BORDERLIGHT value changes the "lower" (shadow) part of IE's border.

Basically these values just let you toy with the 3D effect on IE table borders. Listing 9.7 shows another example using the preceding line of code.

Listing 9.7

Border colors with IE tables

```
<TABLE BORDER=1 CELLSPACING=2 CELLPADDING=2 BORDERCOLOR=blue
BORDERLIGHT=lightblue>
<TR><TH>JOB</TH><TH>MONDAY</TH><TH>TUESDAY</
TH><TH>WEDNESDAY</TH>
<TR><TH>Clean</TH><TD>Mike</TD><TD>Bill</TD><TD>Sue</TD>
<TR><TH>Cook</TH><TD>Sue</TD><TD>Mike</TD><TD>Bill</TD>
<TR><TH>Wash</TH><TD>Bill</TD><TD>Sue</TD><TD>Mike</TD>
</TABLE>
```

It doesn't show up well in black and white, so it won't do much good for me to include a screen shot—play with the color values for your table, and then check them out in an HTML 3.2-compatible browser.

10

Please Fill Out This Form...

● **In this chapter:**

- ● The purpose and use of forms

- ● A form's relationship to a CGI script

- ● The form tags and what they do

- ● What makes a good form?

- ● Beyond the basics: Client-side forms

While links and imagemaps enable users to move among Web sites, forms enable users to truly participate in your Web site. They are a great way of gathering instant feedback. . . . . ●

A form on the Web is almost exactly like a form in real life: It's made of up spaces to enter text information, lists of choices to check off, and options to select. But while a paper form must then be turned in or mailed, a Web form is instantly submitted—and often instantly responded to. In more technical terms, forms are the "front end" to CGI scripts, and together they expand the power of the Web tremendously, making it truly interactive.

First, there's something called CGI

Before you get started on forms, there's something important to keep in mind. Forms are fun to design, and they look great. But by themselves they don't do anything. You can put a form on your Web site, and your reader can have a wonderful time filling in the blanks and clicking all the nice buttons. But when they hit the Submit button (or whatever you choose to call it), something has to happen to the data they've supplied. The only way to make something happen—to direct the data to you—is to design a CGI script.

 TIP **Actually it's not the only way...just the most common by far. At** the end of this chapter I show you how to send form data to yourself via e-mail—just in case your ISP or administrator won't let you run your own CGI scripts.

A **form** in HTML is the front-end to Web interactivity. It's where the user enters text and makes selections, while the back end, the actual processing of data, is done on the Web server by **CGI scripts**. For more information about CGI scripting and how it relates to forms, see Chapter 11, "Introduction to CGI."

 Plain Enxglish, Please!

CGI stands for **Common Gateway Interface**—it's the standard way that browsers and Web servers communicate. Using a basic protocol, it's possible for a Web browser to send information to the Web server for processing. CGI is the name for that protocol. **99**

Okay, back to forms themselves

Forms help your site look professional and be interactive. Their power lies in the different ways they can accept and organize the user's input. Including forms in your Web site makes it something other than a simple one-way presentation.

You can get a good idea of the vast number of uses for forms just by browsing around on the Web for awhile. Businesses and organizations use forms for conducting surveys, taking online shopping and product orders, as well as for service registration. Many personal home pages have guest books that users can "sign" by simply filling in a form. To see how widespread they've become, check out the large forms on the White House site (**http:// www.whitehouse.gov/**).

Here are the basic elements of a form

There are four form tags, and they're used just like any others in HTML. The first, <FORM>, is a container that defines the beginning and end of a form and how and where the information collected will be sent. The other three— <TEXTAREA>, <SELECT>, and <INPUT>—make up the part of the form the user sees and interacts with: the actual text entry areas, menu selections, and push buttons.

 TIP **Most of the HTML editors available on the Net support form** creation. If you like, use them. What you're about to learn in the next few sections can almost all be at least partially automated with one of these editors. Of course, it's sometimes good to know how things work, first, and then play with a timesaving tool.

The very first thing—the *FORM* tag

The <FORM> tag is used to mark the beginning of a form, and its complement, </FORM>, is used to mark the end. All the other form tags are ignored outside of a <FORM>/</FORM> pairing, so you must be very clear about where your form begins and where it ends.

TIP Add a </FORM> immediately after you create a <FORM>, and then go back and fill in the contents. This helps eliminate accidentally leaving the end-form tag off after you've finished. (HTML editors with forms creation features add the tags for you.)

The <FORM> tag has two attributes that define how a particular form behaves. While the contents of the form are set by the remaining tags, these two options determine where the information entered by the user goes and how it is sent there.

The first is ACTION. A form's ACTION defines the URL that the information entered into a form is sent to. It appears inside the FORM tag, as follows:

```
<FORM ACTION="URL">
...
</FORM>
```

URL may be any URL, though for the data entered into the form to be processed correctly, URL should point to a CGI script that was designed to handle that particular form. If an ACTION is omitted, the URL of the page containing the form is used by default.

The FORM tag's second option is its METHOD. A form's METHOD defines how the information collected by that form will be sent to the ACTION URL, and may be one of two choices: "GET" or "POST". The "GET" method is the simpler of the two, but "POST" allows far more data to be transmitted. Which METHOD you choose depends entirely on how the CGI script that will process the form data is written, but a well-written CGI will handle both. METHOD has no effect on the form itself, only how the gathered information is sent.

TIP It's always a good idea, when writing CGI scripts, to use a library that **parses** (translates into something useful) form data automatically no matter which METHOD you use. These libraries are covered in Chapter 15, "Scripting Your Page."

The METHOD option is used inside the FORM tag like this:

```
<FORM METHOD="POST">
...
</FORM>
```

CAUTION **Although it's possible to leave off a form's** METHOD **and have it** work perfectly well, it's not generally a good idea. You should be as explicit as you can with your HTML, both to remind you of what you intended to do in a specific case and to avoid relying on defaults that may change in the future or be different for different browsers.

So, which of the two methods should you use for your form? While the "GET" METHOD is simpler for CGI scripts to handle, it limits the amount of data that can be sent, usually to slightly less than one kilobyte. That makes it great for very simple queries, such as, for instance, keyword search engines. If there is any chance that your form will generate more data than that, though, you should use the "POST" METHOD.

You generally set both attributes at the same time. Here's an example:

```
<FORM ACTION="http://my.server.com/cgi-bin/form.sh" METHOD="GET">
...
</FORM>
```

Let 'em write: Allowing users to input free-flow text

The **TEXTAREA** tag enables users to enter free-form text information in an open-ended edit field. TEXTAREAs are defined with a beginning <TEXTAREA> and a closing </TEXTAREA>, with default text held between them, as follows:

```
<FORM ACTION="/cgi-bin/form.sh" METHOD="POST">
    Type your comment here:<BR>
    <TEXTAREA>
Everything was wonderful!
    </TEXTAREA>
</FORM>
```

This code sample produces Figure 10.1.

CAUTION **No HTML tags used inside a** TEXTAREA **pair are interpreted. In many** ways, TEXTAREA acts like an editable <PRE> section with a fixed-width font being used and all line breaks being preserved.

Like FORM, TEXTAREA also has attributes that may be set inside the initial tag.

Fig. 10.1
A TEXTAREA can be
created with hopeful
defaults: "Everything
was wonderful!"
However, users can
very easily type over
this text with less
enthusiastic comments.

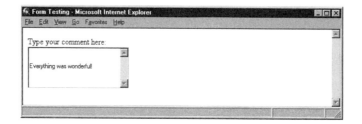

The first attribute is NAME, and it is required. The name of the TEXTAREA is what
will be paired with the contents of the area when the user submits the form.
You must always give a NAME, as this is how the form element is identified and
its value retrieved by the CGI script.

The other two options are ROWS and COLS, each defining how big the TEXTAREA
is to be in character heights and widths. If left off, ROWS is set to one and COLS
is set to 20, allowing for only a very small typing area. You can boost that a
bit, though, as shown in the following example:

```
<TEXTAREA NAME="comment" ROWS=4 COLS=60>
I love your product!
I wish I had found it sooner.
</TEXTAREA>
```

This snippet of HTML results in Figure 10.2.

Fig. 10.2
This TEXTAREA is
named "comment,"
and is 60 columns
wide and four rows
tall.

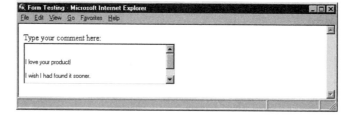

Q&A ***What if I have no idea how much text the user will
want to type?***

A TEXTAREA allows users to type in as much as they like. The specifications
for row and column only determine how big the TEXTAREA appears in the
Web browser. If the user types past the right "margin," a horizontal
scroll bar will appear; if the user types more lines than there are rows, a

vertical scroll bar will appear. Note that TEXTAREA does not include a word-wrap feature, users must hit the Return key if they want to wrap their sentences to the next line.

Giving users choices

While TEXTAREAs enable users to enter free-form text information, it is often a better idea to allow them to make limited choices from a predefined list—just what the **SELECT** tag was designed to do.

The SELECT tag itself is simple, just a <SELECT></SELECT> pair with three attributes:

- NAME, as with TEXTAREA, defines a name that will be paired with whatever value the user selects.

- SIZE defines the height of the list of selections to show the user. If it's left off or if it's set to one, the user is shown his choices as a pop-up menu, as shown in Figure 10.3.

- MULTIPLE takes no value and simply defines if this SELECT group allows multiple selections at one time. If omitted, the user can only make one choice from the list; if included, the user can make any number of choices, including zero. Also, as a side effect of specifying MULTIPLE, the list is shown as a scrollable list (not a pop-up menu) even if SIZE is set to one.

Fig. 10.3
Only the current selection is shown if SIZE is set to 1. The other options appear when the pop-down menu is clicked on with the mouse.

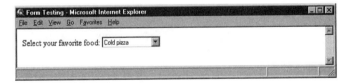

After the SELECT tag is defined, OPTION must be defined within it. The OPTION tag defines each individual choice that the user will see and is only recognized inside a <SELECT></SELECT> pair. Like the <LI> tag, an OPTION's text does not need to be closed with </OPTION>, though it doesn't hurt. Here's an example:

```
<FORM METHOD="GET">
    Select your favorite food:
    <SELECT NAME="food">
        <OPTION>Cold pizza
        <OPTION>Cold Chinese
        <OPTION>Cold fried chicken
    </SELECT>
</FORM>
```

The OPTION tag itself has two attributes:

- VALUE is what is associated with the SELECT NAME if that option is chosen by the user. VALUE is used by the CGI script to identify the option, but it does not need to correspond to the text the user sees. Creative use of this can make selections easier to deal with from the CGI side of a form. If VALUE is omitted, it is defaulted to the text that follows the OPTION.

- SELECTED defines which OPTION(s) are selected by default when the choices are first displayed. If SELECTED is not set on any options, none of them appear chosen by default. Usually, the single most common selection should be SELECTED as the default.

For instance, if you want to enable customers to rate your service people, you might use something like the following:

```
<FORM ACTION="/cgi-bin/service_logger.sh" METHOD="GET">
    Please rate the service you received:
    <SELECT NAME="service">
        <OPTION VALUE="100">Excellent
        <OPTION VALUE="75" SELECTED>Good
        <OPTION VALUE="60">Fair
        <OPTION VALUE="50">Poor
    </SELECT>
</FORM>
```

Note that the VALUEs of the OPTIONs relate to your scoring system rather than the actual text of the OPTION. This example results in Figure 10.4.

Fig. 10.4
Web sites can generate information for you as well as provide information to the people who visit the site.

Gathering *<INPUT>*

Our next tag for HTML forms gives you the opportunity to accept a number of different types of input from the user. The <INPUT> tag follows this format:

```
<INPUT TYPE=type_of_box NAME="variable" SIZE=number
MAXLENGTH=number>
```

Now, technically, the only required attributes are TYPE and NAME. Some other "types" of the input tag also accept the attribute VALUE. But first, let's look at the different types of <INPUT>.

TIP   **By the way, notice that <INPUT> is an empty tag. There's no** </INPUT> element.

Typed *TEXT* from users

The first possible value for the TYPE attribute is TEXT, which creates a single-line text box of a length you choose. Notice that the length of the box and the maximum length entered by the user can be set separately. It's possible to have a box longer (or, more often, shorter) than the maximum number of characters you allow to be entered. Here's an example of a text box:

```
Last name: <INPUT TYPE=TEXT NAME="last_name" SIZE=40
MAXLENGTH=40>
```

When appropriately entered between <FORM> tags, this <INPUT> yields a box similar to the one in Figure 10.5. If desired, the attribute VALUE can be used to give the textbox a default entry, as in the following example:

```
Type of Computer: <INPUT TYPE=TEXT NAME="computer" SIZE=50
MAXLENGTH=50 VALUE="Pentium">
```

Fig. 10.5
Using the TEXT option
with the TYPE
attribute.

TIP Just in case you feel that you can't seem to remember when to use quotes ("") with these form elements, realize that it's okay to put quotes around *every* value. That might make things easier.

What's the *PASSWORD*?

The PASSWORD option is nearly identical to the TEXT option except that it responds to typed letters with bullet points or a similar scheme (chosen by the browser) to keep the words from being read. A sample password box could be:

```
Enter Password: <INPUT TYPE=PASSWORD NAME="password" SIZE=25
MAXLENGTH=25>
```

When characters are typed into this textbox, they are shown on the screen as in Figure 10.6.

Fig. 10.6
PASSWORD hides text
from people looking
over your user's
shoulder.

Recognize that the text is still stored as the text typed by the user—not as bullet points or similar characters.

Q&A ***Does using a password field ensure that the information entered is secure?***

Even though a PASSWORD field prevents your secret data from being read on the screen, it is still passed over the network as plain, unencrypted text. It can even appear in the URL that way. So the answer is no—don't let PASSWORD lull you into a false sense of security.

Yes or no...*CHECKBOX*

This value for TYPE enables you to create a checkbox-style interface for your form. This is best used when there are two possible values for a given choice—and no others. You can also determine whether or not a checkbox will already be checked (so that it must be unchecked by the user if they don't agree), by using the attribute CHECKED. Here's an example of adding checkboxes to a form:

```
Type of computer(s) you own:<BR>
<INPUT TYPE=CHECKBOX NAME="586" CHECKED> Pentium
<INPUT TYPE=CHECKBOX NAME="486"> 486-Series PC
<INPUT TYPE=CHECKBOX NAME="Mac"> Macintosh
```

In this example, it's possible to check as many of the options as are presented. CHECKBOX evaluates each item separately from any others. Figure 10.7 illustrates how CHECKBOX is displayed in a browser.

Fig. 10.7
Notice that Pentium is pre-checked.

Tuning a single choice...*RADIO*

Like CHECKBOX, RADIO is designed to offer your user a choice from predetermined options. Unlike CHECKBOX, however, RADIO is also designed to accept only one response from among its options. RADIO uses the same attributes and basic format as CHECKBOX.

RADIO requires that you use the VALUE attribute, and that the NAME attribute be the same for all <INPUT> tags that are intended for the same group. VALUE, on the other hand, should be different for each choice. For instance, look at the following example:

```
Choose the computer type you use most often:<BR>
<INPUT TYPE=RADIO NAME="Computer" VALUE="P" CHECKED> Pentium
<INPUT TYPE=RADIO NAME="Computer" VALUE="4"> 486-Series PC
<INPUT TYPE=RADIO NAME="Computer" VALUE="M"> Macintosh
<INPUT TYPE=RADIO NAME="Computer" VALUE="O"> Other
```

CAUTION With RADIO, it's important to assign a default value, because it's possible that the user will simply skip the entry altogether. While the user can't check more than one, he or she can fail to choose any of them. So pick the most common value and set it as CHECKED, just so that the form-processing script doesn't have trouble.

Keeping things sorta *HIDDEN*

This <INPUT> type technically isn't "input" at all. Rather, it's designed to pass some sort of value along to the Web server and script. It's generally used to send a keyword, validation number, or some other kind of string to the script so that the script knows it's being accessed by a valid (or just a particular) Web page. The <INPUT TYPE=HIDDEN> tag takes the attributes NAME and VALUE. For example:

```
<INPUT TYPE=HIDDEN NAME="pagename" VALUE="form5">
```

CAUTION This isn't really terribly covert, because an intrepid user could simply View Source to see the value of the hidden field. It's more useful from a programmer's standpoint. For instance, on a large Web site, the hidden value might tell a multi-purpose script which particular form (among many) is sending the data, so the script knows how to process the data.

Erasing the whole thing...*RESET*

The <INPUT> tag has built into it the capability to clear an HTML form. RESET simply creates a push button (named with the VALUE string) that resets all of the elements in that particular FORM to their default values (erasing anything that the user has entered). An example would be the following:

```
<INPUT TYPE=RESET>
```

With a VALUE statement, you could enter the following:

```
<INPUT TYPE=RESET VALUE="Reset the Form">
```

The results are shown in Figure 10.8.

Fig. 10.8
Default and *VALUE-*
attributed Reset
buttons.

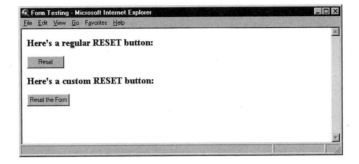

SUBMIT

The `<INPUT>` tag also has a type that automatically submits the data that's been entered into the HTML form. The `SUBMIT` type accepts only the attribute `VALUE`, which can be used to rename the button. Otherwise, the only purpose of the `SUBMIT` button is to send off all the other form information that's been entered by your user. See the following two examples (see Figure 10.9):

```
<INPUT TYPE=SUBMIT>
<INPUT TYPE=SUBMIT VALUE="SEND IT IN!">
```

Fig. 10.9
Creating a SUBMIT
button.

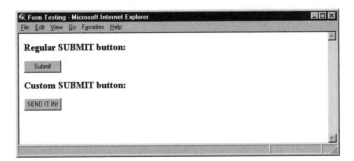

You can use just about anything you want for the `VALUE`, although it's best to remember that really small words, like *OK*, don't look great as buttons. To make a button larger, enter the `VALUE` with spaces on either end, like in the following:

```
<INPUT TYPE=SUBMIT VALUE="       GO       ">
```

Cheating 101: Looking at other people's HTML

One great way to figure out how to build forms is to look at how other people build forms. You can often even use their code, although you'll usually have to do some customizing to suit your particular needs.

If you spend a fair amount of time surfing the Web, you're likely to come across some very well-designed forms or some forms that are different than the usual. You can easily find out how the Web authors created their forms by looking at the HTML source. Most browsers have a "View Source" button, which you can use to get the HTML coded version of the page.

Even if your browser doesn't have that option, you can save the page to your hard disk, and then open it in a text editor or an HTML editor. This is a great shortcut for run-of-the-mill forms as well, especially if you need to get the form up and running in a hurry. You'll still have to write your own CGI script to accept the data, but that's inevitable. You just have to make sure that you change the ACTION URL so that the form gets sent to the right place when the SUBMIT button is clicked.

Note that this method of cheating can be used for other HTML coding aspects as well, but it works especially well with forms because you don't have any special graphics or media files to contend with.

Beyond the basics: Client-side forms

It's a simple trick, and one you may have already thought of yourself. Early in this chapter I said that ACTION can accept nearly any URL, right? Well, it can. Even a mailto:

```
<FORM ACTION="mailto:me@mynet.com" METHOD=POST>
```

When your user hits the SUBMIT button, the results of the form are now forwarded to your e-mail address instead of to a CGI script. And that's great if you don't have access to your Web server's CGI directory. There is one caveat—what to do with the e-mail when it gets to your e-mail box.

The first problem is the fact that the e-mail message is still encoded in that lovely POST format that forms use to send a message to scripts. Figure 10.10 shows an example of a typical received message.

Fig. 10.10
The results of a mailto: form POSTing.

```
results=Mike+Smith%0D%0A1234+Main+Road%0D%0A
Colorado+City%0D%0AC0%0D%0A8 09 00%0D%0A
Desktop+computers%0D%0APeripherals%0D%0A
```

It's not very pretty. The second problem is an extension of the first—you're either going to have to process all of these e-mails by hand or you need to write a program on your computer that interacts with your e-mail program in some way. Either way is probably fine for the small-business or home Web designer—at least, you get the form data from users without requiring access to the server.

TIP

There *are* **utilities available for download that will help you turn** form data into something more useful. I've found more for Mac than Windows—and, of course, there are tons for UNIX. Check out **http:// www.yahoo.com/Computers_and_Internet/Internet/ World_Wide_Web/Programming/Forms/** for a start.

You might also notice one last problem—once the data is sent by e-mail, the page just sits there. You need to include a button on the page to let users get back in the hierarchy. (Perhaps a "Push Me After Submitting the Form" clickable icon, as we discussed in Chapter 4.) Alternately, you could force another page to load when the SUBMIT button is clicked—but only with a little programming of your own. You can learn that in Chapter 15, "Scripting Your Page."

11

Introduction to CGI

● **In this chapter:**

- **CGI and what it does**

- **The languages for programming CGI scripts**

- **How can you use CGI to give your pages extra features?**

- **The information you need to keep in mind while programming CGI scripts**

- **Here's what other CGI artists have done**

The Common Gateway Interface (CGI) is the doorway between your Web server and the computer it runs on. Under-standing CGI, both what it is and how it works, can help you expand the capabilities of your site tremendously. . . . . . . ➤

The problem with creating fill-in forms for your Web pages is that they don't actually do anything. Your readers can fill them in to their hearts' content, but when they click the Submit button, the data won't go anywhere. That's where the Common Gateway Interface (CGI) comes in. By developing CGI scripts, you can make your forms—and other features on your Web pages— truly interactive. CGI scripts bring your static Web pages to life—returning requested data, responding to user input, and making a record of how many people access your site. Interactivity is a large part of the appeal of the Web, and CGI programming is the "back end" that makes it possible.

What is CGI?

Think of CGI as the way in which a Web browser can run programs on the Web server computer. In this way, it's much the same as the way Netscape or Mosaic use helper applications to display picture formats that they don't know about internally. The big difference is that **CGI scripts** appear to run in the browser itself; you don't need an external program to make things happen.

To a user, a link to a CGI program looks like a link to any other URL. It can be clicked and results in new information being displayed, just like any other link.

But, under the hood, a **CGI program** is much more than a normal Web page. When a normal URL is selected, a file is read, interpreted, and displayed by the browser. When a URL to a CGI program is selected, it causes a program to be run on the server system, and that program can do just about anything you want it to: scan databases, sort names, or send mail. CGI scripts allow for complex back-end processing.

CGI changes the definition of what a Web page is. While normal pages are static and unchanging, CGI programs enable a page to be anything you want it to be.

66 *Plain English, Please!*

The terms **CGI programs**, **CGI scripts**, and **CGIs** are used interchangeably in this chapter just as they are on the Web itself. 99

A CGI success story

Imagine Pete's Trucking. Pete and his shipping department need to keep their customers informed about the location of various shipments. Using Pete's current system, a customer phones in a request and a service rep faxes a response. The system works, but only during office hours. It also seems clumsy, requiring a verbal request for a fax that may then have to be scanned back into a computer. Errors and delays crop up often.

By using CGI, Pete can extend the functionality of his Web site. A customer service page might request a customer's name and password. Based on that information, it scans the manifest database and returns a response—in seconds, 24 hours a day, without interrupting the service rep. And, instead of a fax, the customer now has a digital copy of the data he wants and can print it, e-mail it, or save it to disk. By writing a small CGI program, Pete has solved a nagging problem and his customers are happy. The result is shown in Figure 11.1.

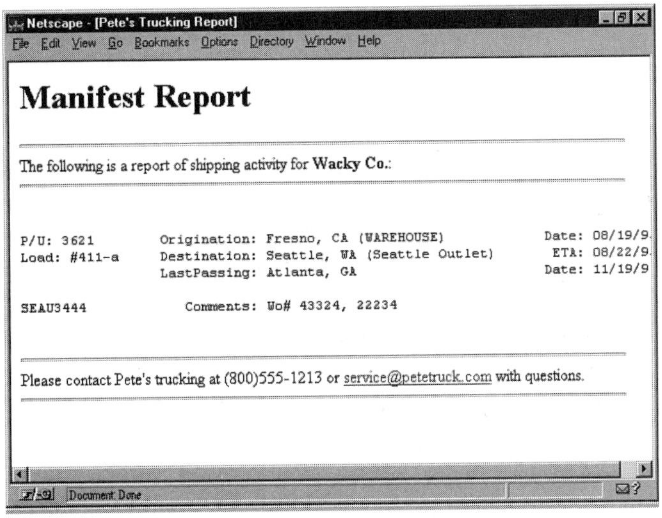

Fig. 11.1
Pete's biggest customer finds out that his driver is very lost.

```
Netscape - [Pete's Trucking Report]                           _ 8 X
File  Edit  View  Go  Bookmarks  Options  Directory  Window  Help

Manifest Report

The following is a report of shipping activity for Wacky Co.:


P/U: 3621       Origination: Fresno, CA (WAREHOUSE)      Date: 08/19/9
Load: #411-a    Destination: Seattle, WA (Seattle Outlet)  ETA: 08/22/9
                LastPassing: Atlanta, GA                  Date: 11/19/9

SEAU3444         Comments: Wo# 43324, 22234


Please contact Pete's trucking at (800)555-1213 or service@petetruck.com with questions.


Document Done
```

Why reinvent the wheel?

CGI programming can be extremely frustrating in the beginning. There are many rules to follow, most of which can be obscure or complex. Even getting a simple script up and running can be a chore.

One of the best ways to get over these first few hurdles and start CGI programming is to look at existing code. By reviewing (or simply using) existing CGI scripts, you can not only save yourself a lot of time, but also teach yourself new techniques.

Existing code almost always makes a good base to expand from. Instead of implementing a new script from scratch, an older program can often be modified to suit your needs. Collections of CGI programs can be found on the Web, and a good starting point is the World Famous CGI Shop (**http://lpage.com/cgi/**).

Most experienced CGI programmers will almost always be happy to share their code and talents with you. They've probably already solved any problem you might have and can save you hours of frustration with a word or a clue. Just ask. (Or look for collections of wisdom like those found at **http://www.yahoo.com/Computers_and_Internet/Internet/World_Wide_Web/CGI_Common_Gateway_Interface/** on the Web.)

And be sure to return the favor when you become an expert. That's part of the fun of being on the Web.

Pick a language, almost any language

You do not write CGI scripts in HTML like you write Web pages. CGI scripts are written in other computer languages, such as UNIX shell scripts, Perl, C, AppleScript, or Visual Basic, and to write them you need knowledge of at least one of these languages. Although a discussion of even one of them is beyond the scope of this chapter, there are strengths and weaknesses to each, and many excellent references exist.

- UNIX shell scripts (or Windows NT or 95 batch files) are a good choice for small or temporary CGI programs. They are easy to write and you can see results immediately. But you're not limited to simple scripts. Your CGI programs can be as complex as you want to make them.

- Perl is a good choice for medium-complexity programs, and most platforms support it. It's fast, easy to program, and it's interpreted, meaning that it doesn't need to be compiled like C. Perl allows you all the advantages of a full computer language and a shell script combined. Also, a Perl library exists that automatically translates any data sent to your CGI program into a usable form. You can get this library from **ftp://ftp.ncsa.uiuc.edu/Web/httpd/Unix/ncsa_httpd/cgi/** and download **cgi-lib.pl.Z** for UNIX users. Information on Perl itself is available all over the Web, including **http://www.yahoo.com/ Computers_and_Internet/Programming_Languages/Perl_BB**, **http://www.yahoo.com/Computers_and_Internet/Internet/ World_Wide_Web/Programming/Perl_Scripts**, and **news:comp.lang.perl** on Usenet. Perl is easily the most popular language for CGIs, so tons of resources are available for reusing ideas or code.

- For very complex data manipulation, it's best to use a full-fledged computer language, such as C. It will give you the fastest response and let you work with your information in the most flexible way. A C library also exists for decoding submitted data, and is available at **ftp:// ftp.ncsa.uiuc.edu/Web/httpd/Unix/ncsa_httpd/cgi/ncsa-default.Z** for a direct download.

- Macintosh Web servers are very popular, and easy-to-create hooks exist between the Web server applications and Mac scripting languages like AppleScript and Frontier. You might start with the AppleScript/Frontier CGI tour at **http://cy-mac.welc.cam.ac.uk/cgi.html** on the Web. MacPerl is an implementation of Perl for the Mac. Check out info from the author of MacPerl at **http://err.ethz.ch/~neeri/macintosh/ perl.html** along with links to other MacPerl sites.

Here are a few CGI examples

The best way to learn what CGI scripts can do and how they do it is by example. The four examples below progress from using CGI programs to display simple static data, to more complex dynamic data, to using server-provided information, and to the ultimate end of CGI: reacting to user input.

First, a simple example

Although CGI programs can become extremely complex, they can also be quite simple. One of the simplest is the UNIX shell script in Listing 11.1 (and shown in Figure 11.2).

Listing 11.1

A simple CGI script

```
#!/bin/sh
echo "Content-type: text/html"
echo ""
echo "<HTML><HEAD><TITLE>Sample</TITLE></HEAD>"
echo "<BODY>This is a <EM>simple</EM> CGI script.</BODY>
</HTML>"
```

Fig. 11.2
The output of CGI scripts can look exactly like HTML.

The first line of this script (`#!/bin/sh`) tells UNIX what shell this program is written for; if the program were a Windows NT batch file, the line could be excluded.

The second line (`echo "Content-type: text/html"`) tells the Web server what type of information is to follow in MIME (Multipurpose Internet Mail Extension) format. **MIME** is a method of delivering complex binary data using only ASCII text characters. There are hundreds of standard MIME formats now registered, but the two most common for CGI applications are `"text/html"` (for HTML output) and `"text/plain"` (for plain ASCII output).

The third line (`echo ""`) is simply an empty space to tell the server that what follows is the data described by the `"Content-type"`.

CAUTION **Be sure to use the correct** `"Content-type:"` **for the type of output** you are generating. If your CGI program outputs HTML but your `Content-type` is listed as `"text/plain,"` none of the HTML tags will be interpreted, leaving your page looking like an HTML source code listing.

Finally, the fourth and fifth lines are the actual HTML data. These are sent through the server to the browser and interpreted just the same as instructions would be if they'd been read from an HTML file.

Installing and referencing a CGI script

While conventions among servers differ, most require that CGI programs be installed in a special CGI directory. This is a subdirectory of the main directory on the Web server computer's hard drive, and is usually called cgi-bin. If you don't have the permissions needed to install your program in that directory, talk to your system administrator. The system administrator will also tell you how to install the script itself, which is usually a matter of copying it from your own computer to the appropriate directory of the main Web server.

After your CGI script is in place, you can reference it from a browser like any other URL. For example, if you installed a program called simple.sh in the cgi-bin directory, its URL would be as follows:

http://my.server.com/cgi-bin/simple.sh

If complex.pl (a more complex Perl program) is installed in cgi-bin/sales/order, a typical directory dedicated to sales orders taken over the Web, its URL would be as follows:

http://my.server.com/cgi-bin/sales/order/complex.pl

These URLs can be used like any others, including as HREFs from other Web pages or as SRC URLs for images.

Q&A *I keep getting errors when I try to run my CGI program. What do they mean, and what's the best way to debug my script?*

The most common error is "500 Server Error." It means that you either forgot to send the "Content-type:" line before your data, or your CGI program failed somehow part of the way through. Both cases mean that you have some debugging to do.

If you get "403 Forbidden," you need to set certain permissions on your CGI script. Talk to your system administrator to correct this problem. (It could also mean the script is currently being edited by someone else with permission to access it. Ask around.)

Now for a dynamic example

Of course, the simple CGI program in Listing 11.1 only outputs static data, and your reader wouldn't be able to tell it from a normal Web page. The real power of CGI scripts can be seen when they go beyond this and start generating dynamic data— something that's impossible for a normal page to do.

The CGI script in Listing 11.2 (displayed in Figure 11.3) displays a new wise saying each time you jump to it.

Listing 15.2

A dynamic CGI script

```
#!/bin/sh
echo "Content-type: text/html"
echo ""
echo "<HTML><HEAD><TITLE>Fortune</TITLE></HEAD>"
echo "<BODY>Words of wisdom:<HR><PRE>"
FORTUNE='/usr/games/fortune'
if [   "$FORTUNE" = "" ]; then
     echo "A wise system administrator installs 'fortune'
     ➥for his users."
     echo "       — Anon"
else
     echo $FORTUNE
fi
echo "</PRE></BODY></HTML>"
```

Instead of just displaying a predefined message, this script— through the UNIX `fortune` command—shows dynamic information each time it is run. If a user were to select the link that ran this script twice in a row, it would produce totally different results. This works because `fortune` has been installed in the games directory of the UNIX computer in advance. If it's not there (check with your system administrator), the script won't do anything at all.

Just about any UNIX utility, or combination of utilities, can be used in place of the `fortune` command in the above example. The real power of CGI scripts is to allow the entire capability of the computer to go into generating the Web page, and this example only hints at the possibilities.

Fig. 11.3
Web users are given new words of advice from the UNIX fortune command each time they jump to this script.

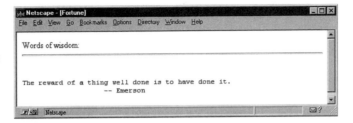

Making use of data provided by the server

Dynamic Web pages can be even more powerful if they use some of the information that the server automatically provides to every CGI program.

When a CGI script is run by the server, several **environment variables** are set, each containing information about the server software, the browser the request came from, and the script itself. These variables can then be read by the CGI program and used in various ways.

For example, the program in Listing 11.3 keeps track of every machine that connects to it and responds with a greeting (see Figure 11.4). Instead of being written as a UNIX shell script, this CGI program is written in Perl, which allows for greater control over how the log information is displayed.

Listing 11.3

A CGI program that uses server information

```
#!/usr/local/bin/perl
print "Content-type: text/html\n\n";
# Find out where they're from
$remote_host = $ENV{'REMOTE_HOST'};
if (length($remote_host) == 0) {
    $remote_host = $ENV{'REMOTE_ADDR'};
}
# Log this access
($sec,$min,$hour,$mday,$mon,$year,$wday,$yday,$isdst) = gmtime;
open(FILE,">>access.log");
if ($mon < 9)   { print FILE "0"; }; print FILE ++($mon),"/";
if ($mday < 10) { print FILE "0"; }; print FILE "$mday/$year";
if ($hour < 10) { print FILE "0"; }; print FILE "$hour:";
if ($min < 10)  { print FILE "0"; }; print FILE "$min:";
if ($sec < 10)  { print FILE "0"; }; print FILE "$sec GMT
    ➥$remote_host\n";
```

continues

Listing 11.3 continued

```
close FILE;
# And output the HTML

print "<BODY>Hello\!  You are connecting from $remote_host.
    ➥</BODY></HTML>\n";
```

Fig. 11.4

This CGI program not only tells users that you know where they live, but it keeps a log of that information, too.

This program uses two environment variables set by the server to find out the name of the machine running the browser: REMOTE_HOST and REMOTE_ADDR. REMOTE_HOST normally contains the Internet host name of the browser's machine, for example, my.server.com. But if, for some reason, this variable is empty, REMOTE_ADDR always contains the Internet address of the browser: 123.45.67.123, for example.

That's what the fourth through seventh lines of the program are doing: getting this information. The rest just gets the time and date, writes them to a file, and returns a message to the user.

There are many variables like these. The most common are shown in Table 11.1.

Table 11.1   CGI environment variables

Variable	Contents
REMOTE_HOST	The Internet name of the machine the browser is running on; may be empty if the information is not known
REMOTE_ADDR	The Internet address of the machine the browser is running on
SCRIPT_NAME	The program currently running
SERVER_NAME	The Internet name or address of the server itself
HTTP_USER_AGENT	The browser software that the user is running

A complete list of CGI environment variables is available at **http:// hoohoo.ncsa.uiuc.edu/docs/cgi/env.html.**

By using these environment variables creatively, you can do all sorts of neat things. Combining SERVER_NAME and SCRIPT_NAME can produce a URL to the currently running script, allowing it to reference itself. HTTP_USER_AGENT can be used to check what browser the user is running and send the appropriate page to the user (i.e., Netscape users get an advanced page, Lynx users get a text-only page, and so on).

Making use of input supplied by your readers

By far the most popular, most powerful use of CGI programs is to transmit information users type into fill-in forms. CGI scripts can take the input that a user provides in a form and process it in any way you choose. This allows your Web site to become truly interactive.

For example, the program in Listing 11.4 is a guestbook, an electronic version of the familiar visitor log used by hotels and museums. It first displays a list of signers, and then uses a form to ask the current user to add his signature. It is written in Perl and uses a form-input **parsing** library called cgi-bin.pl. The guestbook appears in Figure 11.5.

 Plain English, Please!

In English, parsing means to explain the grammatical form or function of a word. In computerese, **parsing** means something more like turning computer gobble-de-gook into something that people (or, at least, programs written by people) can understand.

Listing 11.4

A CGI program that uses user input

```
#!/usr/local/bin/perl
print "Content-type: text/html\n\n";
# Load the library
do "cgi-bin.pl" ¦ die "Fatal Error: Could not load cgi-bin.pl";
&ReadParse;
# Set the location of the guestbook
$guestbk = "guestbk.gbk";
# Get the sign-ins name
```

continues

Listing 11.4 continued

```
$name = $in{'name'};
# Only add to the log if they entered something
if (length($name) > 0) {
    open(FILE,">>$guestbk");
    print FILE "$name\n";
    close FILE;
}
# Show the current sign-ins
print "<HTML>\n<HEAD><TITLE>Guestbook</TITLE></HEAD>\n";
print "<BODY>\n<H1>Guestbook</H1>\n<H2>Current signees:
    ➡</H2>\n<HR>\n<UL>\n";
open(FILE,"<$guestbk") ¦¦ print "You'll be the first\!\n";
while (<FILE>) {
    print "<LI>$_";
}
close FILE;
print "</UL>\n";
# Request new sign-ins
print "<HR>\n<FORM
METHOD=\"GET\"ACTION=\"$ENV{'SCRIPT_NAME'}\">";
print "Your name: <INPUT TYPE=\"text\"NAME=\"name\"SIZE=\
"20\">";
print "<INPUT TYPE=\"submit\" VALUE=\"Sign in\!\"></FORM>\n</
BODY>
    ➡\n</HTML>\n";
```

Fig. 11.5
Guestbook is a nice way to make your site more personal.

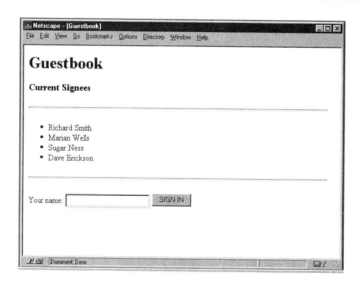

By using the cgi-bin.pl library, the information entered into a form by the user is extracted from the request and stored in a Perl table called in. You can get the VALUES of each form INPUT by asking in for it by its NAME. For instance, if a form INPUT has the NAME "address," the following line of Perl code would return the value the user entered:

```
$addr_variable = $in{'address'};
```

Before you can use in, you must have loaded cgi-bin.pl and *called* the library routine that sets up the table. Both of these procedures are handled in lines four and five in Listing 11.4.

CGI in the real Web world

The power of CGI is being used every day on the Web, from individuals who run small personal sites spiced up with a simple form, to multinational corporations who are using the Web as a new frontier for sales and customer interaction.

Commercial sites

There's a lot to see out there. For instance, it's already possible to place orders over the Web for flowers, pizza, or software. You can buy glasses, stuffed animals, and clothing without having to get out of your seat.

Check out the virtual malls listed on Yahoo (**http://www.yahoo.com/ Business_and_Economy/Companies/Shopping_Centers**). All these shopping sites use CGI scripts to answer requests, process orders, and complete transactions. And while the scope of these commercial sites is probably beyond what you will want to do yourself, there are dozens of professional designers who, for a fee, will set up a site for you that will rival anything else on the Web.

Or, perhaps you're working in a company that will ask you to be a part of the Web design team. Regardless of your ultimate responsibilities, you should be aware of the power of CGIs and what's possible. Surf a little.

The public domain

Don't assume that you need a professionally designed page for professional results. With a little help, almost anybody can put together a great looking, interactive, CGI-based Web site—especially if you take advantage of public domain programs that already exist.

Often rivaling the capabilities of custom scripts, many public domain CGI programs exist free for the taking, and more are being created every day. Even if these scripts are too general for your needs, they can be mined for techniques and methods that you can then use in your own programs.

You can find many public domain CGI scripts at:

> **http://www.yahoo.com/Computers_and_Internet/Internet/**
> **World_Wide_Web/CGI___Common_Gateway_Interface/**
>
> **http://ftp.ncsa.uiuc.edu/Web/httpd/Unix/cgi**
>
> **news:comp.infosystems.www.authoring.cgi**

CGI and security

When creating forms and CGI scripts, you should be aware that, normally, none of the data passed between the browser and the server is encrypted. This means that any private data (credit card numbers, love letters, etc.) can be stolen by machines between the sender and receiver. Thankfully, more and more browsers (such as Netscape) have the capability to automatically encrypt data and make secure data transfer possible.

Another point about security: There are people out on the Web who would love nothing more than to cause you trouble. Purely out of a sense of vindictiveness, they try to make your life as hard as it can be. Your CGI scripts need to take this into account.

For example, cleverly written queries can be used to gain privileges on your server that you never intended to grant. One common trick involves sending a shell command appended to some piece of requested data, so that when the CGI program uses that piece of data in an external command, the **piggy-back** command is executed as well.

Imagine a user entering john_doe@usc.edu;rm -rf / into a form. A badly written CGI script might simply add the UNIX command finger to the front of the request and execute it as a shell command. The ; in the user's entry causes the second command to run as well (rm in UNIX means delete), deleting a lot of files. One good reason to borrow CGI scripts from elsewhere is because other authors have already thought of these things.

You may also find others at the site mentioned earlier in this chapter—especially if you're looking for a site that involves programming in something other than Perl.

The cutting edge

Check out some of the following sites, which make good use of CGI scripts and interactivity:

- **http://www.sci.kun.nl/thalia/funpage/startrek**

- **http://www.hotwired.com**

- **http://www.uroulette.com:8000/** (see Figure 11.6)

- **http://bf.cstar.ac.com/bf**

- **http://bf.cstar.ac.com/lifestyle/**

- **http://www.inference.com/~hansen/talk.html**

- **http://www.usc.edu/dept/garden**

Fig. 11.6
If you're a betting browser, you can take your chances with this CGI. But don't blame me if you're not happy with where you end up.

CGI scripting isn't easy, and increasingly it's handled by specialists. But you can do a great deal on your own, and the results can be both impressive and immensely helpful. In many ways, CGI puts the final touches on your Web site, because it allows you to collect, manipulate, and respond to data, and not just present information.

Part IV: Bells and Whistles

12

You've Been Framed

● **In this chapter:**

- **What's the idea behind these frames?**

- **Creating the frames**

- **A simple frame document for a template**

- **Making your pages appear in frames**

- **Beyond the basics: Advanced targeting**

Netscape raised the bar again when they came up with frames, which allow you to split your user's browser screen into different panels for holding Web pages. Now we're building a serious interface! . . . . ➤

O ne of the most exciting additions to HTML recently has been the frames specification. Now part of the HTML 3.2 proposal, frames are gaining popularity in the Web world, with the latest versions of Internet Explorer supporting them. Originally, they were a Netscape-only technology. But, eventually everyone catches up, it seems.

Frames aren't overwhelmingly difficult to add to your pages, but they do require a slight shift in thought. Although they seem similar to tables at first, frames are considerably more powerful. So much so, in fact, that frames can divide your Web page so that it is accessing more than one URL at a time.

The idea behind frames

Frames are basically another way to create a unique interface for your Web site. Dividing the page into different parts—each of which can be updated separately—creates a number of different interface elements you can offer. Even a simple use of the frame specification lets you add interface graphics or a corporate logo to a site, while the rest of your page scrolls beneath it (see Figure 12.1).

Fig. 12.1
A simple frames
interface.

Using frames in this way takes you one step closer to the ideal Web interface because it makes it as intuitive and universal as possible. Frames are great for the following:

- *Table of contents.* By placing the TOC in a "column" on your Web page, people can click around your site or your documentation pages without being forced to constantly move "back" to the contents page. Because the TOC is always there, users simply click a new content level in the static frame.

- *Fixed interface elements.* As mentioned above, you can force clickable graphics, logos, and other information to stay in one fixed portion of the screen, while the rest of your document scrolls in another frame.

- *Better forms and results.* Frames also enable you to create a form in one frame and offer results in another frame. This is something we're beginning to see extensively with **Web search pages**. With the search text box always available, you're free to change search phrases or pinpoint your search more quickly, without moving back in the hierarchy of the Web pages.

66 *Plain English, please!*

Web search pages (or **search engines**) are the popular sites like Infoseek (**http://www.infoseek.com/**) or Alta Vista (**http://www.alta-vista.com/**) that are used for searching the Web by keyword. Some of these sites are now using frames to divide their interface into different parts.

Creating the frames

Probably most unique among the HTML-style tags so far is the <FRAMESET> tag. This container is required for frames-style pages—and it also replaces the <BODY> tag completely on these pages. When you use frames, then, you're committed to using them completely—you can't just add frames to part of your page. On a typical page, <FRAMESET> is added like this:

```
<HTML>
<HEAD>
...HEAD Markup...
</HEAD>
```

```
<FRAMESET>
...Frames and other HTML markup...
</FRAMESET>
</HTML>
```

The <FRAMESET> tag accepts two attributes: ROWS and COLS. Both attributes accept numerical values (size in pixels), percentages, or a combination of both. The value * can be used to suggest that a particular row or column should take up the rest of the page. The number of rows or columns is suggested by the number of values you give the attribute. These attributes take the following format:

```
<FRAMESET ROWS="numbers,percentages,*"COLS="numbers,
➥percentages,*">
```

The following example creates two rows: one 50 pixels long and another row that takes up the rest of the page:

```
<FRAMESET ROWS="50,*">
```

This would be useful for a page that displays a fixed map or graphic at the top that you know is less than 50 pixels high. The next example creates a Web interface with two columns: one on the left-most 25 percent of the screen and one on the other 75 percent:

```
<FRAMESET COLS="25%,75%">
```

This would be a good way to set up a documentation (or **FAQ**) site that offers contents in the first frame and actual text and examples in the second, larger frame.

Plain English, please!

FAQ stands for **Frequently Asked Questions**, and it's a document format often found on the Internet that uses "Q&A" style to answer common questions. The typical FAQ has an extensive table of contents, which is the perfect candidate for transforming into a frame document. **"**

Each <FRAMESET> statement works with one attribute or the other. That means you can only create a frameset with either rows or columns. In order to create rows *within* columns (or vice versa), you can nest <FRAMESET> statements. For instance, the following creates a page with two columns:

```
<FRAMESET COLS="25%,75%">
   <FRAMESET ROWS="50%,50%">
   </FRAMESET>
   <FRAMESET ROWS="10%,90%">
   </FRAMESET>
</FRAMESET>
```

The first column is divided into two rows that each take up 50 percent of that column. The second column is divided into two rows, the first taking 10 percent and the second taking the rest of that column. Although this doesn't display anything in and of itself, it creates logical breaks in the page. We come back to nesting <FRAMESET> tags as you develop more advanced frame interfaces in this chapter.

Getting stuff to appear in the frames

The <FRAME> tag is used within the <FRAMESET> container to determine what actually appears in a particular frame. Each <FRAME> tag is an empty tag—and it's not unlike the <LI> tags you add to HTML lists. It's simply there, within the <FRAMESET> container, to determine what URL or name is associated with the particular frame it defines. It takes the following format:

```
<FRAMESET COLS/ROWS="numbers">
<FRAME SRC="URL">
...
</FRAMESET>
```

The SRC attribute is used to tell the frame what URL should be loaded in that frame. For instance, the following code creates two frame rows: one that loads the URL MENU.HTML at the top of the Web page and one that loads the URL HELP.HTML at the bottom of the page (see Figure 12.2):

```
<FRAMESET ROWS="20%,80%">
<FRAME SRC="menu.html">
<FRAME SRC="help.html">
</FRAMESET>
```

By using the <FRAME> tag, you create what's known as a **frame window**. Each window corresponds to a "row" or "column" definition in the <FRAMESET> tag, but nothing is drawn or displayed until an appropriate <FRAME> tag is used to define each individual window.

Fig. 12.2
The <FRAME> tag
assigns URLs to each
frame window.

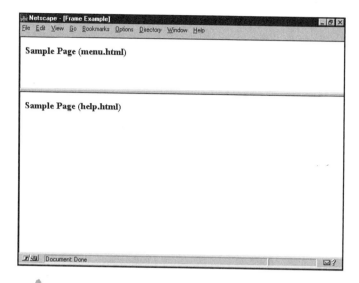

TIP **Here's the trick. When the user clicks a link on one of the pages** you've used as a SRC, the next page will load—in that same frame window. So choose carefully. You want to use one window as a "main viewer" for larger documents. More on that in a moment.

Creating a template

If you like, you can take what we just discussed and create a template of sorts for later use. All frame documents look something like this, although the number of framesets you decide to nest within one another may vary.

Listing 12.1

Simple frame document

```
<HTML>
<HEAD>
<TITLE>Frame Example</TITLE>
</HEAD>
<FRAMESET ROWS="25%,75%">
<FRAME SRC="menu.html">
<FRAME SRC="help.html">
</FRAMESET>
</HTML>
```

While you're at it, you also need to create some files to put in those frames. If you have some HTML documents hanging around, you can rename them to MENU.HTML and HELP.HTML for this example.

If you want to experiment further, try changing the `<FRAMESET>` tag in Listing 12.1 to the following (see Figure 12.3):

```
<FRAMESET COLS="25%,75%">
```

Or, change the percentages to see how that affects your layout.

Fig. 12.3

Loading separate HTML documents into a frame-based page.

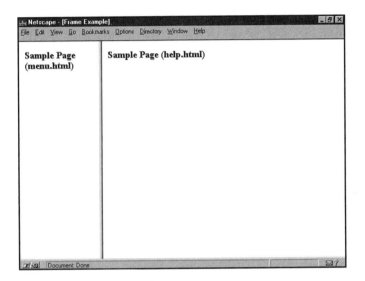

Tweaking your frames

Aside from `SRC`, the `<FRAME>` tag can accept the attributes `NAME`, `MARGINWIDTH`, `MARGINHEIGHT`, `SCROLLING`, and `NORESIZE`. All of these but `NAME` are appearance-oriented. Let's deal with them first and come back to `NAME` in a moment.

`MARGINWIDTH` and `MARGINHEIGHT` are used to control the right/left margins and the top/bottom margins of the text and graphics within a frame, respectively. Each takes a numerical value in pixels, so that the following

```
<FRAME SRC="text.html" MARGINWIDTH=5 MARGINHEIGHT=5>
```

creates a five-pixel border between the contents of TEXT.HTML and the frame edges.

SCROLLING can accept the values YES, NO, and AUTO and is used to determine whether or not scroll bars will appear in the frame window. The default value is AUTO, and this is probably the best to use in most cases. Because users have all different screen resolutions and available browser window space, even short documents sometimes need to be scrolled.

The NORESIZE attribute doesn't require a value and is used to keep the user from resizing a frame window.

Q&A *I only used NORESIZE in one of my FRAME tags, but now some of the other frames won't resize. Did I do something wrong?*

Probably not. NORESIZE actually forces a frame's borders to become rigid—not just the frame itself. That means that any frames that share a border with that frame will also be fixed in size.

An example of SCROLLING and NORESIZE would be:

```
<FRAME SRC="text.html" SCROLLING="yes" NORESIZE>
```

Sending text to our non-frame buddies

The <NOFRAMES> container tag is used to contain HTML markup intended for browsers that do not support the frames specification. Text and HTML tags inside the <NOFRAMES> container are ignored by frames-capable browsers. All others should generally ignore the other frames tags (which they won't recognize) but display the text in between the <NOFRAMES> tags. The following is an example:

```
<FRAMESET ROWS="25%,75%">
<FRAME SRC="menu.html">
<FRAME SRC="index.html">
<NOFRAMES>
<P>This page requires a Frames capable browser to view. If
you'd prefer,you can access our <a href="2_index.html">HTML
2.0 compliant pages</a>to view this information without the
frames interface.</P>
</NOFRAMES>
</FRAMESET>
```

Getting new pages to load in frames

So far, we've seen how to use the frames commands to split a page into two (or more) sections, so, you can have controls or a logo in one frame, and a "main viewer" in the other for looking at documents. Some folks stop right there. All they really worry about is making sure that their company logo or advertisements stay fixed at the top of the page. And that's cool.

But what if you could just leave some controls—like an imagemap or some text links—in the top frame window and load a new document in the other window? It'd be like creating a Web page TV-remote. Just click a link, and a new page loads in the other frame window (see Figure 12.4). You can do just that, if you know a little about **targeting**.

Fig. 12.4

Here's how lots of folks use frames. Click the "remote controls" and a new page appears in the main viewer frame.

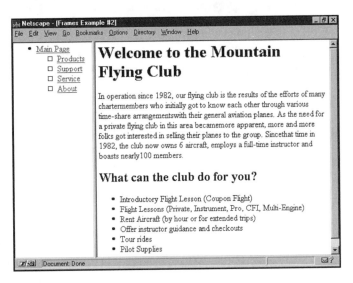

Giving your frames a *NAME*

First, you need to name your frame windows—at least, you have to name the windows you might want to change. This is accomplished with the NAME attribute to the <FRAME> tag, which takes the following format:

```
<FRAME SRC="original URL" NAME="window_name">
```

This shouldn't look too foreign to you, as it's a little like the way that the NAME attribute works for `<A NAME>` links. When the frame window has a distinct name, you can access it directly from other frame windows. An example of this is the following:

```
<FRAME SRC="index.html" NAME="main_viewer">
```

CAUTION **Although you can pretty much name your frame window anything** you want, there is one restriction: You can't start the name with an underscore character (_). If you do, the name will be ignored. But, there's a good reason for that. The underscore is used to signal a number of "magic" target names. We get to those in the section at the end of this chapter.

Sending new pages to named frames

With your frame successfully named, you're ready to target the name with a hypertext link. This is accomplished with the TARGET attribute to a typical `<A>` anchor tag, which follows this format:

```
<A HREF="new_URL" TARGET="window_name">link text</A>
```

The new URL is the new document that you want to have appear in the frame window. The window_name is the same name that you used to name the frame windows with the NAME attribute to the `<FRAME>` tag. An example:

```
<A HREF="products.html" TARGET="main_viewer">View Products
</A>
```

 TIP **Whenever possible, view your pages in a browser to make sure** they're not abnormally wide or that you're not forcing users to scroll constantly to read your pages. If you can, also try to view your pages on different platforms (e.g. Mac, Windows, UNIX) to make sure everything fits well.

Give your users an out (or a back)

First, using a frame-based document as an interface for your Web site makes the Back and Forward buttons on the user's Web browser program nearly useless. As far as the browser is concerned, no completely new pages have been loaded. So, if you click Back, you'll go to the site you visited before you loaded the frames document—no matter how long or far you've been surfing *inside* the frames (see Figure 12.5).

TIP **Actually, the latest versions of Netscape and Internet Explorer do** allow you to move back *within* the frames interface by clicking the Back button. You'll *still* want to create extra interface elements for users of older browsers, though.

The answer to this is simple: Take special care that you're providing your user with enough controls to move around in your Web site. If you're using a specific frame window for controls, remember to give your user as many links in that window as possible. Let your user go directly to the main pages of your site and never bury a user five or six pages deep without giving an easy way back.

 TIP **Also, because the URL doesn't change, you might want to put a** direct URL (in regular text) at the bottom of any pages from your site that are loaded in your main viewer frame, so that users can create a bookmark directly to those pages if they desire.

Fig. 12.5
No matter how many new pages are loaded in the main viewer frame, the URL stays the same. Hit back and you'll move back to a previous Web site.

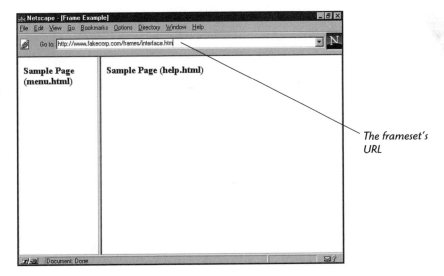

The frameset's URL

An elegant example of frames

Now I'm not a huge fan of using a great number of frames, although I've seen some snazzy implementation of three or four frames on a page. Let's create an example where we use just two different frame windows. One offers a "table of contents" page and one displays the actual information for your site.

Listing 12.2 is the table of contents page.

Listing 12.2

TOC.HTM

```
<HTML>
<HEAD>
<TITLE>Contents</TITLE>
</HEAD>
<BODY>
<H3>My Site:</H3>
<UL>
    <LI><A HREF="index.htm">Main page</A>
    <UL>
        <LI><A HREF="products.htm"TARGET="main_window">Products
</A><LI><A HREF="support.htm" TARGET="main_window">Support</A>
        <LI><A HREF="service.htm" TARGET="main_window">
Service</A>

        <LI><A HREF="about.htm" TARGET="main_window">About</A>
    </UL>
  </UL>
  </BODY>
</HTML>
```

See what I'm getting at here? In one frame we have these simple text links, which we can use to control the main frame window. It gives a nice, easy interface to the whole site. Now let's create the frames page—MAIN.HTML (see Listing 12.3).

Listing 12.3

MAIN.HTM

```
<HTML>
<HEAD>
<TITLE>Frames Interface</TITLE>
</HEAD>
<FRAMESET ROWS="10%, 90%">
   <FRAME SRC="controls.htm" NORESIZE>
   <FRAMESET COLS="30%,70%">
      <FRAME SRC="toc.htm" NAME="toc_window" MARGINWIDTH=3
       MARGINHEIGHT=3>
      <FRAME SRC="index.htm" NAME="main_window" MARGINWIDTH=3
```

```
            MARGINHEIGHT=3>
        </FRAMESET>
    </FRAMESET>

    </HTML>
```

Here's what we've done. The first <FRAMESET> creates two rows on the page. Then a <FRAME> tag is used to add the controls at the top of the browser window. The second <FRAMESET> creates two columns within the second row. The smaller is for the table of contents pages. In the other frame window, you put all of the main HTML documents. Figure 12.6 shows how the whole thing looks in Netscape.

 TIP **To make this work properly, you need to create the documents** listing in TOC.HTM, like INDEX.HTM, PRODUCTS.HTM, SERVICE.HTM, and so on.

Fig. 12.6
A three-way interface is attractive, but it can be tough to manage.

The "TOC.HTM" pages here

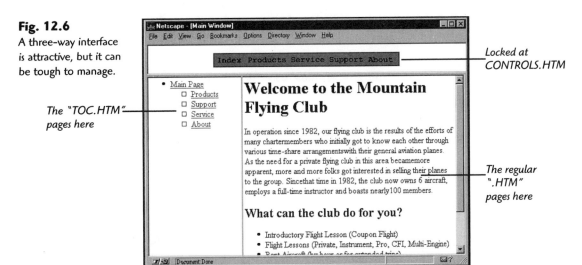

Locked at CONTROLS.HTM

The regular ".HTM" pages here

Beyond the basics: Advanced targeting

Other link-related tags have been updated to accept a TARGET attribute along with the anchor tag. For instance, client-side imagemaps have their AREA tag updated to accept a target window so that an area defined to access a certain link loads that page into the target. This is the format:

```
<AREA SHAPE=shape COORDS="numbers" HREF="URL"TARGET=
"window_name">
```

Likewise, you can add a TARGET attribute to the <FORM> tag. Remember that it's the <FORM> container tag that tells the browser the URL for the script that is required to process the form data. In that same tag, you can also specify a target window for the results that are received from the server. If you want users to be able to use your form repeatedly (to allow them to generate different results), you can leave both the form and the results in separate frames. This attribute takes the following format:

```
<FORM ACTION="Script_URL" TARGET="window_name">
```

Cut down on typing with *<BASE>* targets

What if you want the majority of your links to point to a particular frame window? Back in Listing 12.2, you created a file called TOC.HTML that had lots of hypertext links. Each one of those links required a TARGET attribute that pointed to the main viewer. You could have made that easier with a <BASE> tag in the head of your document. Use this format:

```
<HEAD>
<BASE TARGET="window_name">
</HEAD>
```

A good example of this for the previous example would be:

```
<BASE TARGET="main_window">
```

You don't have to specify the target window in each individual anchor in an HTML document that has this tag in its head. Now all links default to the target defined in the <BASE> tag.

TIP If you *do* use TARGET **attributes, they override the** <BASE> **tag for** that particular link.

Unveiling the "magic" targets

Here's why you can't name frame windows with something that starts with an underscore. The "magic" target names all start with an underscore, which signals to the browser that it should treat this link extra special. The following are some examples:

- `TARGET="_blank"` The URL specified in this link always loads in a new blank browser window.

- `TARGET="_self"` This is used for overriding a `<BASE>` tag and forcing a link to load in the same window that it's clicked in.

- `TARGET="_parent"` This causes the document to load in the current window's parent—generally, the frame window immediately preceding in the `<FRAMESET>` definition. If no parent exists, it acts like `"_self"`.

- `TARGET="_top"` The document is loaded in the top-most frame of the current browser window.

Basically, these magic targets are designed to let you break out of the current `<FRAMESET>` structure in some way. Experiment with them to see how you can move around to different windows.

Ultimate Control: Style Sheets

This upset me when I first heard about it, too. Do we have to relearn HTML for these new style sheets? Nope. Actually, they're pretty easy to add, once you get the gist of 'em . . . ⊳

The age-old debate in the HTML world (okay, so the debate is about two years old) is the push and pull between designers who want control over the display of their pages and the standard bearers who want the widest possible audience for Web pages. Up until now, it's been something of a standoff, with companies like Netscape and Microsoft adding nonstandard HTML-like references to their browsers' capabilities, while the standards organizations have ignored or repudiated those attempts.

The new world order of HTML standard creation may have finally changed that a bit. The W3C now comprises representatives of both camps—both the HTML standard creators and the strongest corporate players in Web creation tools. So, the two philosophies have begun to merge, and **style sheets** seem to be one of their answers.

 Plain English, please!

> **Style sheets** are a clever way to add advanced formatting to HTML pages. You can define things like font faces, font sizes, alignment, and other characteristics—giving your page more of a desktop-published look. But style tags are also designed to be very transparent, so that older browsers can still access and display the pages.

Why add to the confusion?

I think this is a valid point. After all, HTML is plenty complicated as it stands, right? Well, not enough for some folks. For the real artists and designers out there, HTML is a bit too limiting. Style sheets offer a chance for some real control. And, to be honest, they're not terribly difficult to grasp, once you get into the spin of things.

The magic of style sheets is that they can become almost infinitely complicated. You can decide minute details like character spacing, color, font families, and other desktop publishing-type decisions. At the same time, however, not rendering these decisions is up to the individual user and browser, so that minimal information is lost, and the majority of browsers can view your information—even if they're not using the latest and greatest browser (see Figure 13.1).

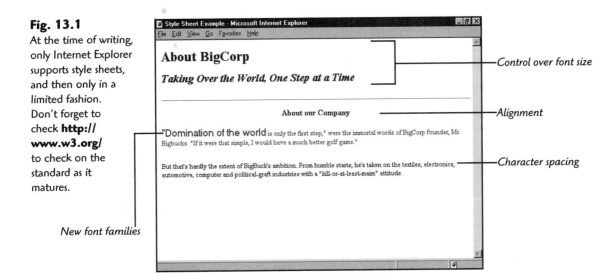

Fig. 13.1
At the time of writing, only Internet Explorer supports style sheets, and then only in a limited fashion. Don't forget to check **http://www.w3.org/** to check on the standard as it matures.

New font families

Control over font size

Alignment

Character spacing

In fact, style sheets are considerably more complicated than nearly any other aspect of HTML. Why? It's my belief that this is laying the groundwork for more advanced programs to make the leap into HTML design.

Right now, the power of most desktop publishing programs is lost on Web design. In a few years, as the style sheet standards formalize and come into practice, I believe you'll begin to see fewer people using text editors for Web creation and more professional-level page layout programs being brought to the game.

Setting your page up for style sheets

It seems to me that the <STYLE> tag is the easiest to understand when it comes to style sheets in HTML, and I'd like to talk about it first. You're in the <HEAD> section of your document now, and you use the <STYLE> container to define some of the style elements you want to add to our Web page. The basic format is the following:

```
<HEAD>
<TITLE>Doc title</TITLE>
<STYLE TYPE="MIME type">
HTML tag.class {special formatting}
...
<SPAN> {special formatting}
</STYLE>
</HEAD>
```

For your purposes, the TYPE attribute of the <STYLE> tag will always accept the MIME-type text/css. That stands for the Cascading Style Sheets standard for Web style, and it is basically just a standard that defines what sort of things we can do to text, images, and background on your Web page. It also defines the special formatting codes you use within your <STYLE> definition.

Creating *CLASS*es

"HTML tag" refers to any of the HTML you've learned thus far. Nearly all of them can be given a **class**, which creates a unique instance of this particular tag. When that class is specified in the body portion of your document, the special formatting is used for that particular instance of the HTML tag.

Let's look at an example:

```
<HEAD>
<TITLE>My Styled Page</TITLE>
<STYLE TYPE="text/css">
  H1.italic { font-style: italic }
  P.red_caps { color: red; font-style: small-caps }
    .blue_Helv { font-family: Helvetica, sans-serif; color:
➥blue }
</STYLE>
</HEAD>
```

CAUTION **Not all browsers will support all CSS styles—for instance, Internet** Explorer 3.0 doesn't support small caps. Of course, you can add the styles anyway; they'll just be ignored by browsers that don't recognize them.

Now, with these style definitions, you've created new classes of the familiar <H1> and <P> tags, named italic and red_caps respectively. When you want these special instances to occur in your HTML document, use the CLASS attribute to the standard HTML tag. Therefore, the following creates the special cases for your HTML tags within the document itself:

```
<H1 CLASS="italic">This header is italicized</H1>
<P CLASS="red_caps">This text should be in red, and all
➥small-caps.</P>
```

The class blue_Helv, which was defined with no particular element in mind, can be used with any element. So that the following works just fine:

```
<OL CLASS="blue_Helv">
    <LI> Item One
    <LI> Item Two
```

```
</OL>
<P CLASS="blue_Helv">The text, like the previous list, will
➥be blue Helvetica.</A>
```

TIP **Class names are completely of your choosing. Keep them short** and descriptive and avoid spaces (use the underscore if necessary). Also avoid common HTML words and tag names, just for clarity.

Defining *SPAN*

Notice that the original example offered another new tag, the <SPAN> tag. <SPAN> is basically a designer-defined tag that enables you to create a special case for emphasizing certain text in your document. It works just like the <EM> tag except for one small detail—it has no HTML 2.0 counterpart. So, browsers that don't recognize style sheets won't interpret the <SPAN> element in any way. If you use a preexisting tag, other browsers will only see half of your formatting.

When I say styles sheets, I mean CSS

Let me make sure that this gets a little more confusing. You see, it turns out that there are a ton of different ways to start adding style sheets to your Web documents in the current working draft—the key is knowing what "type" of style sheets will be understood by the browser. In this chapter we're specifically talking about the **Cascading Style Sheet (CSS)** specification.

But the CSS style sheet definition is only one of an infinite number of possible style sheet definitions. That means that anyone can create a style sheet definition, give it a MIME name like text/bob, and create a browser that includes all of the codes required to render the elements of that style sheet. This can get very tedious to learn and design by hand, which is part of the fodder for

my argument that style sheets are the beginning of the end of simple (unassisted) HTML layout.

Fortunately for us, Microsoft has jumped into the fray by rolling support for the Cascading Style Sheet specification (CSS1) into Internet Explorer. Netscape seems likely to follow suit. With those two supporting CSS, it looks like the rest of the Web probably will, too.

The W3C also recently announced that CSS will be the first standard for style sheets. That, at least, gives you common ground to work with when you set out to design Web pages for the general public. And, of course, the magic of style sheets is that if a browser can't use them, it won't. No basic information is lost.

Consider this example. In the `<HEAD>` section, you define `<SPAN>`:

```
<STYLE TYPE="text/css">
  SPAN { font-style: small-caps }
</STYLE>
```

Now, in the body of your document, you can do the following:

```
<P><SPAN>Welcome to</SPAN> my home page on the Web. I'm glad
you could find the time to drop by and see what we've got
going today.</P>
```

In a style sheet-capable browser, you see small caps used for an attractive, printed-style introduction to your paragraph. In older browsers, the text is unaffected.

So what kinda stuff can you do?

Having seen how certain style elements can be defined for your Web page, you might be interested in learning all of the different style changes you can make to your documents. But there's something important we should discuss first.

The current working draft of the CSS style sheet definition is about 50 pages long—and it's basically full of possible style properties. That means things go much deeper than { `color: red` } in CSS. I'll touch on some of the high points, but if you get very deep into style sheets, you'll want to consult **http://www.w3.org/pub/WWW/TR/WD-css1.html** for the latest CSS Level 1 developments and changes.

Table 13.1 offers some of the more likely CSS defined style properties and their possible values or value types.

Table 13.1 CsS-defined style properties

Property	Value	Example(s)
`font-family`	name of font	Helvetica, Serif, Symbol
`font-size`	number/percentage	12pt, +1, 120%
`font-weight`	number/strength	+1, light, medium, extra bold
`font-style`	name of style	italic, normal
`font`	combination of above	12pt Serif medium small caps

Property	Value	Example(s)
color	word/hex number	red, green, blue, FF00FF
background	color/blend/file	paper.gif, red, black/white
word-spacing	number+units	1pt, 4em, 1in
text-spacing	number+units	3pt, 0.1em, +1
text-decoration	word	underline, line through, box, blink
vertical-align	word/percentage	baseline, sup, sub, top, middle, 50%
text-align	word	left, right, center, justify
text-indent	number/percentage	1in, 5%, 3em
margin	number	0.5in, 2em
list-style	word/URL	disc, circle, square, lower alpha
white-space	pre/normal	pre, normal

You can probably figure out what most of these do, but I want to point out something about a few of them.

The FONT property is basically a shorthand reference for the four that appear above it in the table. You can simply use any of the related values for FONT, effectivly describing its entire appearance in one tag. With any font tag, you probably want to be as generic with font names (like Helvetica or Courier) as possible because the user's browser will have to decide what that font name's closest counterpart is on the user's system.

The possible values for COLOR include black, red, white, green, blue, yellow, brown, gray, orange, and purple. You can also add "light" or "dark" to any of these colors. Also, remember that you're acting on a particular tag (most of the time) and that color most often refers to text color. It can be used with any text-related tag, like <BLOCKQUOTE>, as in the following example:

```
<STYLE TYPE="text/css">
  BLOCKQUOTE.helv_red { font-family: helvetica; color: red }
</STYLE>
```

And, you'd call it just like any other CLASS of an HTML tag:

```
<BLOCKQUOTE CLASS="helv_red">Blockquote class</BLOCKQUOTE>
```

The properties VERTICAL-ALIGN and TEXT-ALIGN give Web designers the much-desired control over centering and justifying text in a document.

The BACKGROUND property is most often used in conjunction with the <BODY> tag, although you can technically change the background of nearly any element. The background can be a color, two colors (blended in the background), or an URL to a graphics file. You can also include both color and file, so that a background color is used if the file isn't found. Here's an example:

```
<HEAD>
<TITLE>Background Page</TITLE>
<STYLE TYPE="text/css">
  BODY.back { background: URL(http://www.bigcorp.com/
  ➥back.gif) white/blue }
</STYLE>
<HEAD>
<BODY CLASS="back">
```

Rolling style sheets into your pages

For the most part, a style sheet should be secondary to the communicative nature of your text and graphics. Ideally, this is a page that would work for both HTML 2.0 users and users with style sheet-capable browsers. Let's put together a small style sheet and HTML page.

Listing 13.1 is a sample of how style sheets work in a typical Web page.

Listing 13.1

Using style sheet with real HTML pages

```
<HTML>
<HEAD>
<TITLE>Style Sheet Example</TITLE>
<STYLE TYPE="text/css">
 BODY.back {background: white}
 H2.ital {font-style: italic}
 H3 {text-align: center}
 P.blue {color: blue}
 SPAN {font: 14pt sans-serif; color: blue}
</STYLE>
</HEAD>
<BODY CLASS="back">
<H1>About BigCorp</H1>
<H2 CLASS="ital">Taking Over the World, One Step at a Time</H2>
```

```
<HR>
<H3>About our Company</H3>
<P CLASS="blue">
<SPAN>"Domination of the world</SPAN> is only the first
step,"were the immortal words of BigCorp founder, Mr. Bigbucks.
"If it were that simple,I would have a much better golf
game."</P>
<P>But that's hardly the extent of BigBuck's ambition. From
humble starts,he's taken on the textiles, electronics,
automotive, computer and political-graft indsutries with a
"kill-or-at-least-maim" attitude.</P>
</BODY>
</HTML>
```

It's really about that simple. Of course, things can get a little more complicated, but it all, ultimately, makes sense. See Figure 13.2 to check out the
listing in Internet Explorer.

Fig. 13.2
Even the simple
commands for
style sheets give us
amazing control.

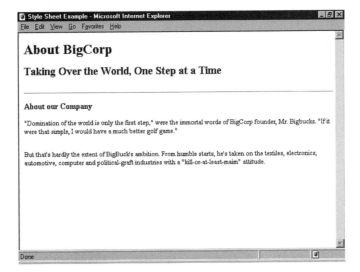

A few other style sheet tags

Aside from what we've already put to use, there are two other basic things
we can discuss concerning style sheets. You may have noticed that we had
to create a class for every instance of a particular style that we wanted to
create—even if we only wanted to use that style once. But we don't have to.

It's possible and acceptable to create something called an **override**—a one-time implementation of a style for a particular purpose. In fact, your whole page could be overrides, if you wanted, but that might be a little tedious.

Style overrides

With a <STYLE> tag defined in the head of your document, you can not only use the currently defined classes for creating styles, but you can also use overrides to change the style of nearly any HTML tag. How does this work? It's similar to defining style classes, but you instead use the STYLE attribute with any legal HTML tag. The following is an example:

```
<P STYLE="text align: center"> This paragraph is centered,
even if it doesn't have a CLASS defined that centers text.
</P>
The following text is <EM STYLE="color: blue">blue and
emphasized</EM>.
<OL STYLE="list-style: lower-roman">
<LI> Each list element
<LI> Is numbered with lowercase
<LI> Roman numerals
</OL>
```

You can see where the flexibility of style sheets is almost getting out of control. Although you can call these overrides for your current style sheet, the truth is that you can use these STYLE-attributed HTML tags anytime that you want to—as long as you've defined the text/css type through a <STYLE> tag in the head of your document.

 TIP **If you prefer to generate your style elements on-the-fly, you can** define an empty <STYLE> tag that does little more than define the TYPE as text/css. Then, use the STYLE attribute to override all the way through your document.

Divisions and the *ALIGN* Attribute

The style sheet standard also creates another tag, the <DIV> (division) tag, which allows you to assign attributes to a particular part of your document. <DIV> is a container tag that applies different styles to anything, including images, placed between the two tags. Ultimately, it gives the designer another level of organization for his Web page. If you think of a <DIV> as one level below the <BODY> tag, you're on the right track.

The <DIV> tag works like this:

```
<DIV CLASS="class_name" ALIGN="direction">
...HTML Markup...
</DIV>
```

Notice that the <DIV> tag can accept the same CLASS attribute that most other HTML tags can take when used with a style sheet. This allows you to create a division of your HTML pages that accepts particular style properties. In addition, the <DIV> tag can take the attribute ALIGN, which accepts LEFT, CENTER, RIGHT, or JUSTIFY.

 TIP **Many browsers began accepting the *DIV* tag and *ALIGN*** attribute early in the original HTML 3.x draft's lifespan. This is the most appropriate way to center a page or portion of the page. When possible, use this tag instead of the Netscape-specific <CENTER> tag.

Let's take a look at the <DIV> tag in action:

```
<DIV ALIGN="CENTER">
<IMG SRC="XJ906.GIF">
<H3>The XJ906 Mega-Notebook</H3>
<P>We can't be more proud of our latest addition to our
notebook line-up,the XJ906. Available with a number of
processors (all daughterboard upgradable) and many memory
configurations (up to 64 MB) the most impressive aspect
of the XJ906 has to be its cutting-edge approach to
multimedia.</P>
<UL>
<LI>6x CD-ROM (internal, sliding-tray)
<LI>2 PCCard 2.0 slots
<LI>16-bit stereo sound and built-in speakers
<LI>Hardware MPEG support
<LI>NTSC Video In/Out Ports
<LI>Available docking station
</UL>
</DIV>
```

Because <DIV> has been supported for quite some time, you can view it in many different browsers—not just the very latest (see Figure 13.3).

Fig. 13.3
The <DIV> tag centers items in Netscape Navigator.

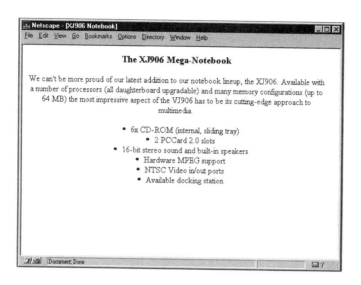

Beyond the basics: *LINK*ing your style sheets

What if you define a really long <STYLE> sheet in the <HEAD> of your document, and then decide you want to use all of those styles in all or many of your Web pages. You have to cut and paste the <STYLE> container into all your documents, right?

Nope. You just use the special <LINK> tag to link any new pages to the page that contains the <STYLE> container. Using the REL attribute for the <LINK> tag, you're essentially adding the <STYLE> elements from the linked page to the current page. Predefined style classes can then be used in the current HTML markup.

This version of the <LINK> tag works like this:

```
<LINK TTTLE="link_doc_title" REL=stylesheet HREF="URL"
➡TYPE="text/css">
```

The TYPE can accept any style sheet type you might be interested in using—we're sticking with CSS. The TITLE should be the same as the remote file's title (the page with the <STYLE> stuff in it) and the HREF URL needs to be an URL to that same document. An example might be:

```
<LINK TITLE="MY STYLE" REL=stylesheet HREF="style.html"
➥TYPE="text/css">
```

So what type of file are you linking to? If you prefer, you can simply link to a common HTML file that defines the style for your Web site. For instance, if you've create an index page (INDEX.HTML) that includes a style definition, you can <LINK> directly to that page and then use the old <STYLE> classes in your new page.

Or, you can create a document that includes nothing but a <STYLE> container and style page definitions. HTML and head/body tags aren't required because the <LINK> tag is essentially "replaced" in the current document with the <STYLE> information. And the <LINK> tag is already in the appropriate place for that <STYLE> information—between the <HEAD> tags. Cool, huh?

14

Going Nuts with Multimedia and Java

● **In this chapter:**

- **How hypermedia links work**

- **Getting and using multimedia documents**

- **How do you embed something in a Web page?**

- **Working with browser plug-ins**

- **Adding Java windows to pages**

How about a Web site that sings and dances? Adding multi-media elements, plug-in documents, and Java windows require just a few extra HTML commands . . . . ▶

Eventually, radio went nuts with all the sort of things they added to what was a pretty straightforward technology. At first, of course, everything was on an AM frequency, with little enough care paid to exactly how rich the sound was or how many speakers it came out of. It was just kind of amazing that the sound got to your set at all.

Then things went crazy. Add-ons, FM bands, stereo, surround sound, tons of speakers, CD-quality, and so on. It's still radio, and it still does basically the same thing. But, now it's—at least ostensibly—a whole lot better.

That's what's going on with the Web right now. Just a few months ago, the Web transmitted text, graphics, and the occasional digital movie. Now, you can "embed" all this stuff in your document, such as QuickTime VR 3-D worlds, Java programs—even presentation software slide shows. And, to do it, you need the right commands . . . and to see it, your user needs the right browser.

 CAUTION **As with any other Web technology, it's always good to warn your** users when you implement something that's specific to a certain Web browser. Even something like "Optimized for Netscape Navigator" is fine. In fact, Netscape and Microsoft encourage you to do this by providing graphics on their site that you can download and use to create clickable graphic links to their sites. It's advertising, after all.

What's a hypermedia link?

A hypermedia link really isn't much different than any other kind of link—instead of linking to another HTML document, you link to a multimedia file. The user's browser, then, has to recognize the kind of file you've linked to, and then load a **helper application**. The helper application takes over from the browser and displays the multimedia file (see Figure 14.1).

66 *Plain English, please!*

A **helper application** is a small program that works with a Web browser to handle all the multimedia files that the browser doesn't feel like showing. Because many browsers aren't equipped to display digital movies, for instance, those files are passed on to a helper movie player. 99

Fig. 14.1
Here's a helper application playing a digital movie.

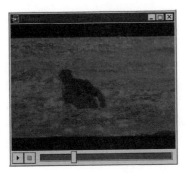

Creating the hypermedia link

Hypermedia links can look like any other hyperlink—they can be text, clickable graphics, or hot zones on imagemaps. All you have to do different is enter an URL for a multimedia file in place of an URL to an HTML document.

TIP **Whenever you create a hypermedia link, it's a good idea to tell** your user how large the file is that he's about to load. Some users may want to pass on a 1.5MB audio clip, for instance.

If hypermedia links look like other links, they're created like other links, too. Here's an example for a Windows sound file in the WAV format (see Figure 14.2):

```
<A HREF="hello.wav"> Greeting from Todd (89 KB) </A>
```

CAUTION **Unless you have the webmaster's explicit permission, never link** to a multimedia file that's on someone else's Web site. When your users access a file on their site, it may slow down their computers significantly.

Fig. 14.2
To create a hypermedia link, just enter the URL for a multimedia file.

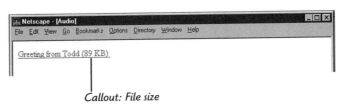

Callout: File size

Now, when your user clicks the link, the file is downloaded to her computer. After that, it's up to the browser and whatever helper applications the user has available.

What files are multimedia files?

So what sort of files are we talking about? Most multimedia files are simply documents that store information outside of the capabilities of HTML. That might mean digital movies, sounds, presentations, or even 3-D worlds. Table 14.1 points out a number of the major types. This list isn't exhaustive, but it should give you an idea of the type of files that can be distributed on the Web.

Table 14.1 Multimedia formats for Web pages

File Format	Type of File	Extension
Sun Systems sound	audio	.AU
Windows sound	audio	.WAV
Audio Interchange	audio	.AIFF, .AIFC
MPEG audio	audio	.MPG, .MPEG
SoundBlaster VOiCe	audio	.VOC
RealAudio	audio stream	.RA, .RAM
CompuServe GIF	graphics	.GIF
JPEG (compressed)	graphics	JPG, .JPEG
TIFF	graphics	.TIF, .TIFF
Windows Bitmap	graphics	.BMP
Apple Picture	graphics	.PICT
Fractal Animations	animation	.FLI, .FLC
VRML	3-D world animation	.WRL
MPEG video	video	.MPG, .MPEG
QuickTime	video	.MOV, .MOOV, .QT
Video For Windows	video	.AVI
Macromedia Shockwave	multimedia presentation	.DCR

File Format	Type of File	Extension
ASCII text	plain text	.TXT, .TEXT
Postscript	formatted text	.PS
Adobe Acrobat	formatted text	.PDF

You may have noticed that I included file extensions in the table. The reasoning behind that is simple: Most Web browsers (and many Web authors) identify multimedia files by their file name extensions. So, it's very important that you name your own multimedia files with these extensions, especially when you're going to make them available to everyone on the Web (see Figure 14.3).

TIP **Even Mac users need to get in the habit of adding file extensions.** Remember it's the browser—not your server—that needs to know the file's extension.

Fig. 14.3
Browsers like Netscape Navigator rely on file name extensions to decide how to deal with a particular multimedia file.

And, even though these are all different file types, each doesn't necessarily require a separate helper application. Many sound helpers play the majority of different sound files, for instance, and some graphics programs can handle multiple file types. For the most part, you need different helper applications for the various video, animation, and formatted text file types. But, more and more browsers are including the capability to view these files without help.

Finding (or creating) multimedia stuff

There are actually books out there that are only about augmenting your Web pages with cool multimedia stuff. Aside from obvious things—such as creating QuickTime movies or recording Windows audio sounds—you can do really amazing stuff like creating Macromedia Director projects (animation, video, sound), building presentation graphics with programs like PowerPoint, or even designing 3-D virtual reality worlds with **VRML**.

Plain English, Please!

The **Virtual Reality Modeling Language** (**VRML**) is a developing standard for creating 3-D worlds for transmission over the Web. A great resource for this emerging application of HTML-related technology is **http://cedar.cic.net/~rtilmann/mm/vrmlup.htm** on the Web.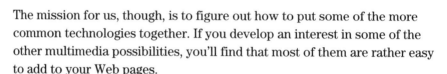

The mission for us, though, is to figure out how to put some of the more common technologies together. If you develop an interest in some of the other multimedia possibilities, you'll find that most of them are rather easy to add to your Web pages.

Making a little sound of your own

A number of programs exist that enable you to create digital sounds; that is, they let you record sounds to a computer file much as you would to a cassette tape. In fact, both Windows and the Mac OS offer these capabilities as included features with the operating system.

Recording sounds in Windows 95

Using Sound Recorder in Windows 95, it's simple to create WAV format sounds for transmission over the Web. Sound Recorder can be found in the Applications menu of the Start menu, under Accessories, Multimedia, Sound Recorder. To use the program, you need a properly configured multimedia system (at least a sound card and microphone). Start up the application by selecting it in the Start menu (see Figure 14.4).

Fig. 14.4
Recording sounds in WAV format with Windows 95 Sound Recorder.

Play   Stop   Record

Sound Recorder uses a familiar interface (with cassette recorder-style buttons) to enable you to record sounds you create through your sound card. To begin, simply click once on the Record button and speak into your microphone. When you're done, click the Stop button.

TIP **With the proper RCA-style jacks, you can plug anything into your** sound card's microphone input for recording—including a cassette player, CD, or an audio feed from your VCR.

To save the new sound, choose File, Save from Sound Recorder's menu. Enter an appropriate file name and choose the folder in which you'd like the sound stored (ideally, choose a folder you're using for your Web site creation). Then click Save. From there, you can use the Windows Explorer to examine the file size of the saved sound file . . . just to make sure it will be a reasonable download for your users.

TIP **Sound Recorder features another command, File, Preferences,** where you can adjust the quality of your recording. Generally speaking, the better the quality, the greater the file size, so try to reasonable compromises for your Web users.

Recording sounds with the Mac OS

Mac users also have a special way to record sounds using Apple-provided tools, but it's a little more limited. Using the Sound control panel, you can create your own recordings using a microphone or any internal sound device (such as a CD-ROM drive). To do so, open the Sound control panel and select Alert Sounds from the pop-up menu. Then, click the Add button (see Figure 14.5).

Fig. 14.5
Recording sounds
with the Mac OS.

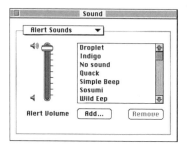

After you record your sounds using the cassette-style interface, click the Save button to save the sounds as a Mac alert. Unfortunately, you'll notice that you haven't actually created a file (complete with its own file name) for use on your Web site.

To do that, you need to head to the System Folder on your Mac and double-click the System file. Scroll to the end of the folder, and you should see the various sound files available, including the one you just created. While holding down the Option key, drag the file on the Desktop or into another folder. It's now a System 7 sound file that you can copy or rename. But there's one more problem—you're limiting your audience if you post a System 7 sound file to the Web!

The answer is a shareware program called SoundApp.

Converting sounds with SoundApp for Macintosh

Available as freeware for download from nearly any major Macintosh archive, SoundApp is among the most popular tools for Web authors (and users). SoundApp's own home is **http://www-cs-students.stanford.edu/~franke/SoundApp/index.html** on the Web.

SoundApp is basically a sound player, but it can also convert files from System 7 sounds to more popular Web formats like .AIFF and .WAV. If you've already created a System 7 sound, use the File, Convert command in SoundApp's menu to convert the file (see Figure 14.6).

After you choose the file in the Open dialog box and select the style of conversion from the pop-up menu, click Open. SoundApp creates a new file in the chosen file format and saves it in a new folder called SoundApp Converted. Open that folder to access the file.

Fig. 14.6
Converting files with SoundApp.

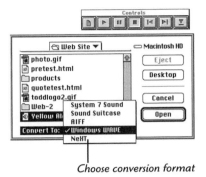

Choose conversion format

 TIP   **Notice that SoundApp doesn't give the new file a different name,** so you need to edit the name yourself (don't forget an appropriate file extension). If you prefer, you can choose Options, Preferences from the SoundApp menu, and then click the Convert icon. In the dialog box, you can check the DOSify Output Filenames checkbox to force SoundApp to create file names with appropriate extensions.

Digging up sounds on the Web

Not all the sounds you will want to use will necessarily be those you create—you might also want to use some recognizable sounds and sound clips from movies, television, or history. Here are some great places to start in the popular Yahoo directory:

http://www.yahoo.com/Entertainment/Movies_and_Films/ Multimedia/Sounds/—Yahoo's guide to popular archives of sounds from television and cinema.

http://www.yahoo.com/Computers_and_Internet/Multimedia/ Sound/—Another Yahoo entry, covers the various types of sound you can add to Web pages.

http://www.yahoo.com/Computers_and_Internet/Multimedia/ Sound/Archives/—Sound archives that focus on (or include) sounds other than TV and movies.

You may also find audio clips on other sites devoted to areas that interest you, such as sites from movie studios, news services, radio and TV stations, and others.

CAUTION **Always think twice about copyright issues before posting an audio** file to your Web site. Many sounds that seem freely available on the Internet are actually owned by certain companies or individuals. It's up to you to secure their permission to replay the clip on your site.

Microwave popcorn? How about digital movies?

A very popular way to add multimedia pizazz to a Web page is through the inclusion of digital movie clips. At the same time, digital movies tend to be rather large and time-consuming downloads for the average user. So, creating videos is a compromise.

It also requires a good deal of equipment. You definitely need special equipment for your Windows or Mac computer, although some models of both include video input ports. You also need special software to **digitize**, edit, and save the video as a computer file (see Figure 14.7).

 Plain English, Please!

As with audio, video must be **digitized**, or turned into computer recognizable ones and zeros, before it can be saved as a computer document. The process of digitizing usually requires special computer hardware that can interpret sounds and video, and then create computer files for playback in special programs.

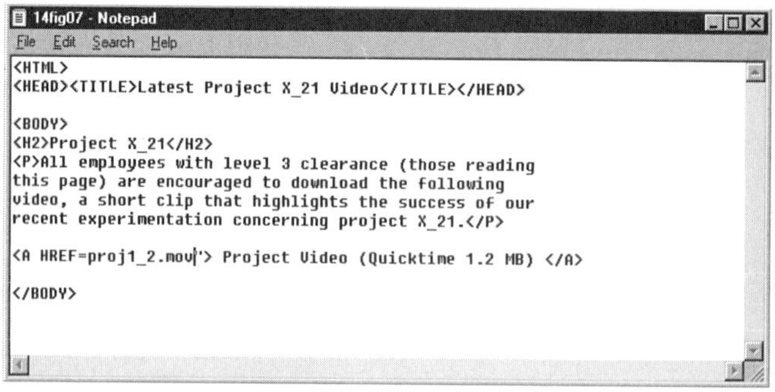

Fig. 14.7
Using common formats like QuickTime or Video for Windows, your Web page can include links to digital video clips.

```
14fig07 - Notepad
File  Edit  Search  Help
<HTML>
<HEAD><TITLE>Latest Project X_21 Video</TITLE></HEAD>

<BODY>
<H2>Project X_21</H2>
<P>All employees with level 3 clearance (those reading
this page) are encouraged to download the following
video, a short clip that highlights the success of our
recent experimentation concerning project X_21.</P>

<A HREF=proj1_2.mov'> Project Video (Quicktime 1.2 MB) </A>

</BODY>
```

Digital video movies are generally in one of three different formats common to the Web: QuickTime, MPEG, or Video for Windows. Any of these is acceptable, although QuickTime and MPEG are both more easily played on computers other than Windows PCs.

Beyond creating your own movies, there are a number of areas on the Web where you can download digital clips. I recommend you start at the Yahoo directory with **http://www.yahoo.com/Computers_and_Internet/ Multimedia/Archives/** where you'll find archived movies and other multimedia files.

Plugging multimedia stuff into the browser window

The two most popular Web browsers on the market—Netscape Navigator and Microsoft Internet Explorer—both feature support for the plug-in technology pioneered by Netscape. What's a **plug-in**? It's a small program that can do something above-and-beyond the capabilities of the browser, such as show a digital movie.

But, instead of loading a helper application, a plug-in shows the multimedia file *inside* the Web browser window, just as if it were part of the page. Basically, the plug-in programs extend the capabilities of the browser.

Currently the plug-in technology is a Netscape-specific standard, but other browsers, notably Internet Explorer, support Netscape plug-ins. In order to add plug-ins to your page, you need to learn a new HTML-like command. This one isn't part of the HTML 3.2 standard, so far.

Embedding files in your document

There's just one simple way to get a multimedia file to play in the browser window, using a plug-in: the <EMBED> tag from Netscape. It's a pretty simple tag, working a whole lot like the <IMG> tag from HTML. It does have a few extra attributes, though.

Here's how the <EMBED> container works:

```
<EMBED SRC="URL"> ... </EMBED>
```

See? It's pretty familiar looking. Even the basic attributes for <EMBED> should look pretty familiar:

- SRC="URL" tells the browser where to find the multimedia document it's going to display. Usually, the browser figures out what plug-in to use based on the file name extension—so you need to include one.

- HEIGHT="number" defines the height (in pixels) of the "window" created for the plug-in.

- WIDTH="value" defines the width (in pixels) of the "window" created for the plug-in.

Knowing that, we find that embedding a sound Macromedia Director file, for instance, could be as easy as:

```
<EMBED SRC="welcome.drc" WIDTH=144 HEIGHT=132>
```

When a Netscape-compatible browser encounters this statement, it runs the Shockwave plug-in (if the user has it installed), which is capable of playing Macromedia Director presentations in the browser window.

TIP   **It's always a good idea to include a link to the company that** distributes any plug-ins that you make use of on your Web page.

Each individual piece of plug-in software needs to be installed on the user's computer—most are available for download on the Web. At the same time, each Web author needs to learn, from the software company that created the plug-in, what special commands, if any, the plug-in requires in the <EMBED> tag.

Q&A   ***I can't seem to get my embedded document to load correctly. What's wrong?***

The most common problem with embedded documents is saving them with the wrong file extension. It's vitally important that you make sure you use the extension that browsers expect for the various types of plug-ins. Also, remember that you need the actual plug-in software installed on your test system.

A quick example: QuickTime movies

Just about every plug-in has different commands and values that are possible—to determine what commands are required for your plug-in document, consult the documentation that accompanies the program that created the plug-in, or, perhaps, instructions can be found on the plug-in company's Web site.

One example is particularly useful: QuickTime videos. A QuickTime plug-in is included with recent copies of Netscape Navigator, and is available for many other modern browsers. Table 14.2 shows some of the possible commands for embedding a QuickTime movie as a plug-in document.

Table 14.2   Possible commands for a QuickTime movie plug-in document

Command	Useful value	What it does...
AUTOPLAY	TRUE	Causes movie to begin automatically
CONTROLLER	FALSE	Hides movie controls
LOOP	TRUE	Movie loops over and over
PLAYEVERYFRAME	TRUE	Plays every frame, even if movie is too slow

Like QuickTime, most plug-in formats have their own little extra attributes. You need to learn these attributes from the particular companies that write the plug-ins.

Working that thing called Java

You've probably heard at least a little something about Java if you've spent much time on the Internet. And you might have wondered why you should care. **Java**, in a nutshell, is a full-fledged computer programming language that's designed to work a lot like some other popular languages—notably a programming language called C++ (many popular Mac and Windows applications are written in C++).

 TIP Programming in Java is well beyond the scope of this book; we'll just be looking at how to add finished Java programs to our pages. For more on Java, check out *Special Edition Using Java* and *Java by Example*, both by Que.

The difference with Java is that it's also designed to run on nearly any sort of computer that might be connected to the Internet. It's popular for programmers who want to write programs for use on the Web because, once the program is downloaded, it can be run by nearly anyone who visits the Web site.

Getting yourself some Java applets

For the most part, Java programs end up being very small when they're used on Web sites, for the same reason that we try to keep everything else small—it takes time to download files across the Internet. These small programs are often called **applets** because, unlike full-sized computer applications, applets generally perform only one specific function (see Figure 14.9).

Fig. 14.9
Here's an example of a single-function Java applet being displayed in Netscape Navigator.

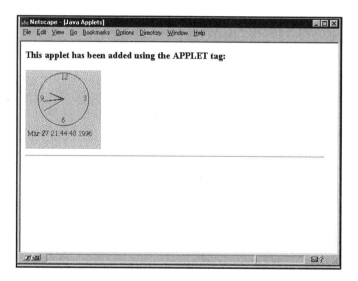

If you're not going to write Java applets yourself (or have someone else do it for you), you might want to check out what the Web has to offer in the way of freeware and shareware Java applets for your site. A good place to start is **http://www.yahoo.com/Computers_and_Internet/Programming_Languages/Java/Applets/** from Yahoo.

Adding Java applets to your page

You add Java applets in HTML 3.2-compatible browsers with the <APPLET> container tag. Along with the <APPLET> tag is the <PARAM> tag, which offers certain parameters to the browser concerning the applet (like the speed at which something should display, initialize, and so on). <APPLET> accepts the attributes CODE, CODEBASE, HEIGHT, and WIDTH.

An <APPLET> tag follows the general format:

```
<APPLET CODEBASE="applet_path_URL" CODE="appletFile.class"
➥WIDTH="number" HEIGHT="number">
<PARAM NAME="attributeName" VALUE="string/number">
...
Alt HTML text for non-Java browsers
</APPLET>
```

CODEBASE is the path (in URL form) to the directory on your server containing the Java applet. (It's basically like an URL without the final document name.) CODE takes the name of the applet. This file always ends in .class to suggest that it's a compiled Java class. CODE should always be just the file name, because CODEBASE is used to find the path to the Java applet.

 TIP Notice that CODEBASE and CODE work together to create a complete URL. So, for a relative URL, CODEBASE isn't required if the applet is in the same directory as the Web page.

The WIDTH and HEIGHT attributes accept the number in pixels for the Java applet on your Web page.

What do people do with Java?

As Java becomes more and more popular on the Internet (and as more folks learn how to program with it), we're seeing a diversification in the sort of programs that are appearing on Web pages. It's a fairly slow process, though, so we can still point to some fairly simple categories.

For the most part, Java applets are either small games, Web communications enhancements, or ways to display data from internal databases on Web sites. It's also typical to see Java applets that are responsible for presenting animated information screens or simple animated cartoons.

The future holds more possibilities for Java, but for now, the applets are still in the infancy stage where a lot of folks are just proving to themselves that they can create a program at all. There are, indeed, a fair number of clocks, calculators, and tic-tac-toe games that have been created.

If you're looking for an online office suite of productivity applications, you'll have to wait a bit longer.

An example of the first line of <APPLET> would be the following:

```
<APPLET CODEBASE="http://www.myserver.com/applets/"
➥CODE="clock.class"
HEIGHT="300" WIDTH="300">
```

<PARAM> is a bit easier to use than it may seem. It essentially creates a variable, assigns a value, and passes it to the Java applet. The applet must be written to understand the parameter's name and value. NAME is used to create the parameter's name; it should be expected by the applet. VALUE is used to assign the value to that particular parameter. It could be a number, bit of text, or even a command that causes the applet to work in a particular way.

 TIP **Understanding the <PARAM> tag might enable you to use freeware/** shareware Java applets on your own pages. By passing your own parameters to general purpose applets, you may find them useful for your particular Web site.

A simple <PARAM> tag is the following:

```
<PARAM NAME="Speed" VALUE="5">
```

In this case, the Java applet has to recognize and know what to do with a variable named Speed with a value of 5.

The alternative HTML markup in the <APPLET> container enables you to offer HTML text to browsers that aren't Java-enabled. A Java-aware browser ignores the markup (and displays the applet window instead), while non-Java browsers ignore everything but the markup. So, an example would be the following:

```
<APPLET CODE="counter.class" HEIGHT="20" WIDTH="20">
<P>You need a <I>Java-aware</I> browser to see this
➥counter!</P>
</APPLET>
```

This displays the text, instead of the applet, when it encounters a browser that doesn't support Java.

15

Scripting Your Page

● **In this chapter:**

- **What is scripting?**

- **JavaScript versus the other guys**

- **How to enter JavaScript**

- **JavaScript functions revealed**

- **Counting, looping, and other programming junk**

- **JavaScript for event handling**

- **Can I use JavaScript to double-check form input?**

If you've gotten this far and you think HTML is a wussy-game without any real programming meat, take on this chapter and try on JavaScript. . . . . ▷

I t seems like only last chapter that we were talking about how to add Java applets to a document for Internet Explorer. Now we're going to talk about JavaScript and some of the other scripting languages that you can use to turn your Web pages into mini-programs. Sound cool? It'll take a little practice—especially if you've never done any computer programming. And, on top of that, there's a lot of extra stuff to enter into our text editors.

But, yeah, it is pretty cool.

Are Java and JavaScript the same?

Let's start by making a distinction between Java and Javascript. Java is a full-fledged programming language in the spirit of C++. It is designed for the more advanced programmer, with its strength being the capability to run in a **virtual machine** that can be created by a Web browser.

 Plain English, please!

This **virtual machine** concept is pretty much the reason for all the hype surrounding Java. Here's the idea: Every computer in the world can pretend to be a less-sophisticated "Java-standard" computer. Instead of programming specifically for Windows or the Mac OS, then, programmers just a write the program for the virtual machine. Because Web browsers can create this machine, it's possible to run the Java program from within the Web browser...which means we can offer cooler stuff on our Web sites. 99

Java, then, is similar to the programming languages used to build full-fledged applications that can be run on PCs, Macs, and UNIX machines. It's well-suited for the Internet, but not necessarily exclusive to the Web.

So what's JavaScript?

JavaScript, on the other hand, is a less complex scripting language similar to AppleScript, Visual Basic Scripting (VBScript), and other scripting languages. JavaScript is also similar in some surface ways to Java, but it doesn't require you to worry as much about some of the underlying structure in a program. It's a bit limited in that way, but still very useful.

Here's another way to think about it: Java applets almost always require a special little window on the Web page to run because they are complete applications all to themselves. JavaScript, on the other hand, is actually part of your HTML code. It doesn't create any special windows or anything—it just makes your Web pages a little more dynamic (see Figure 15.1).

Fig. 15.1
There usually aren't many hints as to whether a page is using JavaScript. In this case, Netscape uses JavaScript (instead of a CGI script) to load new pages with this pop-up menu.

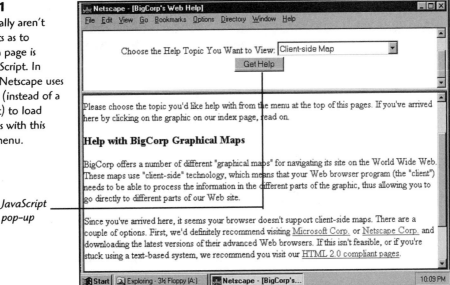

JavaScript pop-up

What about other scripting languages?

JavaScript is easily the most popular among Web scripting languages, which isn't terribly surprising when you consider that it was both first to be marketed and created by Netscape. JavaScript is even being considered for inclusion in aspects of the HTML 3.2 standard, so you can rest assured that the Web world is serious about JavaScript and more browsers will support it in the future.

CAUTION **Netscape and Internet Explorer are currently the only browsers I** know of that support JavaScript (Microsoft calls it JScript). If you decide to create documents that incorporate JavaScript, be aware that only a few of the latest browsers can interpret it.

Entering scripts in your Web documents

You don't need any special new tools for adding JavaScript to your HTML documents; your text editor will work just fine. You will, however, want to test, test, and test again while you're writing JavaScript code, so be sure you've got the 3.0 (or higher) version of Netscape or IE handy for loading these pages.

 TIP   **Actually, you might want copies of both Netscape and IE for this** chapter, just to make sure everything works in both. (The 3.0 versions of both reportedly have slight differences in how JavaScript makes them happy.)

The *SCRIPT* tag

The <SCRIPT> tag is used to add JavaScript commands to your HTML pages. This is done so that Netscape and compatible browsers can determine what text is actually scripting commands and what text should be displayed in the browser window. <SCRIPT> is a container tag that can accept the attribute LANGUAGE, which enables you to specify the scripting language used (Javascript is generally the default). Here's how it works (see Figure 15.2):

```
<SCRIPT LANGUAGE="JavaScript">
Script Code
</SCRIPT>
```

Hiding scripts in your documents

While it's possible that old browsers that don't recognize JavaScript will just skip over the <SCRIPT> tag, it's also possible that the browser will attempt to interpret your script commands or other text as HTML markup. So, you've got to be careful in how you "hide" the script stuff.

For non-JavaScript browsers, surround the script commands with the HTML comment tag. Here's all the stuff you need to enter:

```
<SCRIPT>
<!—
script commands
// —>
</SCRIPT>
```

In order to keep everyone happy, we've got to add all these special commands. You might have even noticed that we have to put two slashes ("//") in front of the closing HTML comment tag. Why? Because JavaScript will choke when it sees --> because it will try to interpret that as scripting code. (To JavaScript, that looks like two minus signs and a greater than sign.) So, you need to comment the comment.

SCRIPT *tag*

Fig. 15.2
Whenever you add JavaScript statements to your page, you need to separate them with the <SCRIPT> tag.

```
Helpform - Notepad                                          _|8|X
File  Edit  Search  Help
<HTML>
<HEAD>
<TITLE>Help Form</TITLE>
<SCRIPT>
<!---
  function changePage(form) {
        var choice=form.helppage.selectedIndex;
        alert (form.helppage[choice].value);
        parent.main_viewer.location.href=form.helppage[choice].value;
        }
// -->
</SCRIPT>
</HEAD>
<BODY>
<DIV ALIGN="CENTER">
<IMG SRC="helplogo.gif"><BR>
<FORM>
Choose the Help Topic You Want to View:
<SELECT NAME="helppage">
<OPTION SELECTED VALUE="maphelp.html"> Client-side Map
<OPTION VALUE="usehelp.html"> Using Our Site
<OPTION VALUE="phonhelp.html"> Contacting BigCorp
<OPTION VALUE="dl_help.html"> Downloading From Our Site
<OPTION VALUE="buy_help.html"> Ordering Products
</SELECT><BR>
<INPUT TYPE="button" Value="Get Help" onClick="changePage(this.form)">
</FORM>
```

 TIP **Two slashes together // are the comment command in JavaScript.**

In fact, it's always a good idea to create comments within your script that document what you're doing in your programming. Using the two slashes, then, you can keep up a running commentary about your script:

```
<SCRIPT>
<!--
script command      // One-line comment
...script commands...
/* Unlimited-length comments, must be
ended with */
// comment to end hiding -->
</SCRIPT>
```

Looks like you can fill a decent-sized page with nothing but comments, eh? Notice that we've solved the HTML comment problem with a *single-line* JavaScript comment. Single-line comments start with two forward slashes and must physically fit on a single line with a return at the end. Multi-line comments can be enclosed in an opening comment element (/*) and a closing comment element (*/).

Creating a scripting page from scratch in Windows NotePad, then, we'd be starting out with something like Figure 15.3.

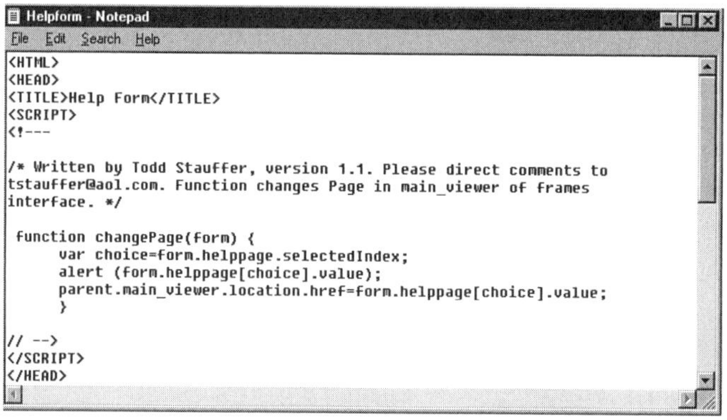

Fig. 15.3
Getting all our commenting out of the way before the real scripting begins.

```
Helpform - Notepad
File  Edit  Search  Help
<HTML>
<HEAD>
<TITLE>Help Form</TITLE>
<SCRIPT>
<!---

/* Written by Todd Stauffer, version 1.1. Please direct comments to
tstauffer@aol.com. Function changes Page in main_viewer of frames
interface. */

function changePage(Form) {
     var choice=form.helppage.selectedIndex;
     alert (form.helppage[choice].value);
     parent.main_viewer.location.href=form.helppage[choice].value;
     }

// -->
</SCRIPT>
</HEAD>
```

Getting JavaScript to function

Did you ever play around with programming languages back when computers did little more than print things out to a printer or to the screen? You know, back before all the windows and icons and pretty little animated things. If you did, you might have used something like BASIC, Fortran, or COBOL—all of which, at least originally, were procedural languages. (Do the first step; then think; then do the next step, etc.)

But that kind of programming meant you got one kind of program that resulted: Q&A-style programs. Remember? You'd get a menu with your choices all in text, or the program would ask you for the next number in the sequence or something. These days, you can click just about any icon you want in a program like Microsoft Word—in any order.

JavaScript, like many of the latest, coolest, most innovative computer programming languages, breaks out of the procedural mold a bit. In

JavaScript, every little thing we do is separated out into a function—for performing a math equation, for instance. The functions can be used in any particular order, just like the icons in MS Word.

So what's a function?

A **function** is basically a "mini-program." Functions start by being "passed" a particular value; they work with that value to make something else happen and then "return" a new value to the body of your program (see Figure 15.4).

Fig. 15.4
Here's (kinda) how a JavaScript program works in your document.

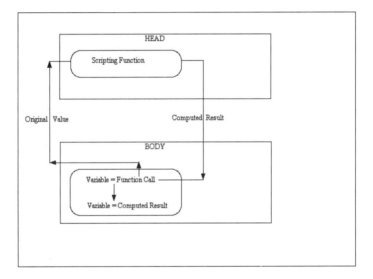

In JavaScript, there are two times you need to worry about functions. First, you need to declare the function. What's declaring? It's when you rear back your head and declare, "Browser, I'm going to have this function, and this is what it's going to do." The browser, when it loads a page, will make note of the different functions that you've declared.

The second step is to call the function in the body of your script. Generally, your script will be just a series of function calls. There isn't a whole lot of calculating done in the guts of your script. You send a value out to a function to be computed and then receive the results back in the body.

Making your function-related intentions known

A good rule, although it's not necessary, is to declare your functions in the HEAD of your HTML document. The function declaration needs to appear between <SCRIPT> tags, but you can have more than one set of <SCRIPT> tags in a document. A single set of <SCRIPT> tags doesn't necessarily define an entire script—it just sets script elements apart from other HTML tags. Function declarations look like the following:

```
<SCRIPT>
<!--
  function function_name(value_name) {
  ...function code...
  return (new_value)
}
// end hiding -->
</SCRIPT>
```

The value_name for the function is just the **variable** name that you assign to the passed value for the duration of the function. When the body of your JavaScript document calls this function, it will generally send along a value. When that value gets to the function, it needs a name. If the function is designed to perform simple math, for instance, you might call the passed value old_num.

66 *Plain English, please!*

> When you create a **variable** in programming, you're really just creating a name for a slot in the computer's memory. You can then assign a certain value to that slot and refer to it by its new name. For instance, if I create a variable called num_1, I could assign the number 5 to that variable. Then I could tell the script to add num_1+10. If I did it right, the script would give me the answer: 15. 99

Also, notice that the entire calculating part of the function is between curly brackets. An example of a function declaration might be:

```
<SCRIPT>
<! —
  function get_square(old_num) {
  new_num = (old_num * old_num)
```

```
    return (new_num)
}
// end hiding -->
</SCRIPT>
```

In the example, we've created a function called `get_square`, which accepts a value, names it `old_num`, and then squares that value and assigns it to a variable named `new_num`. At least, that's what the function is supposed to do. It won't do it yet, because this is just a declaration. It doesn't even know what actual values to work with until you call the function.

TIP **By the way, all the extra spacing in these JavaScript commands** and functions is for the benefit of humans, not computers. I like to add spaces to make things a little easier to read. But you don't have to count the spaces on the page to make sure you get things right.

Get the function going with a call

You **call** the function from the body of your script, which is generally in the body of the Web document. It doesn't really matter where you declare functions (although, as mentioned, it's best to declare them between the <HEAD> tags), but it is best to put the function calls of your script close to the parts of your document where they're needed (this will become more obvious as we work with JavaScript). A function call always appears between <SCRIPT> tags, and it looks something like this:

```
function_name(value);
```

In this function call, the `function_name` should be the same as the function name that you use in the function declaration, but the `value` can be anything you want to pass to the function. You can put most anything in the parentheses—a variable name, an actual number, or a string of text—as long as the function is designed to accept such a value. For instance, our `get_square` function works equally well if we use:

```
<SCRIPT>
num = 5;
num_squared = get_square (num);
</SCRIPT>
```

See what we're doing here? We've assigned the value 5 to the variable num. Then that variable (and hence the 5) is passed to the function get_square, which we declared in the previous section. When that number gets up there to the function, it's renamed old_num in our example, and then it's squared mathematically by the commands in that function.

CAUTION   **Remember, though, that you should be passing a value that the** function expects. If you pass a string of text to a function designed to perform math functions, you won't get anything useful.

So how do we get the answer from the function?

Our story so far...

```
<HEAD>
<TITLE>Testing</TITLE>
<SCRIPT>
<! —
  function get_square(old_num) {
  new_num = (old_num * old_num)
  return (new_num)
}
// end hiding -->
</SCRIPT>
</HEAD>

<BODY>
HTML stuff
<SCRIPT>
<! —
num = 5;
num_squared = get_square (num);
// end hiding -->
</SCRIPT>
```

Down there in the BODY of the Web document, notice that our function call is in the same place where it has been—on the right side of an equal sign. In JavaScript (and in most programming) that's actually an **assignment**. What we're telling the script is, "Set the variable num_squared equal to the value of the function get_squared when we send it the value num."

> ## ❝ *Plain English, please!*
>
> In JavaScript, the equal sign is used to **assign** values to variables. So when you type num = 5, it isn't a question—you just put the number 5 in the variable num. This is in contrast to a comparison, which is two equal signs ==. You use the comparison when you want to script to decide whether or not two values are equal, as in, "does 5==4? ❞

This may take a little leap of thought, but JavaScript does two things with function calls. First, the call is used to pass a value to the function. We already know that part. Then, when the function returns a value, it *takes the place* of the original function call.

Look at the following example:

```
num_squared = get_square (5);
```

After the math of the get_square function is completed and the value is returned, the entire function call (get_square (5)) is given a value of 25. This, in turn, is assigned to the variable num_squared.

Are you still awake?

JavaScript's bold statements

Before we can get any deeper into creating scripts for our Web page, we need to back up a bit and take a look at some of the other little commands you can use in JavaScript—if you've ever done any programming before, some of this should look familiar. Just skim it and move on to the fun stuff in the section called "Event handling with JavaScript." (Just that title kinda gets your blood racing, doesn't it?)

JavaScript includes the conditional statement if...else and the loop statements for and while. You'll also get to know some of the associated JavaScript operators.

 TIP In most cases, you use these statements in functions. These are the commands in JavaScript you use to actually process data.

The key to many of these statements is something called the **condition**, which is simply a bit of JavaScript code that needs to be evaluated before your script decides what to do next. So, before you look at JavaScript statements, let's look at the conditions that JavaScript recognizes.

 Plain English, please!

In programming a **condition** is a quick statement that is either true or false. Let's say you were writing a script that decides whether or not your user has entered all five digits for a zip code. In a function, you could create a condition that says, "If the user has entered five digits in the zip code box, tell them, 'Good job.' If they haven't, make them try again." The function determines whether or not they've complied with your demands and acts appropriately. **"**

Conditions and their operators

Conditions are generally enclosed in parentheses, and they are always a small snippet of code that is designed to evaluate as true or false. For instance, the following is a conditional statement:

```
(x == 1)
```

If x does equal 1, then this condition is true. (I've been lead to understand that programmers will say things like, "This condition evaluates to true.")

And this is why it's important to recognize and use the correct operators for conditions. Look at this one:

```
(errorLevel = 1)
```

Wrong! It's always true because it's an *assignment*. Although it may seem to make sense to use an equal sign in this instance, you actually need to use the comparison operator == for this condition. (See Table 15.1 for a listing of the comparison operators.)

Table 15.1 Comparison operators in JavaScript

Operator	Meaning	Example	Is true when...
==	equals	x == y	x equals y
!=	not equal	x != y	x is not equal to y
>	greater than	x > y	x is greater than y

Operator	Meaning	Example	Is true when...
<	less than	x < y	x is less than y
>=	greater than or equal to	x >= y	x is greater than or equals y
<=	less than or equal to	x <= y	x is less than or equals y

Realize, too, that conditions are not necessarily limited to numerical expressions. For instance, look at the following:

```
(carName != "Ford")
```

This returns the value `false` if the variable `carName` has the value of the string `Ford`.

AND, OR, NOT comparisons

The other operators common to conditional statements are the **boolean** operators. In English, these operators are AND, OR, and NOT. In JavaScript, AND is &&, OR is ¦¦, and NOT is !. An example of a condition would be the following:

```
((x == 5) && (y == 6))
```

This condition evaluates to `true` only if each individual comparison is true. If either comparison is false—or both comparisons are false—the entire conditional statement is false.

On the other hand, the following conditional statement uses the OR operator:

```
((x == 5) ¦¦ (y == 6))
```

In this case, if either of the conditions is true, then the entire statement is true. The statement is only false if both of the conditions are false.

Finally, the NOT operator changes the result of an expression, so that, if the value of x really is five, you could create the following conditional:

```
(!(x == 5))
```

NOT simply reverses the result of the conditional statement. In this example, the entire condition is false, because (x == 5) is true, and the NOT operator reverses that.

if...else

"Or else I'll...I'll..." Ever had parents? Then you know what a conditional statement is. JavaScript offers the `if...else` conditional statement as a way to create either/or situations in your script. The basic construct looks like this:

```
if (condition) {
  script statements }
else {
  other statements }
```

The condition can be any JavaScript that evaluates to either true or false. The statements can be any valid JavaScript statements. For example:

```
if (x == 5) {
  return;
  }
  else {
  x = x + 1;
  }
```

 CAUTION **Notice the little curly brackets around the statements? Every** conditional statement needs the little brackets around them to know when the "if" part ends and the "else" part begins. Forget to type the brackets and your script won't work correctly.

The else and related statements are not required if you simply want the if statements to be skipped and the rest of the function executed.

Loop statements

The next two statement types are used to create **loops**—script elements that repeat until a condition is met. These loop statements are FOR and WHILE.

FOR loops

You generally start a FOR loop by initializing your "counter" variable. Then, you evaluate the counter to see if it's reached a certain level. If it hasn't, the loop performs the enclosed statements and increments your counter. If the counter has reached your predetermined value, the FOR loop ends. For example:

```
for (x=0; x<10; x=x+1) {
  y = 2 * x;
```

```
document.write ("Two times ",x," equals ",y,"<BR>");
}
```

You start by initializing a counter variable (x=1), and then evaluating the counter in a conditional statement (x<10). If the condition is true, the loop performs the enclosed scripting. Then it increments the counter—in this case, adds 1 to it. When the counter reaches 10 in our example, the loop ends.

WHILE loops

The WHILE loop is similar to the FOR loop, except that it offers a little more freedom. WHILE is used for a great variety of conditions.

As long as the condition evaluates to true, the loop will continue. For example:

```
x = 0;
while (x <= 5) {
    x = x +1;
    document.write (X now equals ",x,"<BR>")
    }
```

Q&A *My conditional statements always seem to be true (or always seem to be false), even though they clearly shouldn't be. Is JavaScript just wrong?*

It seems like, in almost any modern programming situation, the first place to look is for accidental assignments in conditions. Go back and look very carefully. Did you say = when you meant ==? Now go back and look again. (I've made three editing passes through this chapter and I'm still finding them.)

Writing the first script

So much for Programming 101. If you read and understood those last few sections, you can at least take heart in the fact that those are fairly useful concepts in computer programming—even in advanced programming languages like C++ and Java. So, it's not knowledge wasted on lowly JavaScript.

Just so we can feel good about ourselves, let's create a simple script. It'll be a "Hello World" program—sort of a tradition when you learn to program. I just have to throw one quick command at you for the purpose of getting your first

JavaScript page to work. It's `document.write`, and it's something called a method in JavaScript. A **method** is basically a variable that does something automatically. In this case, it prints text to your Web page.

Here's the full listing for our script:

```
<HTML>
<HEAD>
<TITLE>Hello World JavaScript Example</TITLE>
</HEAD>
<BODY>

<SCRIPT LANGUAGE="JavaScript">
<!—
/* Our script only requires
one quick statement! */
document.write("Hello World!") // Prints words to Web
document
// end hiding—>
</SCRIPT>
</BODY>
</HTML>
```

Save this document, and then load it in a JavaScript-aware browser (Netscape or IE 3.0). If everything goes as planned, you'll see something that looks like Figure 15.5.

Fig. 15.5
The results of a simple but successful script.

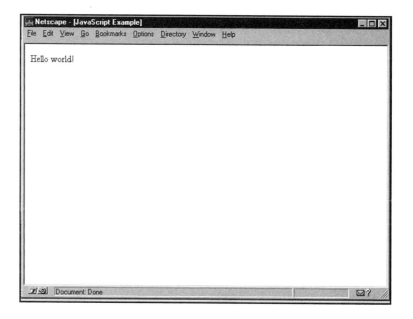

Handling events from users

Well, you've created a complete script, but it can't do much. That's because the strength of JavaScript, more than anything else, is in **event handling**. That is, it's best at responding to something a user does on your page. This is generally done in response to some HTML tag. Here's the basic format for an event handler:

```
<TAG event_handler="JavaScript code">
```

<TAG> can be just about any form or hyperlink tag. Most other tags don't have the capability to accept input from the user. The event_handler is the browser's code for some action by the user. The JavaScript code will most often be a function call.

For instance, you could use an input textbox to send data to a function you've written, as with the following code:

```
<INPUT TYPE="text" NAME="number" SIZE="4">
<INPUT TYPE="button" NAME="Calculate" onClick="result =
compute(this.form.number.value)">
```

In this example, you're responding to the event created when the user clicks the input button. When that happens, the value `this.form.number.value` is sent to a function called `compute`. Notice that the variable `this.form.number` `.value` is JavaScript's object-oriented way of storing the value of the textbox named "number" in the first statement.

Returning values from functions

Let's dig a little deeper into how the object-oriented storage thing works. Your average object is usually just a bunch of grouped variables. For instance, a typical browser has a JavaScript object called `this`, which (in the above example) means "variables for this page." Within `this` is a subcategory called `form`, which means "the form variables." So, the name `this.form` is basically where "the form variables for this page" are stored.

 TIP **Actually, `this` is a special keyword in JavaScript used to refer to the** current object. In the case of our example, the current object is, in fact, where the "variables for the page" are stored. I'm sorry they called it "this" because that's a commonly used pronoun in the English language. Try to think of `this` as a completely different word for a few more paragraphs.

When you use the NAME attribute to an <INPUT> tag (for an HTML form), you're creating another variable within this object. For instance, NAME="mynumber" creates this.form.mynumber. The value of that form variable is stored at this.form.mynumber.value.

Let's look at that last example again:

```
<INPUT TYPE="text" NAME="number" SIZE="4">
<INPUT TYPE="button" NAME="Calculate" onClick="result =
compute(this.form.number.value)">
```

Now, the neat trick here is that you don't necessarily have to pass the specific value to a function in order to use it. All you need to do is send the name of the object that you want the function to concentrate on. That way, it can deal with more than one value from that object.

Consider something. You've just gathered this.form.number.value from the <INPUT> textbox. Now you want to send whatever the user typed to a function. You can make the function call like:

```
<INPUT TYPE="button" NAME="Calculate" onClick="result =
compute(this.form)">
```

You've also cleverly designed the function to work with the <INPUT> value. So, your function will look something like the following:

```
function compute(form) {
  new_number = form.number.value;
  new_number = new_number * 2;
  return (new_number);
}
```

The function received what's known as a "pointer" to the object responsible for storing information in the form. After the function has its hands on that pointer (which the function calls form), it's able to access data within that function by using the object variable scheme, as in form.number.value. Get it?

But this gets even cooler. If the function knows the pointer to the data storage object, it can also create new variables within that object. So, you can change a few more things:

```
<INPUT TYPE=text NAME="number" SIZE=4>
<INPUT TYPE=button NAME="Calculate" Value="Click Me"
onClick="compute(this.form)">
<INPUT TYPE=text NAME="result" SIZE=8>
```

Now (in the second line), you're just telling the browser to run the `compute()` function when the Calculate button is clicked. But you're not assigning the function to a value. So how do you get an answer for your user? By using the object pointer. Here's the new function:

```
function compute(form) {
  new_number = form.number.value;
  form.result.value = new_number * 2;
  return;
}
```

In line three of the function declaration, notice the new variable `form.result.value`. What happens now is the function call sets the function in motion and passes it the object pointer. The function creates its own new variable within the object, called `result`, and gives it a new value. When the function returns, the next line of script is activated. That line is:

```
<INPUT TYPE="text" NAME="result" SIZE="8">
```

Notice the NAME. Because there's already a value assigned to this NAME, that value will be displayed in the textbox (just as if it were default text). In your case, it happens to be the answer (see Figure 15.6). Here's the complete code again:

```
<HTML>
<HEAD>
<TITLE>Compute A Number</TITLE>
<SCRIPT>
<!--
function compute(form) {
  new_number = form.number.value;
  form.result.value = new_number * 2;
  return;
}
// -->
</SCRIPT>

</HEAD>
<BODY>

<FORM>
<INPUT TYPE="text" NAME="number" SIZE="4">
<INPUT TYPE="button" NAME="Calculate" Value="Click Me"
onClick="compute(this.form)">
<INPUT TYPE="text" NAME="result" SIZE="8">
</FORM>
</BODY>
</HTML>
```

Fig. 15.6
Your textbox script,
complete with a result.

Events you might want to handle

There are a number of different events that a typical browser will recognize and for which you can write handlers. Even the simplest handler should call a function you've declared previously, and then elegantly return to that point in the Web document. Table 15.2 shows you some of the events for which there are associated handlers (according the Netscape's JavaScript documentation).

Table 15.2   Events and their event handlers

Event	Means...	Event handler
blur	User moves input focus from form box	onBlur
click	User clicks on form element or link	onClick
change	User changes a form value	onChange
focus	User gives a form box input focus	onFocus
load	User loads the page in Navigator	onLoad
mouseover	User moves mouse over a link	onMouseOver
select	User selects form input field	onSelect
submit	User submits a form	onSubmit
unload	User exits the page	onUnload

You can probably figure out what most of these do from the table. And it should also make you realize how scriptable your Web page really is. You can create alert dialog boxes, for instance, that tell your user that a particular field is required—or that it needs to be filled with a certain number of characters. You can even say "Goodbye" to users as they leave your page, perhaps displaying a phone number of other useful (albeit intrusive) information.

Checking data in forms and alerting users to errors

You may have noticed that JavaScript events tend to be very closely connected to form elements. Why is that significant? Because one of the most meaningful ways to use JavaScript is to check to make sure users are entering the right data. If they don't, you have the option of explaining that to them in an alert box and asking them to go back and change things around a bit.

For the sake of simplicity, I'll post all of the HTML code in the following example. Our form, then, starts out looking like Figure 15.7.

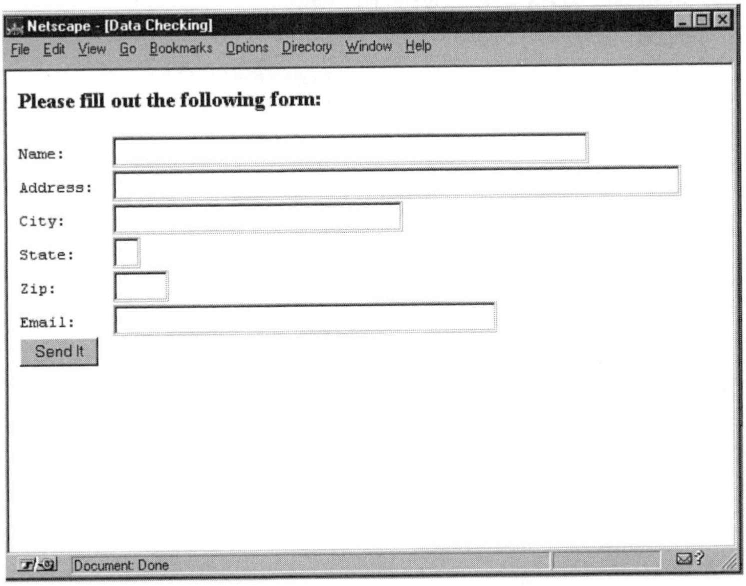

Fig. 15.7
You can start with a typical form page—eventually you'll add the error-checking script elements by hand.

Writing the form checking function

One of the best uses of event handling seems to be for verifying form data. You can use JavaScript to hand off your data object pointer to a function, which can then take a close look at what your user has entered and determine if it's correct.

We'll try it for a zip code. You're simply going to make sure that the user has entered five numbers. To do that, we need to write a function that can tell if a particular string is five characters long or not. I'll cheat a little and tell you how to do that without making you look it up in the JavaScript documentation—it's done with a method called length, which you can add to any variable.

Here's the raw HTML for the function:

```
<HTML>
<HEAD>
<TITLE>Data Checking</TITLE>
<SCRIPT>
<!--
  function zip_check (form) {
  zip_str = form.Zip.value;
  if (zip_str == "") {
     alert("Please enter a five digit number for your Zip
     ➥code");
     return;
     }
  if (zip_str.length != 5) {
     alert ("Your Zip code entry should be 5 digits");
     return;
     }
  return;
  }
// end hiding -->
</SCRIPT>
</HEAD>
```

So we've got two new concepts in this one. First, we've got the alert command, which displays a simple little dialog box when invoked. In the alert box will be the message between quotes (see Figure 15.8).

Fig. 15.8

The alert box occurs when users don't enter the correct number of digits for a zip code.

I've also introduced our new method: `length`. In the function declaration, you may have noticed the following line:

```
if (zip_str.length != 5) {
```

`variable.length` is a method that enables you to determine the length of any variable in JavaScript. Because JavaScript does no variable *typing* (it doesn't explicitly require you to say "this is a number" or "this is text"), then any variable can be treated as a string. In this case, even though the zip code could be interpreted as a number, `zip_str.length` tells you how many characters long it is.

Writing the form checking script

Next we need to jump into the page and create the event handlers for each of the form elements we're dealing with. The only sections we really need to change are the `<INPUT>` tag for the Zip box and the `<INPUT>` tag for the Submit button. Here's the full HTML for the rest of our form:

```
<BODY>
<H3>Please fill out the following form:</H3>
<FORM ACTION="http://www.fakecorp.com/cgi-bin/address_form">
<PRE>
Name:    <INPUT TYPE="TEXT" SIZE="50" NAME="Name">
Address: <INPUT TYPE="TEXT" SIZE="60" NAME="Address">
City:    <INPUT TYPE="TEXT" SIZE="30" NAME="City">
State:   <INPUT TYPE="TEXT" SIZE="2" NAME="State">
Zip:     <INPUT TYPE="TEXT" SIZE="5" NAME="Zip"
         ➥onChange = "zip_check(this.form)">
Email:   <INPUT TYPE="TEXT" SIZE="40" Name="Email">
<INPUT TYPE="SUBMIT" VALUE="Send it" onClick = "zip_check
         ➥(this.form)">
</FORM>
</BODY>
</HTML>
```

This event handler checks an entry in the Zip box by using the `onChange` handler to determine when the user has moved on from Zip's textbox (either by pressing Tab or clicking in another textbox with the mouse). Notice that it's a good idea to place the Zip textbox before the E-mail box, because the user could just click the Submit button and skip past your error check.

Also, by adding the `onClick` event to the Submit button, we're able to catch them if they happen to skip the Zip code box completely. Now we've double-checked their entry. Figure 15.9 shows the error checking in action.

Fig. 15.9
Error checking with
JavaScript.

For more information...

Although JavaScript is a fairly easy language, it still can become very involved, and there's no way you can cover the entire thing in a chapter. If you
don't have any programming experience, you might be better off picking up
a book designed to teach you JavaScript from the ground up. Both *Special
Edition Using JavaScript* and *JavaScript By Example* are excellent titles
from Que.

TIP **If you'd like to learn more about JavaScript, I suggest starting**
with the *JavaScript Authoring Guide* by Netscape Corporation at **http://
home.netscape.com/eng/mozilla/3.0/handbook/javascript/
index.html** on the Web.

16

Designing for Netscape 3.0 and Internet Explorer 3.0

● **In this chapter:**

● **What are the benefits of designing for specific browsers?**

● **Netscape's multicolumns and text additions**

● **Plug-ins that work great for Netscape**

● **Internet Explorer's additions**

● **The soon-to-be-a-standard** *object* **tag**

Version 3.0 of Netscape Navigator and version 3.0 of Internet Explorer give you design choices above and beyond other browsers. You can take advantage of them to give your pages more dazzle . . . . ▶

O nly a couple of years ago, all you had to worry about as an HTML author was learning HTML and putting it to use. But then, near the beginning of 1995, Netscape Navigator first appeared and changed all that. Because Netscape supported several tags and elements that weren't part of the official HTML standard, and some that hadn't even been proposed as standards, writing pages for Netscape was different from writing pages for other browsers.

Isn't HTML supposed to be a standard?

Today, the gap between official HTML and browser-specific HTML has widened further. Netscape Navigator remains the champion of nonstandard HTML, but others, specifically Microsoft, have joined the fray. Internet Explorer, Microsoft's entry into the browser game, offers many HTML-like additions of its own—and things are only getting crazier over time.

In this chapter, we take a brief look at designing for version 3.0 of both Netscape Navigator and Internet Explorer. The new HTML possibilities aren't endless, but they are significant. At the very least, you should know about them. And if you want your Web pages to be looked at, you should start designing for them as well.

The benefits and drawbacks of proprietary HTML designs

As soon as you see some of the great pages designed for Netscape and Internet Explorer, you'll want to incorporate the new features into your own site. Before you do, though, keep a few things in mind. They're important if you're hoping to satisfy the largest possible number of readers.

Whether or not you use these special tags in your Web pages is completely up to you. I'll try to refrain from value judgments, although I must say the <BLINK> tag is annoying. Aside from that, though, I'll just leave you with the following thoughts:

- *Netscape-only tags should go hand-in-hand with a "Netscape-only" warning.* Tell your users when you've used tags that can only be viewed in Netscape—or any other browsers. In fact, you should tell users you're using HTML 3.2 tags or MS Internet Explorer commands, as well. Both Microsoft and Netscape let you add special buttons to your site that say "Download IE 3.0" or "Netscape 3.0 Now!" Both also show you the HTML to use so that your visitors can click those icons and be transported directly to the browsers' download sites (see Figure 6.1).

- *Consider creating alternate pages.* It's not overwhelmingly difficult to create two versions of your site: an HTML 2.0-compliant site and a site with Netscape, IE, or HTML 3.2 additions. You can also create a "front door" that allows users to choose which they would prefer to view.

The problems of success

Because of its unique coding tags (like CENTER, BLINK, VALIGN, and others), Netscape has been blamed for undemocratizing the Web. Because Netscape makes it possible for authors to create nicer looking pages, they do so—but these pages can't be viewed by non-Netscape users. To an extent, this is certainly true. Many Web sites bear a label stating that the pages have been "enhanced for Netscape," and some sites more or less tell anyone without Netscape to get lost.

The same also holds true for Internet Explorer—in fact, both Microsoft and Netscape encourage Web designers and authors to add special "Best Viewed In—" icons to their pages. The fact is, Netscape and IE so completely dominate the browser market (that they have incredible sway in the HTML standard.) Most of what they implement eventually gets included.

But Netscape and Microsoft are only the current culprits. Earlier, the same charges were leveled against NCSA Mosaic, the browser that changed

the world. Because Mosaic could display images, images became the core of many Web pages, and Lynx users got miffed. Some have even claimed that the Web stopped advancing with the release of Mosaic because people started designing pages with magazines, rather than computers, in mind.

Netscape 3.0 and IE 3.0 offer even more enhancements. Most users with graphical access use it as their browser. Some of the new features are being proposed by the W3C for inclusion in HTML 3.2, but others, such as multicolumn text, haven't even made it that far along the path of universal acceptance.

Mosaic's success caused significant problems for the Web and its developers. Netscape and Microsoft's success has done the same. What's important to keep in mind is that not everyone uses these programs and that you have to decide whether or not you'll try to accommodate all users. It's entirely up to you.

Fig. 16.1
Get the Netscape
button from **http://
www.netscape.com/
comprod/mirror/
netscape_now_
program.html** and
the IE icon from
**http:/microsoft.
com/ie/logo/** on the
Web.

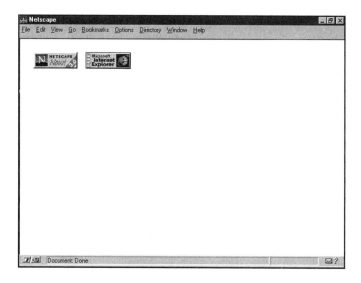

 TIP   **You might want to make your HTML 2.0 site a low-graphics site,** too, so that lower bandwidth users can choose that one over your highly graphical Netscape- or IE-only site.

- *Use HTML 3.2 whenever reasonable.* It's difficult to keep up with the HTML 3.2 standard, which is why many people just keep listening to Netscape. But, when you have the opportunity (e.g., using style sheets for creating strikeout text versus using the <STRIKE> tag), use the standard tags.

- *Make sure you don't lose information.* Frankly, most Netscapisms do very little to communicate information; they, instead, format it a bit more attractively. If you do use Netscapisms, make sure you're not using them in a way that means your other users are missing out on something important. Microsoft is guilty of this as well—only IE-compatible users can see text scrolling across the screen using the <MARQUEE> tags, for instance.

Finally, don't expect a pat on the back from everyone out there for your innovative design work. There's still a large contingent of conservative Internet users out there, and they demand adherence to standards—not to someone's well-intentioned whims. If you design for a nonstandard browser, expect to get some mail that tells you exactly what they think.

What's up in Netscape 3?

For the most part, Netscape's additions in version 3.0 have everything to do with how things appear on the page and little to do with other browsers. That's how it works, after all.

Actually, it's interesting to note that the Netscape part of the chapter is a bit thin because many Netscape-specific tags have either been rolled into the HTML 3.2 standard (like tables and font sizes) or have been so overwhelmingly received by the browser world (like frames) that there's no point in setting them apart anymore.

But, with a new version comes some new tags. Let's check them out.

Adding newspaper-style columns

In Chapter 9 we discussed using the table tags to lay out a document in such a way that the cells could be used to hold graphics, text, and various types of multimedia—making things look more like a newspaper or newsletter.

Netscape 3.0 goes that scenario one better by offering the `<MULTICOL>` tag. Using this tag, you can easily add multiple columns to your page (see Figure 16.2). Here's an example:

```
<MULTICOLS COLS=3 GUTTER=15 WIDTH=600>
Lots of text and graphics
</MULTICOLS>
```

`<MULTICOL>` is a container with three major attributes: `COLS`, `GUTTER`, and `WIDTH`.

- `COLS` is required. It tells Netscape how many columns to create.

- `GUTTER` determines how many pixels of space appear between columns. The default value is 10.

- `WIDTH` determines the overall width of your entire multicolumn format, in pixels. If no `WIDTH` is used, the columns will stretch (or squeeze) to fill the available screen space.

CAUTION   **If you decide to use `WIDTH`, you probably shouldn't go over about 600 pixels in order for the entire layout to fit on a typical VGA (640x480) screen. If you do go over that number, you'll be forcing some of your readers to scroll the screen horizontally in order to read your text.**

Fig. 16.2
With a single container tag, it's possible to have text and graphics flow nicely along in columns.

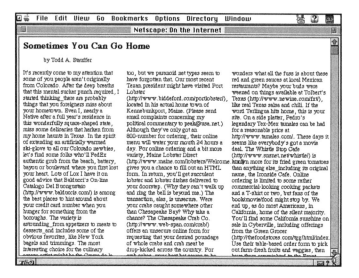

Sometimes you just need your space

A new tag called <SPACER> allows you to create different types of white space in your document, with more precise control. The idea here is that using <BR>, <P>, or even <PRE></PRE> tags isn't enough control over spacing between words or lines. So, enter <SPACER>.

The key to <SPACER> is the attribute TYPE. It allows you to do three very different things with the tag, based on the value you give the TYPE attribute:

- *horizontal*—Inserts horizontal space between words. Another attribute, SIZE, determines how much space.

- *vertical*—Inserts vertical space between lines. Just like <P>, a vertical spacer automatically ends the current line of text, and then the vertical space is added before the beginning of the next line. The height of the space is determined by SIZE.

- *block*—Netscape describes this one as "behaving almost exactly like an invisible image." This type of spacer focuses on WIDTH, HEIGHT, and ALIGN attributes (SIZE is ignored). The attributes work just like they would for the <IMG> tag.

Here are examples of the horizontal and vertical types:

```
This line has text here<SPACER TYPE-horizontal SIZE=50>and
text over here.<P>
This line ends now<SPACER TYPE=vertical SIZE=50>And another
line begins down here.<P>
```

The third type, *block*, would probably be most effective aligned to the left or right margins, with text flowing around it. An example would be:

```
<SPACER TYPE=block HEIGHT=50 WIDTH=30 ALIGN=LEFT>
```

Figure 16.3 shows the different types of <SPACER> in action.

Fig. 16.3
There's no question that these tags give you considerably more control than <PRE> or <P> over the spacing of your text.

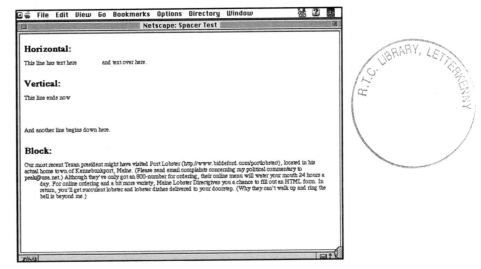

Netscape's own little text styles

This is really little more than a quick note. Netscape has enhanced support for strikeout and underlined text in Navigator 3.0 by including some shortcut tags for strikeout and actually making underlining work.

Striking out

Aside from supporting the <STRIKE> tag for "strikeout" text, Netscape now supports the <S> tag, while maintaining support for the <STRIKE> tag as backward compatibility. Both are container tags (see Figure 16.4).

```
<STRIKE>This text has been struck!</STRIKE>
<S>This text has been s'ed</S>
```

Fig. 16.4
Here's how strikeout text works.

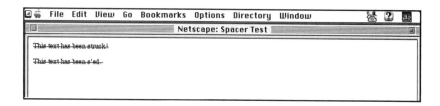

Making Netscape text annoying

<BLINK> is also a container. As a tag, it's designed to make text more annoying by forcing a cursor-style reverse field to blink on and off on top of words contained by this tag. The following is an example:

```
<BLINK>Real Hot Sale Item!</BLINK>
```

Unfortunately, I can't show it to you in a browser because a picture in this book can't show you the blinking. Too bad, huh?

To break or not to break

The <NOBR> tag prevents text from wrapping when it meets with the end of the browser screen. This is occasionally useful, especially in situations where your user might be confused by a line wrap. (It is also supported in IE 3.0.) This is a container tag that accepts text and markup between its tags. It's format is as follows:

```
<NOBR>test and markup</NOBR>
```

Now, this doesn't necessarily mean that users will need to scroll their browser window in order to see the text—in many cases, they just need to expand the browser window. (Or, make it considerably smaller to force the entire length of <NOBR> text to the next line.) This might be useful for addresses, programming code, a line of numbers, or similar text. The following is an example:

```
<NOBR>1234 Main Street * St. Louis, MO * 29000</NOBR>
```

The <WBR> tag is used in conjunction with the <NOBR> container for creating a line break when you know *exactly* where you want one to occur (if it needs to be broken by the edge of the Navigator window). It can also be used outside of the confines of the <NOBR> tag to let Netscape know where it's okay to break up a particularly long word.(IE 3.0 supports <WBR>, too).

<WBR> doesn't usurp the responsibilities of
—it's only a suggestion. If Netscape needs to break a line of text (or a particularly long word), it will do so. If it doesn't need to break at the <WBR>, it won't. An example would be:

```
<P>When I move this Web site the new address will be
http://www.fakecorp.com<WBR>/main/mperry/public/index.html.
Look for a hyperlink soon!</P>
```

Because Netscape Navigator would interpret that address as one word, it allows you to suggest where it should be broken if the address would otherwise overlap the browser window.

TIP   **For lines that always break where you want them to, the <PRE> tag** is still your best bet (e.g., lines of poetry). The <BR> tag might work well, too, if you're not trying to line things up visually.

Netscape plug-ins

In Chapter 14 we discussed using the <EMBED> tag to add plug-in documents to your Web pages. Navigator 3.0 has built-in support for a number of different file formats, thanks to a couple of cool technologies that come with the browser:

- *LiveAudio*   This plug-in is capable of playing AIFF, MIDI, WAV, and AU sound formats. (Works on these platforms: Windows 3.x, Windows 95, Macintosh OS.)

- *Live3D*   This plug-in is a high-performance VRML viewer that enables Netscape users to view embedded 3-D worlds that have the .WRL extension. (Windows 3.1, Windows 95, Macintosh PowerPC.)

- *LiveVideo*   Plug-in to play AVI movies. AVI is the Microsoft video format for Windows. (Windows 3.1, Windows 95.)

- *QuickTime*   This plug-in automatically plays QuickTime movies (.MOV files), including movies with text, MIDI, and other kinds of data. (Use commands in Chapter 14 concerning QuickTime.) (Windows 3.1, Windows 95, Macintosh OS.)

TIP **In general, QuickTime movies can reach a wider audience than** can AVI (Video for Windows) movies. If you store or embed digital movies on your Web site, keep that in mind.

And now for Internet Explorer 3.0

Not to be outdone by Netscape, and always seeking a proprietary path in software development, Microsoft Corporation has developed Internet Explorer 3.0 to offer some additional attractive features. Why should this concern you? Because Internet Explorer is being distributed with Windows 95 (and on the Web for free at **http://microsoft.com/ie/**), and as such it promises to challenge Netscape Navigator as the premier browser—at least for the Windows users crowd (and it *is* a crowd).

These days, IE might even be adding more doo-dads than Netscape. Things like style sheets and the <OBJECT> tag (discussed below) have been supported by IE first. Does this mean we're seeing a switch in momentum in the browser wars?

Give your pages some musical accompaniment

By now, you're used to giving your HTML pages a nice background graphic. Background graphics personalize your work, and they give the reader something nice to look at. Better than the old standard gray, that's for sure.

Well, why not give the readers background music as well? They read your pages, they catch a bit of Mozart, they feel cozy, rested, and willing to stay and listen. Or, if you like, hit 'em with a distorted grunge chord and make 'em wish they'd turned off the speakers. Either way, you get their attention.

The <BGSOUND> tag tells Internet Explorer to play an audio file when the page opens. Obviously, you don't want a huge file (painful downloading), but you can get people's attention with a sound or music snippet, and you can **loop** the file (play it repeatedly) as often as you want. You can use WAV, AU, or MIDI files for this purpose.

To include a background sound, you need the following HTML coding:

```
BGSOUND SRC="mozart.mid" LOOP=8>
```

On your marquees, get set, go!

Internet Explorer 3.0 tries to make your pages move in several ways, one of which is the scrolling marquee. This is nothing more than a string of text that scrolls by itself across the screen, but the effect is much stronger than, say, the <BLINK> command of earlier HTML. You can draw attention to a particular sentence or phrase, or, of course, you can overdo the thing entirely and end up with a jumble of moving lines of text.

To create a scrolling marquee, enclose the text inside the <MARQUEE> </MARQUEE> container. For example, the following code causes the string of text "Watch me move!" to move from the right border of the page to the left border and then start over again when it's finished—*ad infinitum*.

```
<MARQUEE>Watch me move!</MARQUEE>
```

Real-time videos

Although this sort of thing is pretty well covered by plug-ins, these days, IE has the built-in capability to play video files in the AVI format (the standard Microsoft Windows format) using a special extension to the <IMG> tag.

The code for incorporating an AVI video file is as follows:

```
<IMG DYNSRC="videofile.avi">
```

Notice that this is similar to HTML's calling of graphics files, <IMG SRC>. DYNSRC means dynamic source and is used instead. In practice, though, you should offer both possibilities so that readers without Internet Explorer will see something as well. This would be coded as follows:

```
<IMG DYNSRC="videofile.avi" SRC="graphicfile.gif">
```

Internet Explorer will play the AVI file, while other browsers will display the GIF file.

There aren't many options for the DYNSRC element, but they're important. First, you can specify when the AVI file starts playing. FILEOPEN tells it to begin as soon as the page is retrieved; MOUSEOVER tells it to start playing when the reader moves the cursor over the video image.

The other major option lets you place video controls at the bottom of the video image to let the reader take charge of what displays. The default is to have no controls; to include them, you must use the CONTROLS element:

```
<IMG DYNSRC="videofile.avi" CONTROLS>
```

Backgrounds that don't move

Another HTML addition within Internet Explorer is the watermark background. These are the same as the background graphics you're used to except that they don't scroll when your readers use the scroll bar.

The code for watermark backgrounds is quite simple: add the BGPROPERTIES=FIXED element to the usual <BODY BACKGROUND> component.

```
<BODY BACKGROUND="mypattern.gif" BGPROPERTIES=FIXED>
```

The new, improved *OBJECT* tag

This one is new to Internet Explorer, but it's under consideration by the W3C, and it might make it to a future version of HTML. The point of <OBJECT> is to take the place of more proprietary (Netscape-created) tags like <APPLET> and <EMBED>. It works in a couple of different ways. Here's how you'd embed a Video for Windows movie:

```
<OBJECT DATA=movie.avi TYPE="application/avi">
<IMG SRC="still.gif" ALT="Still image">
</OBJECT>
```

The <OBJECT></OBJECT> tag is a container with a number of different attributes. DATA is used to let the browser know that this particular object is going to want to embed or hand over a multimedia file to a helper application. TYPE tells it what the MIME type is for that data, so the browser can figure out quickly if this is a file it can handle.

Notice the <IMG> tag in the middle? That's what the <OBJECT> tag displays if the user's browser can't deal with this type of multimedia document.

In another example, you can see that OBJECT supports some of the other typical attributes for images and multimedia:

```
<OBJECT DATA=shocknew.dcr
        TYPE="application/director"
        WIDTH=288 HEIGHT=200 ALIGN=left>
```

```
<IMG SRC=shocknew.gif ALT="Best with Shockwave">
</OBJECT>
```

How about Java applets? Instead of DATA, we use CLASSID. And the Java applet can't end with .class. If we don't include a CODEBASE (like you would with <APPLET>), <OBJECT> assumes that you're using a relative URL and you want it to look for the Java applet in the current directory. Here's an example:

```
<OBJECT
   CLASSID="java:program.start"
   HEIGHT=100
   WIDTH=100
>
   You need a Java-aware browser to see this applet.
</OBJECT>
```

Notice that the text contained by <OBJECT> is designed to appear in non-Java browsers.

Want one more? The <OBJECT> tag can also support Microsoft's applet technology, ActiveX. If you've got an ActiveX control you want to add to your page, then there's some extra junk you need to add to the <OBJECT> tag…but it'll work. Here's an example:

```
<OBJECT
   id=clock1
   classid="clsid:663C8FEF-1EF9-11CF-A3DB-080036F12502"
   data="http://www.acme.com/ole/clock.stm"
>
fall back ...
</OBJECT>
```

Now if that doesn't make you want to run over to **http://www.microsoft.com/workshop/** and learn all about ActiveX, I don't know what will.

Beyond the basics: Client-pull

The client-pull tag and attributes, currently supported by just advanced browsers like IE and Netscape, enable you to automatically load another HTML page after a predetermined amount of time. You can also use these tags to reload or "refresh" the same HTML document over and over.

The client-pull concept is based on the <META> tag, which is used in the head of your document. For client-pull, the <META> tag takes the attributes HTTP-EQUIV and CONTENT. Client-pull follows the format:

```
<HEAD>
<META HTTP-EQUIV="REFRESH" CONTENT="seconds; URL="new URL">
</HEAD>
```

Unfortunately, this is a little messy compared to most HTML tags, so we'll have to wade through it. The HTTP-EQUIV attribute always takes the value "REFRESH" in client-pull; it only loads a new document if the CONTENT attribute includes an URL. Otherwise it refreshes (reloads) the current document.

The CONTENT attribute accepts a number for the amount of time you want the browser to wait before the next page is loaded (or the current page is refreshed), then a colon and the statement URL=, followed by a valid URL for the page that should be loaded automatically.

Here's an example that just refreshes the current page after waiting 10 seconds:

```
<HEAD>
<META HTTP-EQUIV="REFRESH" CONTENT="10">
</HEAD>
```

And, in this example, we use client-pull to load a new page after waiting 15 seconds:

```
<HEAD>
<META HTTP-EQUIV="REFRESH" CONTENT="15; URL="http://
www.fakecorp.com/index.html">
</HEAD>
```

One of the best uses for client-pull is as part of a "front door" page to your site. You can assume that a user's browser that accepts the client-pull commands is also capable of rendering Netscape- or IE-specific commands. Users with browsers that don't recognize client-pull can click another link on the page to allow them to view regular HTML 2.0 pages.

Part V: My Site's Ready, What Can I Do Now?

17

My Site is Ready, What Can I Do Now?

● **In this chapter:**

- **How do I get my work online?**

- **Announcing your Web pages on the WWW**

- **Talking up your site on Usenet**

- **Virtual "storefronts" on the Web**

- **Maintaining your Web pages**

Now that you've created your very own Web site, it's time to take the plunge: Publish your work on the World Wide Web and see what people think! . . . . ➤

This is what it all comes down to—actually showing the world the fruits of your labor. Ready? Then let's go. But what do you actually need to do to get online and onto the World Wide Web? That's what this chapter lets you know.

Why can't my friends see my Web pages?

The greatest Web site in the world is no good to anybody if it's not being served to the Web. Served? Yep, served. For a Web site to be accessible by any computer other than the one it's actually stored on, it has to be placed on a computer that is set up as a World Wide Web server. This computer will host your site.

So where do you find a Web server? The following are the options:

- *Use your existing Internet account.* If your Internet provider or the place where you work already has a Web server, find out from them if they will host your Web site, and how you need to go about uploading your documents and files.

- *Rent Web space from an Internet presence provider.* Several firms have set themselves up as **presence providers** and host Web sites for a monthly or yearly fee. You can find many of these in the Yahoo listings (**http://www.yahoo.com/Business_and_Economy/Companies/ Internet_Presence_Providers/**).

66 *Plain English, Please!*

An **Internet presence provider** (IPP) is an Internet company that makes Web server space available online. Some IPPs also provide Internet connections (so, they're ISPs), but others are only in it to give you a presence on the Web. 99

- *Put your site on a commercial online service.* The major commercial online services (Prodigy, America Online, Microsoft Network, and CompuServe) offer Web hosting services to their members. Log in to your account and check out the membership information. In fact, the Web services are often free.

- *Turn your own computer into a Web server.* If you're connected to the Internet through an Ethernet connection or a SLIP or PPP connection, you can often establish your own computer to serve your Web. Your machine will need its own unique, static IP (Internet Protocol) number, and you should have a 24-hour connection. If you're ambitious, you can do all this through a modem, but it means having a separate phone line and a 24-hour account. The most common direct way to serve a Web site this way is to have your computer networked (over a fairly fast connection, like ISDN or Ethernet) to an organization that in turn has a high-speed Internet connection.

Finding a Web provider

The first step for new Web authors is to find a provider who can maintain your files on its Internet host computer. Chances are you aren't going to set up your own host on the Internet—this requires a substantial amount of hardware and money (including monthly fees based on the speed of your rented connection). Instead, it makes sense to rent space on an existing server.

When you're considering signing up with an Internet provider, ask them the following questions:

- Can I serve my Web site from your computers?

- If so, does it cost extra?

- How many megabytes of file storage is included?

- Will I be charged for heavy traffic?

- Do you offer Web creation services?

- Does your server handle imagemaps and forms?

- Can someone help me write CGI scripts?

If you get a "yes" answer to everything, and if the cost is reasonable (about $10 per month for standard Web storage, up to $75 for advanced storage and assistance), consider it a good deal.

Using your basic Internet account

The cheapest and easiest option for publishing your Web pages is to add the service to your existing Internet account. Many providers use low cost WWW home pages as an incentive for enrollment, while others charge a marginal fee for their users to have a noncommercial Web presence. Unless you are interested in running a business online or advertising a commercial product, this option may be the best bet for you.

If your provider does not allow you to have a Web page, there are many Internet hosts that are giving people free pages for noncommercial use. You don't even have to buy your basic service from them! One well-known and popular service is Turnpike Metropolis (**http://turnpike.net/turnpike/ metro.html**).

Announcing your arrival

When you know how, publishing information on the Web is easy. It only takes some time and energy (and money if your provider isn't free). Great content is work, but it's work you can do without anyone else's cooperation. Having people look at your work, on the other hand, can't be done alone. Although you can give people all of the opportunities to see your Web work, it's up to them to choose to do so.

The WWW is all about opportunities, and it's up to you to take advantage of them. One way you can do this is to let people (preferably those who might be interested in reading your information) know where it is. This takes more work, but it's well worth the trouble.

Use the newsgroups

Usenet newsgroups cover thousands of special interest discussions. One of these is for new Web page announcements. Called **comp.infosystems. www.announce**, it's a forum where people post notices of new pages and of new content to existing pages.

The **www.announce** group follows a specific format for posting new messages. At the bottom of every posting is an e-mail address where you can get guidelines and other information about the group. The moderator also posts the group's guidelines regularly—it is highly recommended that you read these before sending in a posting for the first time.

TIP **The comp.infosystems.www.announce newsgroup is very busy,** often posting over a hundred new messages a day. The moderator may need up to a week to process new posts, so make sure you give him plenty of time to handle your request when you decide to announce your new Web pages.

You may find that your Web pages center around specific topics of interests, such as Japanese literature or beach volleyball. Usenet has a separate discussion group for nearly every topic and issue conceivable. Use your Usenet newsreader (or a browser like Netscape Navigator, which includes support for newsgroups) to search the list of current groups.

TIP **The DejaNews service (http://www.dejanews.com/) is a great way** to search Usenet newsgroups for particular topics.

It's a big list—as many as 8,000, depending on how your news server is configured—so be prepared to wait while your software retrieves the master list. When you have it, use the program's text search capabilities (if available) to search on your keywords.

Subscribe to the groups you find interesting and read some of the **threads** or discussions that have been posted recently. Make sure that this group is talking about the same things you want to share via your Web pages—many groups are created to ridicule their subjects, so don't wander into a target range by accident. Barney the Dinosaur lovers should stay out of the **alt.barney.die.die.die** discussion group or risk being skewered along side the big purple lizard!

After you are comfortable that you've found the right group, consider participating in the discussions as well as posting a general message about your new Web resources. It's a great way to establish yourself in the online community, which will attract more readers to your site.

Web page directories

One of the most difficult aspects of the World Wide Web is that it lacks organization—it reflects the open and unstructured qualities of the Internet. How do you find what resources are available, and how do you make sure others can find yours? Probably the most popular service on the Web today is directories. These are listings of Web pages that you can search through and link directly to them from the directory entries. Web directories are becoming a big business—the most well-known directory, Yahoo, went commercial after being started by two students at Stanford University. It now sports a redesigned interface and corporate sponsorship.

Other similar directories have experienced the same type of interest and growth. Their success is a direct result of the Web community's reliance on them for finding information on the WWW. Table 17.1 shows some of the most often used directories.

Table 17.1   World Wide Web directory of services

Directory name	URL
Yahoo	**www.yahoo.com**
Web Crawler	**webcrawler.com**
Lycos	**www.lycos.com**
Whole Internet Catalog	**gnn.com/gnn/wic/index.html**
HotBot	**www.hotbot.com**
Alta-Vista	**www.alta-vista.com**
InfoSeek	**www.infoseek.com**

Getting listed on these directory services can be time-consuming. Each has a submission process and listing format to which you have to adhere (see Figure 17.1).

These directories can take up to a week to process new entries. After your listing is added, many will notify you by e-mail. Check your entry to make sure you did not overlook any misspellings, and definitely try out the link to make sure it is pointing to the right Web page. The last thing you want is for users to link to the middle of your content and not understand where they are or how to use your pages.

Netscape has created an advanced HTML feature called **Bulletin** that is used in conjunction with automated programs (called **robots** and **spiders**) that can go out and search the Web for new information. When these programs come across your Web page, they can tell if you made any recent changes to the content from the Bulletin information embedded in your pages. They can then report back to a directory or to users and let them know what's now available. This will be a great way to automate updating your directory listings in the future. For more information about Bulletin, refer to Netscape's home page at **http://www.netscape.com/**.

Fig. 17.1
Yahoo has a special page that includes instructions and an HTML form to let you announce your site.

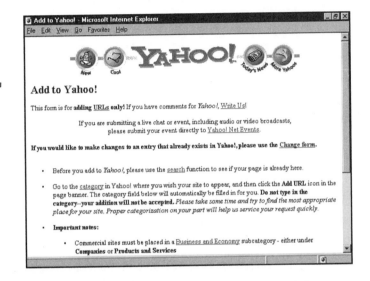

Submissions master

You could spend hours filling in submissions for each of the directories on the list above. Wouldn't it be great if there was a one-stop Web page that would take your information once and send in properly formatted entries to every directory on the list? There is. The service is called Submit It! It is available at **http://www. submit-it.com/submit-it/**. You provide all of your pertinent information into the services form and then choose which directories you want to

be listed on. Submit It! then shows you how each format looks before sending it in.

As each directory takes new listing submissions in different ways, sometimes Submit It! sends you to the directory itself, but your information is prefilled in their submission form. Follow their instructions to return to Submit It! and process the next submission. By using this service, you can get through a dozen submissions in the time it may have otherwise taken you to do just a few.

Your ad here

The WWW is just coming into its own as a commercial environment. The market size is growing. Just this year, another three to four million people in the U.S. alone will join the Internet, either through a commercial service like America Online or through an Internet provider. How can you, as an individual or as someone with a small business or Internet information service, get the kind of recognition you can get in the "real world"?

Marketing opportunities are growing on the Internet. The World Wide Web, as a multimedia environment, provides better marketing opportunities than the text-based services, such as Gopher and e-mail. The truth is, the advertising market is still finding its feet, trying to gauge the levels of participation and the costs that companies should pay for different kinds of representation. Basically, there are three ways you can advertise your business or service:

- Post messages in the commercial Usenet forums. These were created so businesses could advertise without creating a backlash against them from the Internet community. The drawback comes from the fact that most users do not choose to read the forums with any regularity.

- Find Web pages that are willing to include a link to your information in return for a similar link from your pages to their own. This kind of small business co-op arrangement makes sense when your audience would be appropriate for their Web content and vice versa.

- Sponsor a popular Web service. Sites like Yahoo are finding corporate sponsorship to be a lucrative opportunity and are willing to jump on that bandwagon. Other sites might charge lower rates, but if they're related to your Web topics, they might be a good idea for advertising (see Figure 17.2).

Of the three, sponsorship is the most visible and probably will give you the best return for your investment. So how do you find Web pages willing to be sponsored? Begin by visiting the Web sites you would associate with your preferred audience. These may be pages related to the information or services you are marketing, or to common services that people use daily on the Web. Look at the various "What's New" directories and online malls.

Some Web services may be willing to barter a month's advertising in exchange for your services. Do a little research into co-op advertising on the larger and more popular services like *Wired Magazine's* Hot Wired service. The sites that are open to advertising will most likely have rate sheets that you can use to measure your options and how far your budget will get you.

Fig. 17.2
If you find a well-trafficked site that might be visited by folks who would enjoy your page, ask about advertising rates.

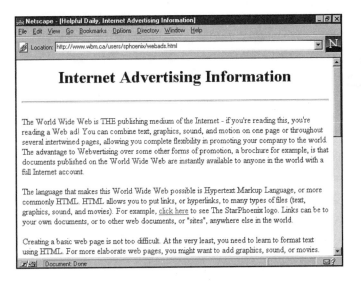

CAUTION **Advertising for the sake of increasing your business is a good** thing, but don't overlook that increased traffic on your Web pages may result in a much higher bill from your provider. Most charge you by the amount of information that users retrieve from your Web site (called "throughput"). The per megabyte rates can vary, so make sure you know how your provider is charging you for your Web service, and plan accordingly.

Choose your Web neighbors

Just as you want to explore your advertising options on the World Wide Web, you may also want to look into associating yourself and your Web pages with other people and businesses online. Besides trading links with other pages (as discussed above), you can also look to join a **virtual mall** on the Web. These electronic storefronts are a growing way for businesses and services to band together to increase their overall visibility.

The mall association may provide co-op advertising or other advantages beyond your own listing in the mall. These storefronts can vary in price, depending on the size of the mall and the quality of its tenants. A good example of this is the Branch Mall (**http://www.branch.com/**).

Choose your Web associates

Just as there are professional associations in your community that you can belong to, there are also virtual associations that may be valuable for networking (making contacts, not hooking up your computers). One such association that was formed in 1994 is the HTML Writer's Guild, an association of WWW developers and authors. The Guild's purpose is to promote HTML development and encourage a level of professionalism and ethics among its members. For more information about the HTML Writer's Guild, go to **http://www.hwg.org/** on the Web.

Web page upkeep

The point has been made before, but it's important enough to stress again: Revise your content! Keep it fresh and interesting. Remove any material that has "expired." A statement like "order before March 31, 1996" looks pretty silly by Christmas of the same year, and it looks like you don't care enough to pay attention to what's on your own Web pages. Add links to new Web sites that are related to your topic. Be current in your field—know what your competitors and colleagues are doing.

If you adapt your content to include new information, events, or news, people will start to rely on you as a source of knowledge, and they will come back to see what else you have for them. Don't let your Web pages sit still and grow stale—they need to move forward and change.

It may seem like this is opening the door on a long road of maintenance and work, but it's all a labor of love. At least, it should be. The World Wide Web is your opportunity to express yourself, to blaze your own trail, and there are no virtual limits to what you can do or how you can touch other people's lives. The Web is a brand new community, and if we all work at carving our own niches, it will become a community we can be proud of and content being a part of.

Beyond the basics: *META* for search engines

Ever see those pages where people put a long line of the same text over and over again, like:

Books Books Books Books Books Books Books Books Books

Those HTML authors are doing that because they believe it influences Web search robots to categorize their site as one that's "very strongly" about a particular subject. (Our example is clearly a book seller of some sort.)

There is another, more attractive way to get search engines to recognize your site by the keywords that *you* choose. Not all of them will be looking for this trick, but most of the major search engines do.

It has to do with the <META> tag in the HEAD of your document. (You might not otherwise have one, so you'll be adding a new line up there.) There are two fairly common <META> tags that search robots look for:

```
<META NAME="description" CONTENT="Write your description
here">
<META name="keywords" content="Write your keywords here, in a
comma separated list">
```

The first <META> tag is used by robots to describe your site in the Web directory's listing. For the CONTENT attribute, descriptions should be between 50 and 200 words, depending on the search robot (shorter is probably best). An example might be:

```
<META NAME="description" CONTENT="Covers books, reader
questions, errors, news, and the Peak Computing Radio Show.">
```

That's an entry I'd probably use for my personal Web site.

The other <META> tag is for keywords that you want the search robot to associate with your site. The idea is, if a user enters these keywords at a major search engine, it's more likely to present your page as an alternative. Here's a sample, again for my page:

```
<META NAME="keywords" content="HTML By Example, AOL, creating
Web pages, books, computers, talk radio, technology, Macintosh
books, Que, Peak Computing, writer, Colorado writer">
```

Make sure you stop by the major Web search services to make sure they haven't added any new twists to the <META> tag, and then sit back and rest assured that you're being categorized correctly.

18

Helpers and Editors for Easier HTML

● **In this chapter:**

● **The pros and cons of stand–alone editors**

● **Why add on an add-on?**

● **What do you want? What do you need? What's the best Web editing tool for you?**

● **Pass or fail—giving Web editors the grade**

Authoring tools put the building blocks of HTML at your fingertips, allowing you to create sophisticated and accurate Web pages with ease. . . . . ▶

As a current WWW designer, you've probably already explored some editing programs and add-ons. Even if you haven't yet, you'll soon see that the Internet community has been bombarded with HTML tools in the past year or so.

Both stand-alone programs and software that act as add-ons to common productivity applications exist for all platforms (most as shareware). This chapter describes the various tools being used by today's HTML authors and helps you select the editor that will satisfy your authoring needs.

Stand-alone editing tools (like HotDog)

Stand-alone editors are separate HTML construction programs; that is, they do not require any supplementary applications for functioning. Table 18.1 displays the pros and cons of stand-alone Web editors.

CAUTION   **Some of these helpers and editors will shield you from the HTML** codes, which can be a good thing, but might also limit what you can do to the HTML functions that the programmers want to include. They could also keep you from learning the HTML discussed in the rest of this book, which is still very important if you plan to develop pages professionally, do any Web programming or scripting, or if you just want to be on the HTML cutting edge.

Table 18.1   The pros and cons of stand-alone editors

Advantages	Disadvantages
Best interfaces and workspaces with toolbars	Lack of standardization among programs requires users to become familiar with individual software idiosyncrasies
WYSIWYG displays and familiar tools	Some editors look just like word processors. Unfortunately, not all of HTML can be finicky, and documents can look different in different browsers

Shareware and freeware programs allow user feedback	Must load document into browser for true display
Low cost (usually under $50)	Constant updating and lack of support for older versions

Add-On editing tools (like Internet Assistant for Word)

Add-on Web editors are supplementary programs that function as complements to existing applications (usually word processing mechanisms). Again, there are both pro and con considerations for incorporating this editing style, as shown in Table 18.2.

Table 18.2   The pros and cons of add-on editors

Advantages	Disadvantages
Extension of *familiar* software	Large size—consume disk space and decrease program performance
Document conversion from standard format to HTML makes page translation easy	High cost for word processing or other initial applications (often $200 or more)

An interesting twist on HTML tools

This chapter is all about the programs you can add to your Windows, Mac, or UNIX machine to get up and running quickly with a Web site. And all that's well and good. But what if I told you that you can create your HTML documents online, at someone else's Web site.

Sure, this is a bit experimental, but Ray Daly has written a Web site—completely in JavaScript—that's designed to enable you to create your own Web pages online. It's pushing JavaScript (which we discussed in Chapter 16) to its limits, but it's fun to play around with.

To create your own Web page from a Web page, check out **http://www.cris.com/~raydaly/htmljive.html** on the Web.

Table 18.2   Continued

Advantages	Disadvantages
Macros and template additions may be modified to add support for new HTML elements	Not easily transportable— add-on remains attached to home program

ASCII editors (WordPad, vi, or SimpleText)

When HTML first came to the Internet, the only editors you could get were tagged with standard HTML codes, and these ASCII editors remain the most widespread form of Web creation currently available (see Table 18.3). Tagged editors only read information that is complemented with a specific set of regulated codes. Lists of these codes are available in the tag menu of most editors.

Table 18.3   The pros and cons of ASCII tag editors

ASCII advantages	ASCII disadvantages
Speedy screen updates	New users often require support material for code manipulation
Most tagged editors supply ing features requiring users to simply fill in the middle data	Most editors lack syntax the middle and end tagscheck-
Users may insert custom tags	Editors provide little or no documentation for codes

What-You-See-Is-What-You-Get editors (FrontPage, Netscape Gold)

WYSIWYG stands for **W**hat **Y**ou **S**ee **I**s **W**hat **Y**ou **G**et—an interface that presents your WWW pages without the standard HTML codes. WYSIWYG provides an aesthetic approach to document creation, allowing concrete layout and formatting—in word processing style (see Table 18.4).

Table 18.4 The pros and cons of WYSIWYG

WYSIWYG advantages	WYSIWYG disadvantages
Graphic representation provides better page layout	Absorb large amounts of disk space to verify tags, fonts, and display
Built-in syntax checks	Lack most recent tag support
Reduced need for previews and browser verification	Internal interpretation is not always correct

MyInternetBusinessPage (Windows 95/NT)

MyInternetBusinessPage boasts the capability to build or edit World Wide Web pages in the actual HTML environment, directly on-screen, without learning or typing any HTML tags. Pull-down menus, pop-up menus, and a toolbar give the user the ability to build or edit World Wide Web pages fast and efficiently in its advanced what-you-see-is-what-you-get format. Most specific HTML commands are contained in simple floating menus that appear when you click your right mouse button—a function that reduces screen clutter and simplifies the Web construction process.

This Web editor supports viewing of GIF, JPEG, BMP, TGA, PCX, and TIF images directly on-screen. The Pro series is compatible with Microsoft Windows 95 and Microsoft Windows NT complete with "long" file names in true 32-bit mode.

Exciting updates to the Pro version will include imagemap creation and editing directly on-screen, full table manipulation, and on-screen image resizing. Software licenses for the full version of MyInternetBusinessPage are available at its home page, **http://www.mybusinesspage.com/**, where a trial version should be available for download.

Web Weaver (Mac)

Formerly known as SuperEdit, this WYSIWYG Web editor supplies HTML authors with floating element lists, balloon help, and an icon toolbar that supports HTML 2 and some HTML 3.x features. Web Weaver's default element lists include Netscape-specific features like BLINK, definable font size, and it will even create custom lists of your favorite HTML codes. This modular approach to Web construction is very similar to HTML Editor's main interface, but it is carried out with greater elegance and harmony among the elements. Web Weaver can be retrieved from **http://www.miracleinc.com/**.

BBEdit HTML extensions (Mac)

Written by Charles Bellver, BBEdit shareware extensions transform this popular Macintosh text editor into a functional HTML editor. Building on BBEdit's strengths as a text editor, HTML extensions support HTML 2 tags and may be customized for HTML 3.2 and Netscape-specific coding. Head to **http://nti.uji.es/software/bb-html-ext/** to download the extensions. After you've got them unarchived, place them in the BBEdit Extensions folder.

BBEdit or BBEdit Lite can be downloaded from a number of different Mac archives (like Info-Mac or the AOL mirrors at **ftp://mirrors.aol.com**) or directly from its owners, BareBones Software at **http:/www.barebones.com/** on the Web.

Webtor (Mac)

Webtor supports HTML 2.0 standards and provides users with a syntax checking mechanism that, while configurable and generally very good, is a bit unstable (this is most true with missing tags or extra closing tags). Webtor displays the structure of the Web page in basic coded outline format, which is particularly useful for new HTML authors. The Webtor home page is at **http:// www.igd.fhg.de/~neuss/webtor/webtor.html** on the Web.

Designer HTML (Windows 3.1, 95, NT)

Designer HTML is a simple HTML editor designed for folks who are reasonably clear on how HTML works, and are willing to get their hands a bit dirty. Now with support for tables, targets, and centering, it's improving slowly. It's only $5 to register, however, because it's written by an individual ("Weasel") at Lawrence University for his own use. It's available for download at **http:// gaigs.cmsc.lawrence.edu/designerHTML/HTMLJAVA.html-ssi** on the Web.

HTML.edit (Mac)

Virtually all of HTML.edit's editing power may be accessed through the program's floating toolbars. This interface design is highlighted by the program's logical but jarring file management methods. HTML.edit divides files into two categories with title and headings in one area and the document's body in another. Because most users neglect the title header of a Web page under construction, this interface separates the elements to simplify the file.

HTML.edit is a fairly typical World Wide Web page editor, providing support for all the usual HTML tags including forms and tables, and a preview command that launches a specified browser directly from the toolbar. Created in HyperCard, it also uses AppleScript hooks to make uploading your Web pages easier, through the popular FTP utility Fetch. It's available on the Web at **http://www.stonehand.com/murray/htmledit.html** and, perhaps most exciting, it's freeware.

HotDog (Windows 3.1, 95, Mac)

The brainchild of Sausage Software, a newcomer to the HTML tools arena, HotDog is a code-only editor that aims to replace all other HTML Web construction programs. This editor provides HTML 2 and HTML 3.2 standards as well as some of the Netscape and IE nonstandard HTML extensions, pull-down menu options for nearly every conceivable HTML component, and color definition options. HotDog even converts existing HTML documents to plain text files by stripping out the HTML characters from Web pages and leaving the text layout intact.

The HotDog Web editor is customizable, allowing you to create document templates and define special boilerplate HTML strings. The program's toolbar supports context-sensitive help (leave the mouse over a button for a few seconds and a message pops up describing its function), and the editor provides "Handy Hints" upon startup that may be disabled when you become familiar with the software. Most importantly, two versions of the HotDog Web editor have been designed—one with Windows 95 features (for the most advanced user), and one that's fully compatible with Windows 3.1 in order to accommodate a larger audience.

A Mac version is due in late 1996.

TIP **Pay close attention to the installation instructions for HotDog—** especially the Windows 9.5 (32–bit) version. You need to install some special add-on files for Windows 95 to make it work correctly, then install HotDog.

HotDog provides additional document management and customizing options, unlimited file sizes, a spell checker, and some WYSIWYG editing features. Both programs may be accessed from the Sausage Software site at **http:// www.sausage.com/**.

SoftQuad HoTMetaL (Windows 3.1, 95, NT, Mac, UNIX)

HoTMetaL has taken off with rave reviews from around the industry. The latest version now supports most conceivable Web-related functions, including tables, frames, Java, sounds, and drag-and-drop editing. A special callout in HoTMetaL's ability to import common word processing documents, then spit them back out, has full-fledge HTML. Demo versions are available at **http://www.sq.com/**.

HTMLed (Windows 3.1, 95)

Another code-only Windows utility, HTMLed provides pull-down menus and permanent toolbars that contain the primary functions of Level 2 HTML coding. Written by I-Net Training & Consulting, HTMLed provides even the most timid beginner with a clean, straightforward interface and workspace.

TIP **HTMLed's button bar displays a mixture of icons and text to make** document creation a clear and simple process. For example, the new document button is represented by an icon of a blank page, but to add a heading, you access a button labeled heading.

Some features have recently been changed to make them more Windows-friendly (in the past, HTMLed had struck its own path with hotkeys and other interface elements). HTMLed also features some extras aimed at beginners— like special help in creating forms and tables, but the results tend to be a bit rudimentary. Head over to download a demo or get more information. HTMLed can be downloaded from **http://www.eucanect.com/ software/htmlinfo.html**.

HTML Writer (Windows)

Another fairly generic HTML editing program is the stand-alone HTML Writer. Though it supports the usual suite of HTML elements, including forms, it does not handle tables. The most commonly accessed HTML tags are readily available from the program's toolbar, and users may define templates so you don't have to retype common Web page layouts. But perhaps the most impressive feature of HTML Writer is its ability to drag and drop highlighted text. More information about HTML Writer is available at **http://lal.cs.byu.edu/people/nosack/index.html**.

Internet Assistant (Windows 3.1, 95, Mac)

Internet Assistant is an HTML template and formatting stylesheet in the guise of a word processor. The trick to Internet Assistant is that you may never have to leave Microsoft Word to accomplish all of your HTML creation, previewing, and Web browsing functions. The browsing capability is provided by a custom implementation of BookLink's (now America Online's) InternetWorks stand-alone browser.

IA orders all of its editing options in pull-down menus and icon-based toolbars. The software supports all HTML 2 and some common HTML 3 features, such as forms. IA also manages your HTML assets (image files and information links) with detailed dialog boxes and property sheets. Its WYSIWYG feature allows you to visualize content as you create it, a feature more common with add-ons than with stand-alone editors. See **http://www.microsoft.com/workshop/** for more information. Internet Assistants exist for other Microsoft products as well, like Excel and PowerPoint.

Netscape Composer (Window 3.1, 95, Mac)

Netscape has rolled WYSIWYG abilities into its famous browser with the Netscape Composer (formerly Netscape Gold) edition, making it a simple thing to create, and then preview, pages in the browser. The editor is feature complete, with visual commands for creating frames, tables, forms, and other HTML 3.2 elements. At the same time, there is (obviously) complete support for Netscape extensions (see Figure 18.1).

Fig. 18.1
Netscape Composer's
advanced features
really do make creating
Web pages a little like
word processing.

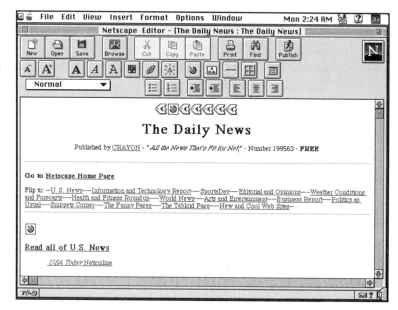

Test-drive versions of Netscape (and, often, beta versions of the newest releases) are available for download from **http://www.netscape.com/** on the Web. Once you've gotten through this text, Netscape Composer is a great way to quickly generate new Web pages.

Adobe PageMill (Windows 95, Mac)

Released initially for the Mac, PageMill jumped out into the HTML arena with a WYSIWYG browser that tried to be the PageMaker of the Web world. Over 100,000 copies were sold at about $100 a piece, and Adobe has rolled that success into a new version for both Windows 95 and Macintosh. Complaints about the way PageMill 1.0 handled HTML have changed Adobe's approach a little bit, and the latest version handles HTML very well (see Figure 18.2).

The graphical interface makes creating frames, tables, and other elements easy. Built-in tools handle client-side imagemaps, graphic transparency, and resizing images. Drag-and-drop editing allows you to instantly create hyperlinks, add plug-in multimedia documents (with native support for QuickTime movies), and add animated GIFs. A PageMill demo (and beta versions, when available) can be downloaded from **http://www.adobe.com/** on the Web.

Fig. 18.2
The PageMill interface is designed for creating entire Web sites, enabling you to drag-and-drop hyperlinks, graphics, and multimedia between pages.

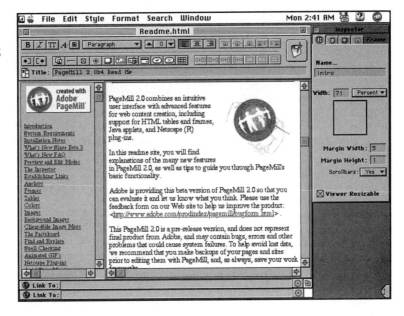

Microsoft FrontPage 97

Microsoft FrontPage 97 is a WYSIWYG environment for creating Web pages that includes drag-and-drop integration with Microsoft Office, templates for common types of Web pages, and graphical tools designed to help you manage your site in the FrontPage Explorer (see Figure 18.3).

Fig. 18.3
FrontPage is both an editing and a site management tool.

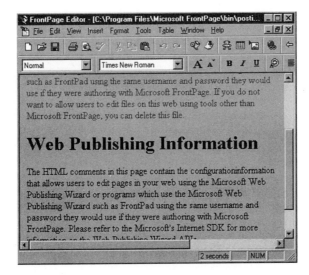

FrontPage is especially useful for Web developers interested in using Microsoft's Web technology like VBScript and ActiveX controls. Support for Java, JavaScript, and Netscape plug-ins also comes along for the ride.

FrontPage sells in retail version for prices ranging from $50 to $150, depending on your upgrade status and whether you already own other Microsoft Office products. Demo or beta versions of FrontPage are often available for free downloading at **http://microsoft.com/frontpage/** on Microsoft's Web site.

Part VI: Appendixes

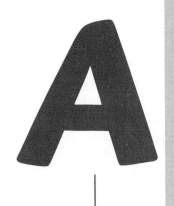

A

HTML 3.2 Elements Reference

This appendix presents the HTML 3.2 elements as they currently stand and are supported by available Web clients. HTML 3.2 is a work-in-progress standard and is subject to change, see **http://www.w3.org/** for details and announcements. Other browser-extensions that are included have been noted as specific to certain programs or companies.

The standard format of an entry is as follows:

ELEMENT

Element description

Container or empty element

Syntax of usage

Attributes

Attribute description

Syntax of usage

Attribute option and option description

Usage

Legal uses of current element

The following is an example:

<P>

Inserts a paragraph break at the current point in the document, beginning with the next line of text or inline graphic against the left margin two lines beneath the current text.

Empty element, requiring no closing tag. (HTML 3.2 offers optional closing tag, `</P>`.)

Syntax

`<P>`

Attributes

ALIGN HTML 3.2 revision of P element, using it as a container and applying alignment to all of the content within the container.

Syntax

<P ALIGN=center> ... </P>

Usage

Body section—stand-alone and within lists, preformatted text and forms containers.

Whole Document Elements

<BODY></BODY>

Defines the body section in an HTML document.

Container element, requires </BODY> closing tag.

Attributes

BACKGROUND HTML 3.2 extension to the standard HTML, specifying a graphic image to be used for the background of the current document.

Syntax

<BODY BACKGROUND=*URL*> (where *URL* is a graphic URL)

BGCOLOR HTML 3.2 extension specifying a color to be used for the current document.

Syntax

<BODY BGCOLOR=*value*> (where *value* is a color notation)

Color notation

"#XXYYZZ" (where *xx* is the value for the red color component, *yy* is the value for the green color component, and *zz* is the value for the blue color component; values range from 00–FF in hexadecimal)

TEXT HTML 3.2 extension specifying a color to be used for the body content text.

Syntax

<BODY TEXT=*value*> (where *value* is a color notation)

Color notation

"#XXYYZZ" (where *xx* is the value for the red color component, *yy* is the value for the green color component, and *zz* is the value for the blue color component; values range from 00–FF in hexadecimal)

LINK HTML 3.2 extension specifying a color to be used for body content hyperlinks.

Syntax

`<BODY LINK=value>` (where value is a color notation)

Color notation

"#XXYYZZ" (where xx is the value for the red color component, yy is the value for the green color component, and zz is the value for the blue color component; values range from 00–FF in hexadecimal)

VLINK HTML 3.2 extension specifying a color to be used for visited body content hyperlinks.

Syntax

`<BODY VLINK=value>` (where *value* is a color notation)

Color notation

"#XXYYZZ" (where *xx* is the value for the red color component, *yy* is the value for the green color component, and *zz* is the value for the blue color component; values range from 00–FF in hexadecimal)

ALINK HTML 3.2 extension specifying a color to be used for active body content hyperlinks.

Syntax

`<BODY VLINK=value>` (where value is a color notation)

Color notation

"#XXYYZZ" (where *xx* is the value for the red color component, *yy* is the value for the green color component, and *zz* is the value for the blue color component; values range from 00–FF in hexadecimal)

Usage

Enclose all HTML content that is a part of the document's body data that is to be displayed by Web clients, including text, inline images, and hyperlink anchors.

Comment Coding

Nonstandard HTML container for inserting hidden comments in HTML documents, which are not displayed in Web viewers.

Container element, requires closing tag.

Syntax: <! — ... —>

Attributes
None

Usage
Any document section and in containers if required.

<HEAD> </HEAD>

Defines the head section in an HTML document.

Container element, requires </HEAD> closing tag.

Attributes
None

Usage
Encloses all HTML content that isn't a part of the body data in a document, including the document's title and link relationships.

<HTML></HTML>

Defines the HTML content in a document on a Web server.

Container element, requires </HTML> closing tag.

Syntax: <HTML>...</HTML>

Attributes
None

Usage
Encloses all content in a document that should be recognized as HTML by Internet applications (such as Web viewers).

Head Section Elements

<BASE>

Indicates the URL of the current document. This helps Web viewers process relative hypertext links within the document.

Empty element, does not require a closing tag.

Syntax
<BASE HREF=*URL*> (where *URL* is specific for the current document)

Attributes
HREF Accepts URL for base address.

Usage
Head section only, not within containers.

<ISINDEX>

Indicates that the current Web page can be searched with the Web client's search feature. Requires server-side index search capabilities.

Empty element, does not require a closing tag.

Syntax
<ISINDEX>

Attributes
PROMPT Netscape extension, customizes text message in search dialog box or window.

Syntax
<ISINDEX PROMPT="*value*"> (where *value* is the new text message)

Usage
Head section only, not within containers. Requires the server-side capability to service searches.

<LINK>

Establishes a relationship between the current document and another document. Can be used more than once to define multiple relationships.

Empty element, does not require a closing tag.

Syntax

`<LINK attribute HREF=URL>` (where *attribute* is the applicable relation-ship, and *URL* is the other party in the relationship)

Attributes

REL Defines the relationship between the current document and the URL.

Syntax

`<LINK REL=relationship HREF=URL>` (where *relationship* is the type of relationship being defined)

Options:

PRECEDE. The current document precedes the resource in the *URL* value.

PREV. The *URL* value resource precedes the current document.

USEINDEX. The *URL* document is a related index used in searches in the current document.

USEGLOSSARY. The *URL* document is an index used for glossary queries in the current document.

ANNOTATION. The *URL* document provides secondary information (such as margin notes) for the current document.

REPLY. The *URL* document provides primary information for the current document.

PRECEDES. Defines the ordered relationship between the two docu-ments, where the current document comes before the *URL* document.

SUBDOCUMENT. Defines the hierarchical relationship between two documents, where the current document is higher than the *URL* docu-ment.

PRESENT. States that whenever the current document is retrieved, the *URL* document must be retrieved as well (but not vice versa).

SEARCH. States that when the *URL* document is accessed, a search is carried out on it before its content is retrieved.

SUPERSEDES. The *URL* document is a previous version of the current document.

HISTORY. The *URL* document contains a documented history of the versions of the current document.

MADE. The *URL* value is the e-mail address of the creator of the current document.

OWNS. The *URL* value defines the owner of the current document.

INCLUDES. The current document includes (as a grouping) the *URL* value.

REV   Defines the relation between the URL and the current document (the reverse relationship of REL).

Syntax
<LINK REV=*relationship* HREF=*URL*> (where *relationship* is the type of relationship being defined)

Options: Use the same as with REL, but reverse the defined relationships.

Usage
Head section only, not within containers.

<META>

Contains additional information about the current document that isn't displayed by Web viewers, but may be used by Web browers or external programs.

Empty element, does not require a closing tag.

Syntax
<META NAME="*value*" CONTENT="*value*">

Attributes
NAME   Gives META information a unique name.

CONTENT   Text or other values to associate with the META name.

Usage
Head section only, not within containers.

<TITLE> </TITLE>

Indicates the document's title, which is displayed in Web viewers but not in the body of the document text.

Container element, requires </TITLE> closing tag.

Syntax
<TITLE>...</TITLE>

Attributes
None

Usage
Head section only, not within containers.

Body Section Elements

<A></A>

Indicates a document anchor, used to create links to other resources or to define a location that can be linked to.

Container element, requires </A> closing tag.

Options:

Creating a hyperlink to a WWW resource:

Syntax
<A HREF= "*URL*">...</A> (where *URL* describes a valid WWW resource)

Attributes
None

Usage
Body section, stand-alone or within text, form, and table containers. Text between the anchor tags is clickable and appears in the viewer's currently defined link color. Clicking the link text activates the link and accesses the specified Web resource.

Defining a named anchor location:

Syntax
<A name="*value*">...</A> (where *value* is a unique anchor name for the current document)

Attributes
None

Usage

Body section, stand-alone or within text, form, and table containers. Text between the anchor tags is not highlighted or clickable.

Creating a hyperlink to a named anchor:

Syntax

`<A HREF= "URL#value">...</A>` (where *URL* describes a valid WWW document and *value* is a named anchor within that document)

Attributes

None

Usage

Body section, stand-alone or within text, form, and table containers. Text between the anchor tags is clickable and will appear in the viewer's currently defined link color. Clicking the link text activates the link and accesses the specified location in the specified Web page.

Creating a hyperlink to a named anchor in the same document:

Syntax

`<A HREF= "#value">...</A>` (where *value* is a named anchor within the same document)

Attributes

None

Usage

Body section, stand-alone or within text, form, and table containers. Text between the anchor tags is clickable and will appear in the viewer's currently defined link color. Clicking the link text activates the link and accesses the specified location in the same Web page.

<ADDRESS></ADDRESS>

Defines the address of the document author and is displayed in Web viewers.

Container element, requires `</ADDRESS>` closing tag.

Syntax

`<ADDRESS>...</ADDRESS>`

Attributes

None

Usage

Body or form sections, stand-alone, or within containers.

\<B>\</B>

Formats the container text as bold text. Requires HTML break elements for text breaks. Can be combined with active HTML style elements.

Container element, requires \</B> closing tag.

Syntax

\<B>...\</B>

Attributes

None

Usage

Body section, stand-alone, and within list and form containers.

\<BASEFONT>

Defines the default document text size to a value from 1–7 (3 is the common default). Requires Netscape support. Affects relative FONT element use.

Empty element, does not require a closing tag.

Syntax

\<BASEFONT SIZE=*n*> (where *n* is a font size value from 1–7)

Attributes

None

Usage

Body section, stand-alone, and within list and form containers.

\<BLINK>\</BLINK>

Makes the container text blink on and off in the WWW client window. Requires Netscape support. Can be combined with active HTML style elements.

Container element, requires \</BLINK> closing tag.

Syntax

`<BLINK>...</BLINK>`

Attributes

None

Usage

Body section, stand-alone, and within list and form containers. Support is very limited and the element is unpopular with readers. Use sparingly.

<BLOCKQUOTE></BLOCKQUOTE>

Defines the container text as a quotation from another source, using the viewer's current text settings. Retains all natural line and paragraph breaks in the text and indents both right and left margins. Can contain active HTML style elements.

Container element, requires `</BLOCKQUOTE>` closing tag.

Syntax

`<BLOCKQUOTE>...</BLOCKQUOTE>`

Attributes

None

Usage

Body section, stand-alone, and within list and form containers.

Inserts a line break at the current point in the document, beginning with the next line of text or inline graphic against the left margin one line beneath the current text.

Empty element, does not require a closing tag.

Syntax

`<BR>`

Attributes

CLEAR Netscape 1.0 extension, defining where the content can begin the next line in the document.

Syntax

`<BR CLEAR=value>` (where *value* is a valid option)

Options:

LEFT. The content can continue on the next available line whose left margin is clear.

RIGHT. The content can continue on the next available line whose right margin is clear.

ALL. The content can continue on the next available line where both margins are clear.

Usage

Body section—stand-alone and within lists, preformatted text and form containers.

<CENTER></CENTER>

Aligns the container text relative to the current container. Netscape addition, supported by HTML 3.2. Can be combined with active HTML style elements.

Container element, requires `</CENTER>` closing tag.

Syntax

`<CENTER>...</CENTER>`

Attributes

None

Usage

Body section, stand-alone, and within list and form containers. Will be superseded by HTML 3.2's `ALIGN` attribute to the P and H elements.

<CITE></CITE>

Defines the container text as a text citation, using the viewer's current text settings. Requires HTML break elements for text breaks. Can be combined with active HTML style elements.

Container element, requires `</CITE>` closing tag.

Syntax

`<CITE>...</CITE>`

Attributes

None

Usage

Body section, stand-alone, and within list and form containers.

<CODE></CODE>

Defines the container text as computer code text, using the viewer's current text settings. Requires HTML break elements for text breaks. Can be combined with active HTML style elements.

Container element, requires </CODE> closing tag.

Syntax

```
<CODE>...</CODE>
```

Attributes

None

Usage

Body section, stand-alone, and within list and form containers.

<DD>

Formats subsequent body text as a text definition. Provides additional space when it is superseded by a new element. Can contain active HTML elements.

Empty element, does not require a closing tag.

Syntax

```
<DD>
```

Attributes

None

Usage

Body section, a component of definition lists (DL), generally following a definition term (DT).

<DFN></DFN>

Defines the container text as definition text, using the viewer's current text settings. Requires HTML break elements for text breaks. Can be combined with active HTML style elements.

Container element, requires </DFN> closing tag.

Syntax
<DFN>...</DFN>

Attributes
None

Usage
Body section, stand-alone, and within list and form containers. Support by current Web viewers is inconsistent (not recommended for use).

<DIR></DIR>

Formats the container text as a file directory list. Contains list items (LI). Can contain active HTML elements. Intended to format text in compressed columns, but viewer support is rare.

Container element, requires </DIR> closing tag.

Syntax
<DIR>...</DIR>

Attributes
None

Usage
Body section, stand-alone, or within other list, form, and table containers.

<DL></DL>

Formats the container text as a definition list. Contains definition term (DT) and definition text (DD). Provides a double-spaced closing text break.

Container element, requires </DL> closing tag.

Syntax
<DL>...</DL>

Attributes

COMPACT Tells browser to show definition list with less whitespace.

Usage

Body section, stand-alone, or within other list, form, and table containers.

<DT>

Formats subsequent body text as a definition term. Provides additional space after the term. Can contain active HTML elements.

Empty element, does not require a closing tag.

Syntax

<DT>

Attributes

None

Usage

Body section, a component of definition lists (DL).

<EM></EM>

Defines the contained text as emphasized, using the viewer's current text settings. Requires HTML break elements for text breaks. Can be combined with active HTML style elements.

Container element, requires </EM> closing tag.

Syntax

<EM>...</EM>

Attributes

None

Usage

Body section, stand-alone, and within list and form containers.

<FONT></FONT>

Formats the container text to the specific or relative font size indicated. Netscape addition, supported by HTML 3.2. Does not affect the use of any other HTML elements.

Container element, requires `</FONT>` closing tag.

Syntax

`<FONT SIZE=value>...</FONT>` (where *value* is an absolute or relative font size)

Attributes

None

Usage

Options:

Absolute font size. Font will be displayed at a specific size ranging from 1–7 (one being the smallest font and seven the largest).

Syntax example: `<FONT SIZE=5>...</FONT>`

Relative font size. Font will be displayed at a size relative (using the plus and minus symbols) to the current base font, which is normally a size 3.

Syntax example: `<FONT SIZE=-2>...</FONT>`

Usage

Body section, stand-alone, and within list and form containers.

<Hn> </Hn>

Defines the container text as a heading, using the viewer's current text settings. Requires HTML break elements for text breaks. Can be combined with active HTML style elements.

Container element, requires `</Hn>` closing tag.

Syntax

`<Hn>...</Hn>` (where *n* corresponds to the heading level)

Level values of 1–6 are valid and each will have unique text definitions; in general, the lower the level number, the larger and more prominent the display text will be.

Attributes

ALIGN HTML 3.2 revision of H element, applying on-screen alignment to all the content within the container.

Syntax

<HnALIGN=*value*>...</Hn> (where *value* is a valid alignment option and *n* corresponds to the heading level)

Options:

LEFT. The content is aligned against the left text margin.

RIGHT. The content is aligned against the right text margin.

CENTER. The content is centered between the left and right text margins.

Usage

Body section, stand-alone, and within list and form containers. Headings define logical relationships; for example, H2 is a subheading of H1 and a superheading of H3. Alignment options are relative to the current container.

<HR>

Displays a horizontal rule in the WWW client window. The rule fills the current container from the left to the right margin. Does not affect other HTML elements in use. Netscape attributes are now supported by many browsers.

Empty element, does not require a closing tag.

Syntax

<HR>

Attributes

WIDTH Netscape extension, defines the actual or window percentage length of the horizontal rule.

Syntax

<HR WIDTH=*value*> (where *value* is a pixel measurement or a percentage, as in 50 percent)

SIZE Netscape extension, defines the height or thickness of the horizontal rule.

Syntax

<HR SIZE=*n*> (where *n* is a pixel measurement)

NOSHADE Netscape extension, displays the rule as a solid black line with no drop shadow.

Syntax

```
<HR NOSHADE>
```

ALIGN Netscape extension, aligns the horizontal rule relative to the current container.

Syntax

`<HR ALIGN=value>` (where `value` is a valid alignment option)

Options:

    LEFT. The rule is aligned against the left text margin.

    RIGHT. The rule is aligned against the right text margin.

    CENTER. The rule is centered between the left and right margins.

Usage

Body section, stand-alone, and within text containers.

<I></I>

Formats the container text as italicized text. Requires HTML break elements for text breaks. Can be combined with active HTML style elements.

Container element, requires `</I>` closing tag.

Syntax

`<I>...</I>`

Attributes

None

Usage

Body section, stand-alone, and within list and form containers.

<IMG>

Displays inline images and imagemaps in the document body.

Empty element, does not require a closing tag.

Syntax: `<IMG SRC="URL">` (where `URL` describes a valid graphic image file)

Attributes

SRC Defines the source of the associated image file.

ALT Defines a text string to be displayed by a WWW client if inline graphic support is not available. Many browsers also display this text before the associated graphic has been downloaded.

Syntax

`<IMG SRC="`*URL*`" ALT"`*value*`">` (where *URL* is a valid graphic file and *value* is a text message)

ISMAP Defines the inline image as an imagemap.

Syntax

`<IMG SRC="`*URL*`" ISMAP>` (where *URL* is a valid graphic file)

ALIGN Applies a specific alignment to text on the same line as the current inline graphic.

Syntax

`<IMG SRC="`*URL*`" ALIGN=`*value*`>` (where *URL* is a valid graphic file and *value* is a valid alignment option)

Options:

TOP. Aligns the top of the image with the line's text.

MIDDLE. Aligns the middle of the image with the line's text.

BOTTOM. Aligns the bottom of the image with the line's text (default).

LEFT. Netscape 1.0 extension, aligns the graphic along the left-hand margin and allows text to flow beside the image.

RIGHT. Netscape 1.0 extension, aligns the graphic along the right-hand margin and allows the text to flow beside the image.

TEXTTOP. Netscape 1.0 extension, aligns the top of the image with the top of the tallest text on the line.

ABSMIDDLE. Netscape 1.0 extension, aligns the middle of the image with the middle of the line's text.

BASELINE. Netscape 1.0 extension, aligns the bottom of the image with the baseline of the line's text.

ABSBOTTOM. Netscape 1.0 extension, aligns the bottom of the image with the bottom of the line's text.

HSPACE Netscape 1.0 extension, defines the space along the horizontal edges of an inline graphic between the graphic and the adjacent text.

Syntax
`<IMG SRC="`*URL*`" HSPACE=`*n*`>` (where *URL* is a valid graphic file and *n* is the measurement of the blank space in pixels)

Usage
Often used in conjunction with VSPACE.

VSPACE Netscape 1.0 extension, defines the space along the vertical edges of an inline graphic between the graphic and the adjacent text.

Syntax
`<IMG SRC="`*URL*`" VSPACE=`*n*`>` (where *URL* is a valid graphic file and *n* is the measurement of the blank space in pixels)

Usage
Often used in conjunction with HSPACE.

WIDTH Netscape 1.0 extension, defines the width of the inline image for the convenience of the WWW client; used with HEIGHT.

HEIGHT Netscape 1.0 extension, defines the height of the inline image for the convenience of the WWW client; used with WIDTH.

Syntax
`<IMG SRC="`*URL*`" WIDTH=`*n1*` HEIGHT=`*n2*`>` (where *URL* is a valid graphic file, *n1* is the measurement of the width of the image in pixels, and *n2* is the measurement of the height of the image in pixels)

Usage
The WIDTH and HEIGHT values can be purposefully different than the image's actual measurements to force the image to "scale" to the new dimensions.

BORDER Netscape 1.0 extension, determines the size of the client-provided border for an inline image.

Syntax
`<IMG SRC="`*URL*`" BORDER=`*n*`>` (where *URL* is a valid graphic file and *n* is the thickness of the border in pixels)

LOWSRC Netscape 1.0 extension, defines a "low resolution" version of the inline image to be displayed at initial retrieval of the document, before the primary image is retrieved.

Syntax

`<IMG SRC="`*URL1*`" LOWRSC="`*URL2*`">` (where *URL1* is a valid graphic file and *URL2* is a valid low resolution substitution for *URL1*)

DYNSRC Internet Explorer extension, used to specify an AVI (Video for Windows) multimedia file to be shown inline.

Usage

Body or form sections, stand-alone, or within containers.

<KBD></KBD>

Defines the container text as keyboard input text, using the viewer's current text settings. Requires HTML break elements for text breaks. Can be combined with active HTML style elements.

Container element, requires `</KBD>` closing tag.

Syntax

`<KBD>...</KBD>`

Attributes

None

Usage

Body section, stand-alone, and within list and form containers.

<LI>

Defines a new item in a list.

Empty element, does not require a closing tag.

Syntax

`<LI>...`

Attributes

TYPE Netscape 1.0 extension, now supported by HTML 3.2, defines the current list type (regardless of the list container).

Syntax

<LI TYPE=*value*> (where *value* is a valid type option)

Options:

CIRCLE. Defines the unordered list marker type as filled circles.

SQUARE. Defines the unordered list marker type as filled squares.

DISC. Defines the unordered list marker type as unfilled circles.

A. Defines the ordered list numbering characters as uppercase letters.

a. Defines the ordered list numbering characters as lowercase letters.

I. Defines the ordered list numbering characters as uppercase Roman numerals.

i. Defines the ordered list numbering characters as lowercase Roman numerals.

1. Defines the ordered list numbering characters as numbers (default).

VALUE Netscape 1.0 extension, defines the new beginning sequential value for the container's current and subsequent list items.

Syntax

<LI VALUE=*n*> (where *n* is a sequential value)

Usage

Body section, in ordered lists (OL) and unordered lists (UL)

<LISTING></LISTING>

Defines the container text as a computer text list, using the viewer's current text settings. Retains all natural line and paragraph breaks in the text. Does not recognize internal HTML style elements.

Container element, requires </LISTING> closing tag.

Syntax

<LISTING>...</LISTING>

Attributes

None

Usage

Body section, stand-alone, and within list and form containers. This element is deprecated and support by current Web viewers is inconsistent (not recommended for use).

<MENU></MENU>

Formats the container text as a menu list. Contains list items (LI). Can contain active HTML elements.

Container element, requires </MENU> closing tag.

Syntax

```
<MENU>...</MENU>
```

Attributes

None

Usage

Body section, stand-alone, or within other list, form, and table containers.

<NOBR></NOBR>

Prevents the container text from wrapping in the viewer window. Requires Netscape 1.0 support. Can be combined with active HTML style elements.

Container element, requires </NOBR> closing tag.

Syntax

```
<NOBR>...</NOBR>
```

Attributes

None

Usage

Body section, stand-alone, and within list and form containers.

<OL></OL>

Formats the container text as an ordered list. Sequentially numbers each enclosed list item (LI). Requires HTML break elements for text breaks. Can contain active HTML style elements.

Container element, requires </OL> closing tag.

Syntax

```
<OL>...</OL>
```

Attributes

COMPACT Instructs browser to show list with less whitespace.

TYPE Netscape 1.0 extension, defines the marker type for items in the contained list.

Syntax

`<UL TYPE=value>` (where `value` is a valid marker option)

Options:

A. Defines the numbering characters as uppercase letters.

a. Defines the numbering characters as lowercase letters.

I. Defines the numbering characters as uppercase Roman numerals.

i. Defines the numbering characters as lowercase Roman numerals.

1. Defines the numbering characters as numbers (default).

START Netscape 1.0 extension, defines the starting sequential value for the container's list items.

Syntax

`<OL START=n>` (where *n* is the starting value for the listed items)

Usage

Body section, stand-alone, and within other containers. Uses the `LI` element to identify list items.

<P> (</P>)

Inserts a paragraph break at the current point in the document, beginning the next line of text or inline graphic against the left margin two lines beneath the current text.

Empty element, does not require a closing tag. Closing tag `</P>` is optional in HTML 3.2, but is required for `ALIGN` attribute.

Syntax

```
<P>
```

Attributes

`ALIGN` HTML 3.2 revision of P element, using it as a container and applying alignment to all of the content within the container.

Syntax

`<P ALIGN=value>...</P>` (where *value* is a valid option)

Options:

LEFT. The content is aligned against the left text margin.

RIGHT. The content is aligned against the right text margin.

CENTER. The content is centered between the left and right text margins.

Usage

Body section, stand-alone, and within list, preformatted text, and forms containers. `ALIGN` values are relative to the current container.

<PLAINTEXT>

Defines the subsequent text as unformatted text, using the viewer's current text settings. Retains all natural line and paragraph breaks in the text. Does not recognize internal HTML style elements.

Empty element, does not require a closing tag.

Syntax

`<PLAINTEXT>`

Attributes

None

Usage

Body section, stand-alone. This element has no closing tag, and all subsequent content (including HTML elements) is displayed as plain text. This element is deprecated and support by current Web viewers is *very* inconsistent (not recommended for use).

<PRE></PRE>

Defines the container content as preformatted and is displayed with the viewer's current text settings (usually a standard proportional font). Retains all natural line and paragraph breaks within the text. Can contain active HTML style elements.

Container element, requires `</PRE>` closing tag.

Syntax

`<PRE>...</PRE>`

Attributes

WIDTH Defines the width of a preformatted text container in characters.

Syntax

`<PRE WIDTH=n>...</PRE>` (where *n* is the number of characters per line)

Usage

Body section, stand-alone, and within lists and form containers.

<S></S>

Formats the container text with strikeouts. Requires HTML break elements for text breaks. Can be combined with active HTML style elements.

Container element, requires `</S>` closing tag.

Syntax

`<S>...</S>`

Attributes

None

Usage

Body section, stand-alone, and within list and form containers. Support by current Web viewers is rare (will become more common with the adoption of HTML 3.2).

<SAMP></SAMP>

Defines the container text as sample output text, using the viewer's current text settings. Requires HTML break elements for text breaks. Can be combined with active HTML style elements.

Container element, requires `</SAMP>` closing tag.

Syntax

`<SAMP>...</SAMP>`

Attributes

None

Usage

Body section, stand-alone, and within list and form containers.

<STRIKE></STRIKE>

Netscape 1.0 specific tag defines container text as strikeout text (see <S></S> for usage.)

<STRONG></STRONG>

Defines the container text as strongly emphasized, using the viewer's current text settings. Requires HTML break elements for text breaks. Can be combined with active HTML style elements.

Container element, requires </STRONG> closing tag.

Syntax: <STRONG>...</STRONG>

Attributes

None

Usage

Body section, stand-alone, and within list and form containers.

<TT></TT>

Formats the container text as typewriter-style text (monospaced font). Requires HTML break elements for text breaks. Can be combined with active HTML style elements.

Container element, requires </TT> closing tag.

Syntax

<TT>...</TT>

Attributes

None

Usage

Body section, stand-alone, and within list and form containers.

<U></U>

Formats the container text as underlined text. Requires HTML break elements for text breaks. Can be combined with active HTML style elements.

Container element, requires </U> closing tag.

Syntax
<U>...</U>

Attributes
None

Usage
Body section, stand-alone, and within list and form containers. Support by current Web viewers is inconsistent (will become more common with the adoption of HTML 3.2).

<UL></UL>

Formats the container text as an unordered list. Marks each enclosed list item (LI) with a viewer-defined bullet. Requires HTML break elements for text breaks. Can contain active HTML style elements.

Container element, requires </UL> closing tag.

Syntax
<UL>...</UL>

Attributes
COMPACT Instructs browser to show list with less whitespace.

TYPE Netscape 1.0 extension, defines the marker type for items in the contained list.

Syntax
<UL TYPE=*value*> (where *value* is a valid marker option)

Options:

CIRCLE. Defines the marker type as filled circles.

SQUARE. Defines the marker type as filled squares.

DISC. Defines the marker type as unfilled circles.

Usage

Body section, stand-alone, and within other containers. Uses the LI element to identify list items.

<VAR></VAR>

Defines the container text as a text variable, using the viewer's current text settings. Requires HTML break elements for text breaks. Can be combined with active HTML style elements.

Container element, requires </VAR> closing tag.

Syntax

<VAR>...</VAR>

Attributes

None

Usage

Body section, stand-alone, and within list and form containers.

<WBR>

Indicates a possible break point in the text. Requires Netscape 1.0 support. Is often used with the NOBR container elements.

Empty element, does not require a closing tag.

Syntax

<WBR>

Attributes

None

Usage

Body section, stand-alone and within list and form containers.

<XMP></XMP>

Defines the container text as a preformatted text example, using the viewer's current text settings. Retains all natural line and paragraph breaks in the text. Does not recognize internal HTML style elements.

Container element, requires </XMP> closing tag.

Syntax
`<XMP>...</XMP>`

Attributes
None

Usage
Body section, stand-alone, and within list and form containers. This element is deprecated and support by current Web viewers is inconsistent (not recommended for use).

Table Elements (HTML 3.2 features)

<CAPTION></CAPTION>

Defines the table's caption text. Can contain active HTML elements.

Container element, requires the `</CAPTION>` closing tag.

Syntax
`<CAPTION>...</CAPTION>`

Attributes
ALIGN   Defines the alignment of the caption text with the table.

Syntax: `<CAPTION ALIGN=value>` (where `value` is a valid alignment option)

Options:

TOP. Aligns caption above the table.

Syntax: `<CAPTION ALIGN=TOP>`

BOTTOM. Aligns caption below the table.

Syntax: `<CAPTION ALIGN=BOTTOM>`

Usage
Body section, within table containers only.

<TABLE></TABLE>

Defines the container text as a table. Contains rows (TR), cells (TD), headers (TH), and captions (CAPTION). Can contain active HTML elements, including forms.

Container element, requires </TABLE> closing tag.

Syntax

<TABLE>...</TABLE>

Attributes

BORDER Defines the line weight of the border around the table cells.

Syntax

<TABLE BORDER=*n*> (where *n* is a number representing the chosen line weight)

Usage

If no border attribute is included, table will display cells without borders.

CELLSPACING Netscape 1.1 extension, defines horizontal spacing between adjacent cells.

Syntax

<TABLE CELLSPACING=*n*> (where *n* is the number of pixels between adjacent cells)

CELLPADDING Netscape 1.1 extension, defines vertical spacing between adjacent cells.

Syntax

<TABLE CELLPADDING=*n*> (where *n* is the number of pixels between adjacent cells)

WIDTH Netscape 1.1 extension, defines width of table cells in pixels or as a percentage of the container's width.

Syntax

<TABLE WIDTH=*value*> (where *value* is the number of pixels or the percentage, expressed as *n* percent, of the width of the individual cells)

Usage

Body section, stand-alone, or within other list and form containers.

<TD>

Defines the text in individual table cells. Supports active HTML elements.

Container element, requires </TD> closing tag (convention allows leaving off the closing tag).

Syntax
```
<TD>...</TD>
```

Attributes
ALIGN Defines the text's horizontal alignment within the specific table cell.

Syntax
`<TD ALIGN=value>` (where *value* is a valid alignment option)

Options:

LEFT. Aligns the text with the cell's left edge.

RIGHT. Aligns the text with the cell's right edge.

CENTER. Centers the text in the cell.

VALIGN Defines the text's vertical alignment within the specific cell.

Options:

TOP. Aligns the header text with the top of the cell.

MIDDLE. Aligns the header text with the middle of the cell.

BOTTOM. Aligns the header text with the bottom of the cell.

NOWRAP Instructs the viewer not to wrap the text within the table cell.

Syntax
```
<TD NOWRAP>
```

COLSPAN Instructs the viewer to span the specified number of table columns.

Syntax
`<TD COLSPAN=n>` (where *n* is a number of table columns to span)

ROWSPAN Instructs the viewer to span the specified table rows.

Syntax
`<TD ROWSPAN=n>` (where *n* is the number of table rows to span)

WIDTH Netscape 1.1 extension, defines the width of the specific table cell.

Syntax

`<TD WIDTH=value>` (where *value* is either the number of pixels or the percentage, expressed as *n* percent, of the width of the table header)

Usage

Body section, within table row containers only.

<TH>

Defines header text in a table. Does not support additional HTML elements.

Container element, requires `</TH>` closing tag (convention allows leaving off the closing tag).

Syntax

`<TH>...</TH>`

Attributes

ALIGN Defines the horizontal alignment of the header text within the table cell.

Syntax

`<TH ALIGN=value>` (where *value* is a valid alignment option)

Options:

LEFT. Aligns the header text with the cell's left edge.

RIGHT. Aligns the header text with the cell's right edge.

CENTER. Centers the header text in the cell.

VALIGN Defines the vertical alignment of the header text within the cell.

Options:

TOP. Aligns the header text with the top of the cell.

MIDDLE. Aligns the header text with the middle of the cell.

BOTTOM. Aligns the header text with the bottom of the cell.

NOWRAP Instructs the viewer not to wrap the header text within the table cell.

Syntax
```
<TH NOWRAP>
```

COLSPAN Instructs the viewer to span the specified number of table columns.

Syntax
```
<TH COLSPAN=n>
```
(where *n* is the number of table columns to span)

ROWSPAN Instructs the viewer to span the specified table rows.

Syntax
```
<TH ROWSPAN=n>
```
(where *n* is the number of table rows to span)

WIDTH Netscape 1.1 extension, defines the width of the table header cell within the table.

Syntax
```
<TH WIDTH=value>
```
(where *value* is either the number of pixels or the percentage, expressed as *n* percent, of the width of the table header)

Usage
Body section, within table containers only.

<TR>

Defines a row within a table.

Container element, requires </TR> closing tag (convention allows leaving off the closing tag).

Syntax
```
<TR>...</TR>
```

Attributes
ALIGN Defines the horizontal alignment of the text within the table row.

Syntax
```
<TR ALIGN=value>
```
(where *value* is a valid alignment option)

Options:

LEFT. Aligns text to the left edge in the row's cells.

RIGHT. Aligns text to the right edge in the row's cells.

CENTER. Centers text in the row's cells.

VALIGN Defines the vertical alignment of the text within the row's cells.

Options:

TOP. Aligns the text with the top of the row's cells.

MIDDLE. Aligns the text with the middle of the row's cells.

BOTTOM. Aligns the text with the bottom of the row's cells.

Usage
Body section, within table containers only.

Form Elements (HTML 3.2 features)

<FORM></FORM>

Defines the container text as a form. Contains input fields (INPUT), selection lists (SELECT), and input boxes (TEXTAREA). Can contain active HTML elements.

Container element, requires </FORM> closing tag.

Syntax: <FORM>...</FORM>

Attributes
ACTION Defines the program that will process the current form.

METHOD Defines the procedure for passing information to the ACTION URL.

Syntax
<FORM ACTION="*URL*" METHOD=*value*> (where *URL* is a valid Web resource and *value* is a valid method option)

Options:

GET. Program retrieves data from current document.

POST. Web page sends the data to the processing program.

Usage
Body section, stand-alone, or within list or table containers.

<INPUT>

Defines an input field where the user may enter information on the form.

Empty element, does not require a closing tag.

Syntax
`<INPUT>`

Attributes
TYPE Defines the format of input data.

Syntax
`<INPUT TYPE=value>` (where *value* is a valid type option)

Options:

TEXT. Defines input type as character data.

PASSWORD. Defines input type as character data.

CHECKBOX. Defines input type as a checkbox.

RADIO. Defines input type as a radio button.

SUBMIT. Defines input type as a submit form data button.

RESET. Defines input type as a reset form data button.

NAME Establishes the symbolic name for this input field.

Syntax
`<INPUT NAME=value>` (where *value* is a text name)

Usage
Required for all INPUT types except SUBMIT and RESET.

CHECKED Indicates that this input field is checked by default.

Syntax
`<INPUT CHECKED>`

SIZE Defines the physical size of the input field.

Options:

For single-line input fields:

Syntax
<INPUT SIZE=*n*> (where *n* is the number of characters for the field)

For multiline input fields:

Syntax
<INPUT SIZE=*x*,*y*> (where *x* is the number of characters per line and *y* is the number of lines in the input field)

MAXLENGTH Establishes the maximum number of characters of input that can be entered into an input field.

Syntax
<INPUT MAXLENGTH=*n*> (where *n* is the number of characters allowed in the input field)

Usage
Body section, form container only.

<OPTION>
Defines a selection item in a selection list; does not support HTML elements.

Empty element, does not require a closing tag.

Syntax
<OPTION>...

Attributes
SELECTED Indicates the selection list option that is selected by default.

Syntax
<OPTION SELECTED>

Usage
Body section, form container, within a SELECT list only.

<SELECT></SELECT>

Defines a list of options that can be selected from a pull-down list in the current form; can contain active HTML elements.

Container element, requires </SELECT> closing tag.

Syntax
<SELECT>...</SELECT>

Attributes
NAME Establishes the symbolic name for this selection list.

Syntax
<SELECT NAME=*value*> (where *value* is a text name)

SIZE Defines the number of options or choices that will be available in the selection list.

Syntax
<SELECT SIZE=*n*> (where *n* is the number of available selections)

MULTIPLE Indicates that multiple selections are allowed from the selection list.

Syntax
<SELECT MULTIPLE>

Usage
Body section, form container only.

<TEXTAREA><TEXTAREA>

Defines a multiline input field; does not support HTML elements.

Container element, requires </TEXTAREA> closing tag.

Syntax
<TEXTAREA>...</TEXTAREA>

 NOTE **Default text to be displayed in the input field is filled between the tags.**

Attributes
NAME Establishes the symbolic name for this selection list.

Syntax
TEXTAREA NAME=*value*> (where *value* is a text name)

ROWS Defines the number of rows the input field will display.

Syntax
<TEXTAREA ROWS=*n*> (where *n* is the number of input field rows visible)

COLS Defines the width (in characters) of the text input area.

Syntax
<TEXTAREA COLS=*n*> (where *n* is the number of columns or characters of the input field's width)

Usage
Regularly combined with ROWS to specify the text input field's display dimensions.

Usage
Body section, within a form container only.

HTML Entities

Note: These escape sequences must be entered in lowercase.

Accented Characters

Æ   for uppercase AE diphthong (ligature)

Á   for uppercase A, acute accent

Â   for uppercase A, circumflex accent

À   for uppercase A, grave accent

Å   for uppercase A, ring

Ã   for uppercase A, tilde

Ä   for uppercase A, dieresis or umlaut mark

Ç   for uppercase C, cedilla

Ð   for uppercase Eth, Icelandic

É   for uppercase E, acute accent

Ê   for uppercase E, circumflex accent

È   for uppercase E, grave accent

Ë   for uppercase E, dieresis or umlaut mark

Í   for uppercase I, acute accent

Î   for uppercase I, circumflex accent

Ì   for uppercase I, grave accent

Ï   for uppercase I, dieresis or umlaut mark

Ñ   for uppercase N, tilde

Ó   for uppercase O, acute accent

Ô   for uppercase O, circumflex accent

Ò   for uppercase O, grave accent

Ø   for uppercase O, slash

Õ   for uppercase O, tilde

Ö   for uppercase O, dieresis or umlaut mark

Þ   for uppercase THORN, Icelandic

Ú   for uppercase U, acute accent

Û   for uppercase U, circumflex accent

Ù   for uppercase U, grave accent

Ü   for uppercase U, dieresis or umlaut mark

Ý   for uppercase Y, acute accent

á   for lowercase a, acute accent

â   for lowercase a, circumflex accent

æ   for lowercase ae diphthong (ligature)

à   for lowercase a, grave accent

å   for lowercase a, ring

ã   for lowercase a, tilde

ä   for lowercase a, dieresis or umlaut mark

ç   for lowercase c, cedilla

é   for lowercase e, acute accent

ê   for lowercase e, circumflex accent

è   for lowercase e, grave accent

ð   for lowercase eth, Icelandic

ë   for lowercase e, dieresis or umlaut mark

í   for lowercase i, acute accent

î   for lowercase i, circumflex accent

ì   for lowercase i, grave accent

ï   for lowercase i, dieresis or umlaut mark

ñ   for lowercase n, tilde

ó   for lowercase o, acute accent

ô   for lowercase o, circumflex accent

ò   for lowercase o, grave accent

ø   for lowercase o, slash

õ   for lowercase o, tilde

ö   for lowercase o, dieresis or umlaut mark

ß   for lowercase sharp s, German (sz ligature)

þ   for lowercase thorn, Icelandic

ú   for lowercase u, acute accent

û   for lowercase u, circumflex accent

ù   for lowercase u, grave accent

ü   for lowercase u, dieresis or umlaut mark

ý   for lowercase y, acute accent

ÿ   for lowercase y, dieresis or umlaut mark

ASCII Characters

&#*n*;   (where *n* is the specified ASCII code)

Reserved HTML Characters

<   for < character

>   for > character

&   for & character

"   for " character

®   Netscape 1.0 extension, for registered trademark symbol

©   Netscape 1.0 extension, for copyright symbol

World Wide Web Bibliography

The following bibliographical references are all available over the World Wide Web; they constitute the majority of the information available regarding HTML and the standards process (as well as references to topics, such as Perl, Usenet, and the WWW itself). Some of these documents will change location over time because the Web isn't a fixed environment. If you have trouble finding a specific document listed here, use a Web searching facility (such as Web Search) to see whether the document is maintained elsewhere.

The quality of the information in these documents varies as does the quality of any data on the Internet. Consider the source before you take the accuracy of any information for granted. Many documents also include links to other documents on this list. In this manner, the WWW lives up to its reputation as a sort of spider's web or maze, and it's very easy to find yourself back where you started after a long, convoluted search.

HTML Documentation

http://www.utoronto.ca/webdocs/HTMLdocs/NewHTML/htmlindex.html
Dr. Ian Graham, University of Toronto

World Wide Web Frequently Asked Questions

http://sunsite.unc.edu/boutell/faq/wwwfaq.txt
Thomas Boutell

A Beginner's Guide to HTML

http://www.ncsa.uiuc.edu/General/Internet/WWW/
HTMLPrimer.html
National Center for Supercomputing Applications (**pubs@ncsa.uiuc.edu**)

HTML Quick Reference

http://kuhttp.cc.ukans.edu/lynx_help/HTML_quick.html
Michael Grobe, The University of Kansas

HyperText Markup Language (HTML)

http://www.w3.org/pub/WWW/MarkUp/MarkUp.html
Daniel W. Connolly, World Wide Web Consortium (W3C) in the Laboratory
for Computer Science, MIT

HyperText Markup Language Specification Version 3.2

http://www.w3.org/pub/WWW/TR/WD-html32.html
Dave Raggett, W3C

Cascading Style Sheets, level 1

http://www.w3.org.1/pub/WWW/TR/WD-css1-960911.html
Hakon Wium Lie (**howcome@w3.org**)
Bert Bos (**bert@w3.org**)

A Beginner's Guide to URLs

http://www.ncsa.uiuc.edu/demoweb/url-primer.html
mosaic@ncsa.uiuc.edu

Elements of HTML Style

http://bookweb.cwis.uci.edu:8042/Staff/StyleGuide.html
J.K. Cohen, UC Irvine (**jkcohen@uci.edu**)

Hypertext Terms

http://www.w3.org/pub/WWW/Terms.html

The Common Gateway Interface

http://hoohoo.ncsa.uiuc.edu/cgi/
Rob McCool, NCSA (**robm@ncsa.uiuc.edu**)

Style Guide for Online Hypertext

http://www.w3.org/pub/WWW/Provider/Style/
Overview.html
Tim Berners-Lee, W3C (**timbl@w3.org**)

Entering the World Wide Web: A Guide to Cyberspace

http://www.eit.com/web/www.guide/
Kevin Hughes, Enterprise Integration Technologies

A Basic HTML Style Guide

http://guinan.gsfc.nasa.gov/Style.html
Alan Richmond, NASA GSFC

IETF HyperText Markup Language (HTML) Working Group

ftp://www.ics.uci.edu/pub/ietf/html/index.html

The HTML 3.0 Hypertext Document Format

http://www.w3.org/hypertext/WWW/Arena/tour/start.html

Daniel W. Connolly's Web Presence

http://www.w3.org/pub/WWW/People/Connolly/
Daniel W. Connolly

The WWW Virtual Library

http://www.w3.org/pub/DataSources/bySubject/
Overview2.htmlvlib@mail.w3.org

The World Wide Web

http://www.w3.org/pub/WWW/TheProject.html
Tim Berners-Lee, W3C (**timbl@w3.org**)

Authoring WWW Documents: Overview

http://rsd.gsfc.nasa.gov/users/delabeau/talk/
Jeff de La Beaujardière (**delabeau@camille.gsfc.nasa.gov**)

Bad Style Page

http://www.earth.com/bad-style/
Tony Sanders, (**sanders@bsdi.com**)

Mirksy's Worst of the Web

http://mirsky.com/wow/
Mirsky-Style Productions

The Web Communications Comprehensive Guide to Publishing on the Web

http://www.webcom.com/html/
Web Communications (**support@webcom.com**)

WebTechs and HTML

http://www.webtechs.com/
Mark Gaither, Webtechs (**webmaster@webtechs.com**)

SGML

http://www.w3.org/pub/WWW/Markup/SGML/
Tim Berners-Lee, W3C (**timbl@w3.org**)

Perl FAQ

http://www.cis.ohio-state.edu/hypertext/faq/usenet/perl-faq/
top.html
Stephen P. Potter and Tom Christiansen (**perlfaq@perl.com**)

PERL—Practical Extraction and Report Language

http://www-cgi.cs.cmu.edu/cgi-bin/perl-man
Larry Wall (**lwall@netlabs.com**)

University of Florida's Perl Archive

http://www.cis.ufl.edu/perl/
Steve Potter, Varimetrix Corporation (**spp@vx.com**)

Microsoft Internet Explorer

http://microsoft.com/ie/
Microsoft Corp

Creating Net Sites

http://www.netscape.com/assist/net_sites/index.html
Netscape Communications Corp

JavaScript Authoring Guide

http://home.netscape.com/eng/mozilla/2.0/handbook/javascript/index.html
Netscape Communications Corp

Index

Check out Que® Books
on the World Wide Web
http://www.mcp.com/que

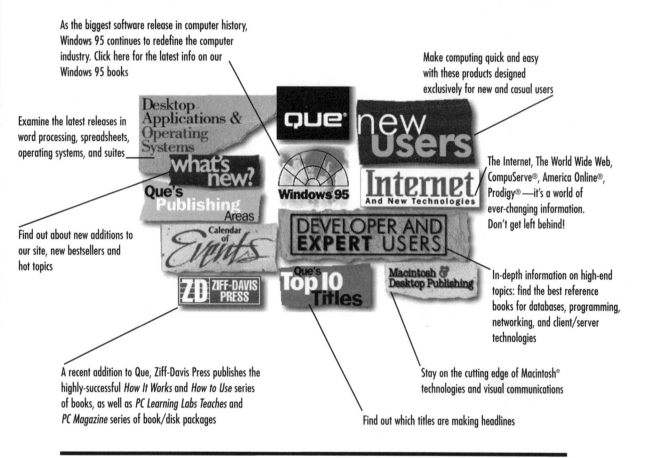

As the biggest software release in computer history, Windows 95 continues to redefine the computer industry. Click here for the latest info on our Windows 95 books

Make computing quick and easy with these products designed exclusively for new and casual users

Examine the latest releases in word processing, spreadsheets, operating systems, and suites

The Internet, The World Wide Web, CompuServe®, America Online®, Prodigy®—it's a world of ever-changing information. Don't get left behind!

Find out about new additions to our site, new bestsellers and hot topics

In-depth information on high-end topics: find the best reference books for databases, programming, networking, and client/server technologies

A recent addition to Que, Ziff-Davis Press publishes the highly-successful *How It Works* and *How to Use* series of books, as well as *PC Learning Labs Teaches* and *PC Magazine* series of book/disk packages

Stay on the cutting edge of Macintosh® technologies and visual communications

Find out which titles are making headlines

With 6 separate publishing groups, Que develops products for many specific market segments and areas of computer technology. Explore our Web Site and you'll find information on best-selling titles, newly published titles, upcoming products, authors, and much more.

- Stay informed on the latest industry trends and products available

- Visit our online bookstore for the latest information and editions

- Download software from Que's library of the best shareware and freeware

Check out Que® Books
on the World Wide Web
http://www.mcp.com/que

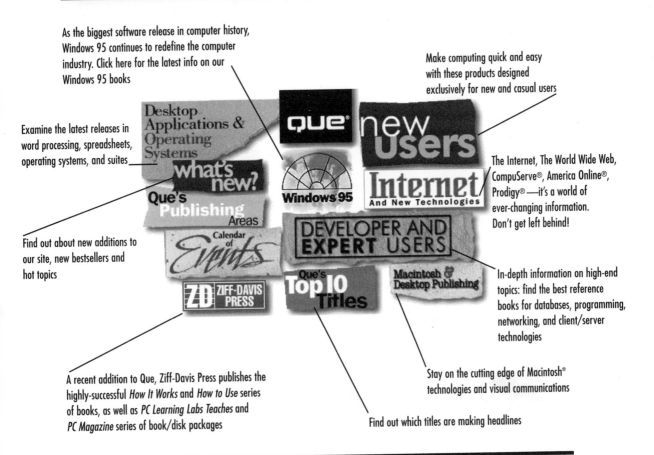

As the biggest software release in computer history, Windows 95 continues to redefine the computer industry. Click here for the latest info on our Windows 95 books

Make computing quick and easy with these products designed exclusively for new and casual users

Examine the latest releases in word processing, spreadsheets, operating systems, and suites

The Internet, The World Wide Web, CompuServe®, America Online®, Prodigy® —it's a world of ever-changing information. Don't get left behind!

Find out about new additions to our site, new bestsellers and hot topics

In-depth information on high-end topics: find the best reference books for databases, programming, networking, and client/server technologies

A recent addition to Que, Ziff-Davis Press publishes the highly-successful *How It Works* and *How to Use* series of books, as well as *PC Learning Labs Teaches* and *PC Magazine* series of book/disk packages

Stay on the cutting edge of Macintosh® technologies and visual communications

Find out which titles are making headlines

With 6 separate publishing groups, Que develops products for many specific market segments and areas of computer technology. Explore our Web Site and you'll find information on best-selling titles, newly published titles, upcoming products, authors, and much more.

- Stay informed on the latest industry trends and products available
- Visit our online bookstore for the latest information and editions
- Download software from Que's library of the best shareware and freeware